President John Quincy Adams' Quarrel with the Freemasons

Also from Westphalia Press

westphaliapress.org

President John Quincy Adams' Quarrel with the Freemasons

John Quincy Adams'
Letters and Opinions of the Masonic Institution

introduced and edited by
Guillermo De Los Reyes

WESTPHALIA PRESS
An imprint of Policy Studies Organization

President John Quincy Adams' Quarrel with the Freemasons

Westphalia Press
An imprint of Policy Studies Organization
1527 New Hampshire Ave., NW
Washington, D.C. 20036
dgutierrezs@ipsonet.org

ISBN-13: 978-1935907213
ISBN-10: 1935907212

Updated material and comments on this edition
can be found at the Westphalia Press website:
www.westphaliapress.org

For Mark Tabbert,
able historian of Masonic
mores and complexities

ANTI-MASONRY IN THE 1820s AND 1830s

PREFACE TO THE NEW EDITION

Freemasonry in America in the early 1820s was robust and growing, and yet it would be tried as much by events as any lodge visitor was ever tried by a suspicious tyler at the door with drawn sword.[i] This could be the best of times for a fraternity recognized as a protector of the national spirit; lodges that enjoyed a reputation buttressed by the Masonic membership of George Washington himself. An enthusiast reiterated that if the capital was a temple to the state religion of republican government, then Masons were the national priesthood.[ii]

These were not the views held by John Quincy Adams. President Adams was no fan of secret societies. Phi Beta Kappa upset him and the Masons, as this collection of his letters makes rather abundantly clear, upset him even more. He put a great deal of energy into trying to persuade people of the evil consequences of Masonry.

He was not the fraternity's first critic. There had been attacks on the Craft during the 1790s, rooted in unfounded accusations about ties with the supposed Bavarian Illuminati, and they had died away.[iii] The contribution of the Masons to the new country was hailed and American and Masonic values

G

seemed virtually identical; Freemasons gave the country a "symbolic core",[iv] and with little social competition, the Grand Lodge played a major part in early Washington.[v]

The role of the Craft was illustrated by the visit of the elderly Marquis de Lafayette to America in 1824-25, when Masons everywhere greeted their brother with extravagant display. Masonic membership in the country, about 16,000 in 1800, was about 80,000 in 1822, roughly five percent of America's eligible male population.[vi] Lafayette, with his stories of campfires with General Washington, was acclaimed as a principal in the now legendary beginnings of the country, but accompanying the celebrations was an undercurrent of suspicions among many Americans about the extremism of French political life.[vii]

In 1826 the supposedly good influences of Masonry on American society were challenged. Criticisms were neither a new development nor the last time the matter would arise. The positive and negative Masonic effects on a culture have been much argued during much of its history, and the rebuttal is often superficial. There are far more volumes dwelling on the easily remarked such as buildings and exposés of initiation ceremonies (–for example the revelations discussed below made by William Morgan) than about a harder to investigate aspect of the movement, one that is subtler if less useful to novelists and Hollywood. There is a temptation to use Masonic terminology to describe this longstanding dichotomy between overt and subliminal as operative and speculative.

H

The anti-Masonic movement of the 1820s and 1830s, as with other anti-Masonic movements, benefited from spotlighting the more public manifestations of the Craft itself and from voyeurism over ritual disclosure. There was ample overt or operative influence of Masonry apparent in the capital and this was and is marked by its public participation in the construction and perpetuation of national traditions, such as cornerstone laying, exhibiting Washington's Masonic trowel in the new Capitol museum, and lending the Washington bible for Presidential inaugurations, [viii] helping maintain the symbolization that the country perhaps needs to forge national unity. This has encouraged extravagant claims about the secret symbolism of the city's streets and monuments, as well as allegations about the supposed influence of Masonry on the government.

It is of course true that an interest in architecture and a great facility with ritual is integral to Masonry, and has contributed to the development of national rituals and political cultures of many nations -- witness the case of Mexico and of Latin American countries.[ix] So this overt material is fair game for opponents. Understanding this role that Freemasonry plays in "ritualization" of national life helps in understanding the uniqueness of America. What is usually neglected is that there is a quieter and ultimately more important influence on ideas about governance and democracy, rooted in Masonry's ties to the Enlightenment.[x]

I

All of this came to a crossroads in 1826. While notable Masonic things were being done in Washington and across the country, that was also the year when William Morgan, a miscreant living in upstate New York who had threatened to expose secrets of the craft, allegedly was murdered, promoting a national hysteria that imperiled Freemasonry in the United States.[xi] Brother Arturo de Hoyos in his monumental study of Masonic exposés, *Light on Masonry,* remarks about Morgan, "He had never been initiated into Masonry, and his entire Masonic experience was built upon deception."[xii]

Nevertheless, the disappearance of Morgan became a national cause célèbre. The charges about Masonic involvement in his kidnaping seemed valid and although a Mason himself, New York's Governor DeWitt Clinton removed from office the sheriff he believed was involved in Morgan's abduction.[xiii] The preponderance of evidence does suggest that he was killed by Masons,[xiv] and the incident ignited a conflagration.

Masonry abjures sectarianism[xv] and the attack on it was led by orthodox religious leaders who objected to its tolerant universalism: "By the 1820s, Freemasonry had expanded beyond its Federalist elite roots and now included many middle-class persons as well as Jeffersonian Republicans. Working together, leader of both parties hoped to limit the influence of Christianity in American public life, Antimasons averred."[xvi] The diversity of Freemasonry, bringing together all sorts of men, was the enemy of religious parochialism which in the 1820s and 1830s coincided with a nativism[xvii] which led the burning of Catholic institutions by mobs and the persecution of Mormons.[xviii]

In contrast with sectarianism, Masonry's tolerance was part of its cosmopolitanism. Cosmopolitanism was the fruit of diversity. Freemasonry embodied these ideals of sociability and cosmopolitanism and it created national icons that brought people together. It was a means by which they participated in the Enlightenment. The American Enlightenment was in fact more open to cultural diversity than was the European version.[xix]

Unfortunately, influences whether overt or subtle, are not always uncontroversial,[xx] and the very success of Enlightenment ideas and of Masonry in early America contributed to the confrontation in the late 1820s and 1830s,[xxi] and to a debate over American beliefs in which Masonry was attacked, its ecumenisms and lack of dogma held against it in a demonstration of how national identities can be bitterly contested.[xxii] The canard about Masonic conspiracies would take on new life, notwithstanding the contributions that the lodges were making to charity, education, and public discourse. Unquestionably. "Antimasonry was more than a political movement; it was a moral crusade. The movement's evangelical middle-class base believed that Masons were an obstacle in their goal to create a more Christian America."[xxiii]

That the Enlightenment has remained alive in America and survived vitriolic attacks perhaps helps explain why the cityscape of Washington as it has emerged over the years is not as chaotic as that of many metropolises. The debate over how to clothe the Republic in icons and symbols has been going on since the American Revolution.[xxiv] Recent changes in sovereignty of emerging nations after the end of the Cold War reminds us of the challenges in early America following severing of ties with Britain. During such upheavals, states are forced to seek a new symbolic vocabulary. The old Russian eagle, after exile, has replaced the hammer and sickle, while the American eagle was never obliged to flee. The symbolic structure laid down in the founding era has survived, although repeatedly challenged.

When J.M. Roberts wrote his classic *The Mythology of the Secret Societies*, he emphasized the dangers of conspiracy theory and in the 1820s in America he was proved right: "The mythology of the secret societies has many different specific embodiments, religious and non religious, liberal and conservative, but it is always an example of the 'puppet' theory of politics. It claims that the real makers of events are not the statesmen who strut before the public, but secret directors who manipulate them, sometimes with, sometimes without, their knowledge."[xxv] Although the consequences can be grave, we can joke about suspicions of Masonry: In the television comic series The Simpsons, Homer joins the Sacred Order of Stonecutters, whose anthem includes: "Who controls the British Crown? Who keeps the metric system down? We do! We do!"[xxvi] Dan Brown is just the most recent observer to conjure up images of dark rooms and strange doings that was part of the 1820s.

An observation about this never-ending speculation rings true: "Such people tend to get the idea first and then seek out the evidence that appears to support their notion. No amount of counter-argument or evidence of the contrary is likely to modify their opinions."[xxvii]

Does the Morgan incident fully explain why such promising times quickly become the worst of times for the American lodges, a nightmare? It was a spark that ignited a fire waiting to be lit but part of a fuller answer is suggested by examining thoroughly the reaction to the grandeur of Lafayette's tour and the major participation of Masons in it,[xxviii] a shrewd suggestion made by historian Mark Tabbert in *American Freemasons: Three Centuries of Building Communities*. The extravagant Masonic-led affection for a foreign aristocrat was regarded as sinister. The displays of mysterious aprons and jewels along with the whispered reference to the Brotherhood, "heightened suspicion of the craft as an international order with secrets and a radical revolutionary past."[xxix]

Another major contribution to the rancor was the confrontation between the followers of John Quincy Adams and Andrew Jackson. Adams was a severe critic of Masonry while Jackson was past Grand Master of Tennessee. New England, where Adams support was high, was where Anti-Masonry was effective. In the South, which was solidly pro Jackson, the effects were much less. [xxx]

The consequences of the Anti-Masonic movement were that "The anti-Masonic depression put some Grand Lodges out of business." In Massachusetts,

"Prior to 1826 new Lodges were being constituted all over the State." In the seventeen years between 1827 and 1844, not a single new lodge was organized. [xxxi] Anti-Masonry for a moment was successful, [xxxii] misconstruing, often deliberately, the blood oaths and rituals as literal rather than metaphoric. [xxxiii] Arthur M. Schlesinger commented, "The Antimasonic movement was rooted in the antagonism of country to town, where most of the lodge were to be found; in objections of the orthodox to the order's diluted Christianity; in lower –class resentment against the well-to-do, who usually composed the membership; and in fear of the boastful claims of Masons to a controlling influence in political and economic life."[xxxiv]

Freemasons had heretofore been unquestionably members of the establishment, patriarchs of the Republic, and now they had become for the moment a persecuted minority.[xxxv] Robert Gould commented: "The hatred of masonry was carried everywhere, and there was no retreat so sacred that it did not enter. Not only were teachers and pastors driven from their stations, children of masons were excluded from schools, and members from their churches. The sacrament was refused to Masons by formal vote of the church, for no other offense than their Masonic connection. Families were divided. Brother was arrayed against brother, father against son, and even wives against their husbands. Desperate efforts were made to take away charter rights from Masonic corporations and to pass laws that would prevent Masons holding their meetings and performing their ceremonies."[xxxvi]

N

Fortunately, even with the support of President Adams, anti-Masons were not able to establish an effective permanent campaign of persecution or to transform public opinion into durable support. [xxxvii] Demonizing Masonry as the source of all evil, they had manipulated relationships between orthodox religious beliefs, Masonry, and civil society. [xxxviii] This would be a recurring case, a seemingly indeterminable contest between maintaining an inclusive civil society and a more narrow and sectarian one, with the Masons on the side of inclusiveness. The Masons in America have not taken a religious or political stand, and never had a quarrel with anyone's church, temple, or faith. But it is not Christian, or for that matter Buddhist or Jewish, and it is aligned with the view of America as a non-sectarian society. The Enlightenment figure Gotthold Lessing remarked, about Freemasonry and civil society, "It may be mother and daughter, or sister and sister; their mutual fate has always worked reciprocally one upon the other. Whatever was the condition of the civic community, so also was Freemasonry in all places and vice versa." [xxxix]

As Jeffrey Croteau points out, "by the early 1930s, the Anti-Masonic Party had essentially become an anti-Jackson party, with Freemasonry serving as a convenient bogeyman which stood in for corrupt political power and threats to democracy." [xl] In 1833, the Anti-Masonic Party claimed 340, 800 adherents,[xli] but it began to fragment and reason returned.[xlii] As the enemies were routed, Masons were able to get about their business.[xliii]

O

Lodges recovered. In fact, in 1847, on May 1, the Masons were invited to place the cornerstone of the Smithsonian Institution. President and Brother James Polk as well as vice president and Brother George Ellis participated. The Grand Master wore an apron given to General Washington by the Grand Lodge of France and presented by Gen. Lafayette, the same one Washington used for the laying of the cornerstone of the Capitol. There was even some Masonic diplomacy when in 1848, the famous Cherokee Chief, William P. Ross, received the degrees in Federal, and conciliation talks among the leaders of the Cherokee Nation were held in the lodge room.[xliv]

The Masons continued to be participants in national rituals. In 1848, on the Fourth of July, the cornerstone of the Washington Monument was laid in Masonic form. Brother and sometime Grand Historian of the Grand Lodge (succeeding Brother Miner in 2011) Paul Dolinksy describes the event as "the greatest parade the city ever saw."[xlv] Robert Mills, a Freemason, designed the Monument. [xlvi] On July 4, 1848, Benjamin B. French, the Grand Master of Masons of the District of Columbia, conducted the exercises in the presence of President Polk, alluding to the influence of Masonry in national symbolism and charging Brother Mills: "I now present to you, my Brother, the square, level, and plumb, which are the working tools you are to use in the erection of this monument. You, as a Freemason, know to what they morally allude ... Look well to the erection of this National Monument; see that every stone is well squared, and that it is placed in its position both level and plumb, that the noble offering of a nation to commemorate greatness, patriotism, and virtue, may stand until the end of time."[xlvii]

Brother French was attired in the same apron and sash worn by President Washington at the Masonic cornerstone laying ceremony for the United States Capitol on September 18, 1793. His chair was the one purchased by Washington himself for Alexandria-Washington Lodge No. 22. The George Washington gavel and the George Washington trowel were both used, and 20,000 people turned out.[xlviii] So the efforts of President Adams came to naught, but this book shows how energetic an opponent he was.

Guillermo De Los Reyes

Q

Notes

[i] John C. Palemer, "The Morgan Affair and Anti-Masonry", *Little Masonic Library*, Book II, Macoy Publishing, Richmond (Virginia), 1946, 241-242.

[ii] Fergus M. Bordewich, *Washington: the Making of the American Capital*, Amistad/HarperCollins, 2008, 151.

[iii] Vernon Stauffer, *The Bavarian Illuminati in America*, Dover, Mincola (New York), 2006 (org.pub. as *New England and the Bavarian Illuminati*, Columbia University Press, New York, 1918), 244, 344-45.

[iv] See Jay Tolson, "Inside the Masons" Posted August 28, 2005, *U.S.News & World Report*, http://www.usnews.com/news/articles/2005/08/28/inside-the-masons.html, Accessed 1 January 2011.

[v] The claim is made that when the British briefly occupied Washington in 1814, Grand Lodge members were able to contact brethren in the British army and navy, and the occupation was perhaps tempered by that "Federal Lodge History", "Taken from the 1976 By-laws", n.a., http://mylodge.net/default.aspx/Federal1/LodgeHistory.html, acc 20 Oct 2010.

[vi] For Grand Lodge membership figures through the years see not only its *Proceedings*, but Paul Bessel, "District of Columbia Grand Lodge Statistics", http://bessel.org/dcstats.htm ac. 4 Jan 2011.

[vii] "... Who were the men involved? Men named Washington, Jefferson, Franklin—Freemasons all! Today, the King of France is in prison, his crown about to roll

R

along with his head. Who are the men behind it? Lafayette, Condorcet, Danton, Desmoulins, Brissot, Sieyès, and the king's own brothers, including the Duc d'Orleans— Freemasons all." Katherine Neville, The Eight, Ballantine Books, New York, 1988, 115.

[viii] See "Washington Bible", http://www. masonicinfo. com/washington_bible.htm ac.23 Feb 2011.

[ix] "Through ritual, people develop their ideas about what are appropriate institutions, what are appropriate qualities in political leaders, and how well the world around them measures up to these standards." David I. Kertzer, Ritual, Politics, and Power, Yale University Press, New Haven and London, 1988, 78-79.

[x] "It is said that existing examples of government did not meet the aspirations of the Founding Fathers and that they may have looked to Freemasonry for inspiration. It would, however, be going too far to say that the American system of government replicated the Masonic system." Robert L.D. Cooper, *Cracking the Freemasons Code: The Truth About Solomon's Key and the Brotherhood*, Atria Books, New York, 2006, 192.

[xi] While a majority believe that Morgan was killed by Masons, the evidence is not entirely conclusive, and there remain at the very least, "...two conflicting explanations of the fate of William Morgan; the one, that under pressure, he consented to leave the country and with five hundred dollars in his pocket, deserted his family, yielded to his new sense of freedom, probably shipped in the crew of some vessel at Montreal, travelled from shore to shore until his end came. The other, that he was brutally murdered; his weighed body thrown into the Niagara River..." John C.

Palmer, "The Morgan Affair and Anti-Masonry", *Little Masonic Library*, Book II, Macoy Publishing & Masonic Supply Co., Richmond (Virginia), 1946, 180. Cf. Mitch Horowitz, Occult America, Bantam Books 2009, 27-29. Thomas Sherrard Roy, *Stalwart Builders: The Grand Lodge of Masons in Massachusetts, 1733-1970*, The Masonic Education and Charity Trust, Boston (Massachsuetts), 1971, 121-125.

[xii] Arturo de Hoyos, *Light on Masonry: The History and Rituals of America's Most Important Masonic Expose*, Scottish Rite Research Society, Washington, D.C., 2008, 36.

[xiii] *Nile's Weekly Register*, 20 October 1827, Baltimore, 115.

[xiv] Numerous original documents are made available in Stephen Dafoe, *Morgan: The Scandal that Shook Freemasonry*, Cornerstone Book Publishers, New Orleans, 2009.

[xv] C.E. Putnam, *Secret Fraternal Societies and Unitarianism: Can a True Christian Belong to Such and Still Honor Christ*, The Bible Institute Colportage Ass'n, Chicago,. 1927, esp. 16-17.

[xvi] Johann N. Neem, *Creating a Nation of Joiners*, Harvard University Press, Cambridge (Massachusetts), 2008, 110.

[xvii] David Brion Davis, ""Some Themes of Counter-Subversion: An Analysis of Anti-Masonic, Anti-Catholic, and Anti-Mormon Literature", *The Missouri Valley Historical Review*, Vol.42 No.2, Sept. 1960, reptd. William D. Moore and Mark A. Tabbert, *Secret Societies in America:*

T

Foundational Studies of Fraternalism, Cornerstone Book Publishers, New Orleans, 2011, 98-118.

[xviii] For a suggestion of these complexities, Terry L. Givens, *By the Hand of Mormon*, Oxford University Press, New York, 2002, 164.

[xix] For the lack of cross-cultural understanding of the French Enlightenment, Henry Vyverberg, *Human Nature, Cultural Diversity, and the French Enlightenment*, Oxford University Press, New York and Oxford, 1989, 205-206.

[xx] See Melissa Dawn Bruzas, "The New Anti-Masonic Movement in America", *Heredom*, Vol.16 2008, 59 ff.

[xxi] See John Robinson, *Proofs of A Conspiracy Against all the Religions and Governments of Europe, carried on in the secret meetings of Free Masons, Illuminati and Reading Societies, Collected from Good Authorities*, Facsimile Reproduction of the Third Edition 1798, Vol. 40, Masonic Book Club, Bloomington (Illinois), 2009.

[xxii] See Mervin B. Hogan, *Mormonism and Freemasonry*, Macoy Publishing, Richmond (Virginia), 1977, 267-68.

[xxiii] Neem, *Creating a Nation of Joiners*, 109-10.

[xxiv] The confrontation between orthodox religion and the Enlightenment predates the struggle over the role of Masonry in American society. See Robert W. Galvin, *America's Founding Secret*, Rowman & Littlefield, Lanham (Maryland), 2002, 78.

[xxv] J.M. Roberts, *The Mythology of the Secret Societies*, Watkins Publishing, London, 208 (1972), 29.

U

[xxvi] Barbara Karg and John K. Young, *101 Things You Don't Know About the Freemasons*, Adams, Avon (Massachusetts), 2007, 225.

[xxvii] Christopher Knight and Alan Butler, *Solomon's Brokers: The Secrets of Freemasonry, The Church, and The Illuminati*, Watkins Publishing, London, 2007, 269.

[xxviii] Cf. Lloyd Kramer, *Lafayette in Two Worlds: Public Cultures & Personal Identities in an Age of Revolutions*, The University of North Carolina Press, Chapel Hill and London, 1996, 189.

[xxix] Mark A. Tabbert, *American Freemasonry: Three Centuries of Building Communities*, New York University Press, New York and London, 2005, 57.

[xxx] William Moseley Brown, *Freemasonry in Virginia (1733-1936)*, Masonic Home Press, Richmond, 1936, 104-105.

[xxxi] Roy, *Stalwart Builders*, 149.

[xxxii] Joel H. Silbery, *The American Political Nation*, Stanford University Press, Stanford (California), 1991, 18.

[xxxiii] Marie Roberts, *British Poets and Secret Societies*, Barnes & Noble Books, Totowa (New Jersey), 1986, 2.

[xxxiv] Arthur M. Schlesinger, "Biography of a Nation of Joiners", *American Historical Review*, Vol.50, October 1944, reptd. Moore and Tabbert, *Secret Societies in America*, 82.

[xxxvi] Qtd, H. Paul Jeffers, *Inside the World's Oldest Secret Society*, Citadel Press, New York, 2005, 87.

[xxxvii] See Geo., D. Rait, *Masonic History of Unaddilla*, RGS Publishing, Bainbridge (New York), 1995, 9-11.

[xxxviii] Anti-Masonry reflected "...a strong reactionary spirit which was almost fanatical in its hatred of the new French ideas and of Unitarianism and freethought in general. " Charles McCarthy, *The Antimasonic Party*, Bibliolife, LaVergne (Tennessee), 2010 (1901), 537-538.

[xxxix] Translations and bibliography of Lessing's *Conversations* appear comprehensively in Robin L. Carr, *Lessing's Masonic Dialogues*, The Masonic Book Club, Bloomington (Illinois), 1991. See p.159.

[xl] Jeffrey Croteau, From Blind Man's Bluff to the Poor Blind Candidate: David Claypoole Johnston's Anti-Masonic Woodcuts for New England Almanacs, 2010 Conference: "History Prints: Facts and Fiction", The *American Antiquarian Society*, November 12-13, 210, Worcester, Massachusetts, 5.

[xli] *New England Anti-Masonic Almanac for the Year of Our Lord 1833*, William Southier Proprietor, Boston, 38. For an extensive analysis of D.C. Johnston's Anti-Masonic Illustrations and a profound discussion of the illustrations included on the New England Anti-Masonic Almanac, see, Jeffrey Croteau, 6-11.

[xlii] The various social movements of the time were linked and possibly reinforced each other.Morgan's widow, Lucinda, became one of the wives of Joseph Smith, the prophet of Mormonism, who introduced Masonic rites

to the new religion. See Mitch Horowitz, *Occult America*, Bantam Books, 2009, 27-28.

[xliii] "Antimasons were not able to translate their activities into a political program or transform public opinion into durable political support. Defining Masonry as the single source of society's ills, they had a single, dubious, and uncompromising objective". Dorothy Ann Lipson, *Freemasonry in Federalist Connecticut*, 1789-1835, Princeton University Press, 1977, 313.

[xliv] See Grand Lodge of District of Columbia *Proceedings*, passim.

[xlv] Paul D. Dolinksy, "The Cornerstone of the Nation", *Scottish Rite Journal*, July-August 2005, http://204.3.136.66/web/journal-files/Issues/jul-aug05/dolinsky.html, ac. 19 Dec 2011.

[xlvi] A Robert Mills was initiated 12 June 1815 in Cassia Lodge No.45, Grand Lodge of Maryland. He was passed on 19 August 1816 and raised on 1 January 1821. See Eric A. Meace, "Of Heroes, Masons, Trowels and Jewels" http://www.scgrandlodgeafm.org/History/LafayetteTrowel.htm, ac. 20 October 2010. Amicable Lodge No. 25 A.F. & A.M. was chartered by the Grand Lodge of Maryland on June 21, 1797. On March 1, 2001 Cassia Lodge No. 45, chartered May 6, 1811 Merged with Amicable Lodge No.25. On November 5, 2002, Centre Lodge No. 108 Chartered May 8, 1859 Merged with Amicable Lodge No. 25. On December 1, 2006, St.John's Lodge No.34 chartered September 8, 1802, merged with Amicable Lodge No.25, and the name of the lodge was changed to Amicable-St John's Lodge No. 25 A.F. & A.M.

[xlvii] Qtd. David Messimer, "Masonic Stones Within the Washington Monument", www.tuckahoe lodge347.org/ wp.../201002%20Masonic%20Stones.pdf, ac.7 Mar 2011. *Site includes excellent colored pictures of Masonic stones in the Monument.*

[xlviii] A good account of the ceremonies is still Frederick Loviad Harvey, *History of the Washington National Monument and of the Washington National Monument Association*, Norman T. Elliott Printing Co, Washington, 1902. In 1998, the Grand Lodge, presided over by Most Worshipful Eldon J. Brown, Grand Master, commemorated the 150th anniversary of this ceremony.

z

LETTERS

AND

OPINIONS

OF THE

MASONIC INSTITUTION.

BY JOHN Q. ADAMS.

PUBLISHED
BY LORENZO STRATTON,
131 MAIN STREET, CINCINNATI.
1851.

PREFACE.

It is now twenty years since there sprung up in the United States an earnest and at times a vehement discussion, of the nature and effect of the bond entered into by those citizens who join the Society of Free and Accepted Masons. The excitement which arose in consequence of the disclosures then made, had the effect, at least for a time, if not permanently, to check the further spread of that association. The legislative power of some of the States was invoked, and at last actually interposed, to prevent the administration of extra-judicial oaths, including of course all such as were constantly taken in the Masonic Order. This was the furtherest point which the opposition ever reached. It did not succeed in procuring the dissolution of the organization of the Order, or even the repeal of the charters under which it had a recognized existence in the social system. From the moment of the adoption of a penal law, deemed strong enough to meet the most serious of the evils complained of, the apprehension of further danger from Masonry began to subside. At this day, the subject has ceased to be talked of. The attention of men has been gradually diverted to other things, until at last it may be said, that few persons are aware of the fact, provided it be not especially forced upon their notice, that not only Freemasonry continues to exist, but also that

other associations partaking of its secret nature, if not of
its unjustifiable obligations, not merely live, but greatly
flourish in the midst of them.

Fully aware of this state of things, a few private citizens who deeply interested themselves in the investigation
of the subject when first agitated, yet feel as if their duty
was not entirely performed so long as they shall have left
undone any act which in their estimation may have the
effect of keeping up among their countrymen a vigilant
observation of the nature and tendency of secret associations. Without cherishing the remotest desire, even if
they could be supposed to entertain the expectation, of
reviving an old excitement, they are nevertheless most
anxious to put in a permanently accessible shape, some
clear and strong exposition of the evil attending similar
ties, as that evil was illustrated years ago in an examination of the Freemason's oath. Such an exposition they
knew could be found in the writings of the Honorable
John Quincy Adams. But although the various papers in
which it was first issued to the public enjoyed an extensive
circulation at the period when it was written, and without
doubt contributed much to the establishment of an im-
proved state of popular opinion, they are believed never to
have been collected together in any one form readily open
to the public examination. This great deficiency, it seemed
to the gentlemen who have been already alluded to, a
desirable object to supply. They accordingly undertook
the task of publishing the present volume, not as a matter
of sale, but solely with the intention of gratuitous distri-
bution. And first of all, they deemed it no more than
proper to communicate with Mr. Adams himself, and to
get his opinion upon the subject. That gentleman very
cheerfully consented to aid the effort, not only by supplying some entirely new documents, which have never

before been printed, but also by promising a recapitulation of his views in the shape of an Introductory Essay. The execution of this last engagement has, however, been prevented by the late much regretted illness which has befallen him. The task of preparing a Preface has, by this unexpected event, been made to fall into other hands, by which it must be fulfilled in a far less comprehensive and satisfactory manner than it would have been by him.

The Institution of Masonry was introduced into the British Colonies of North America more than a hundred years ago. It went on slowly at first, but from the time of the Revolution it spread more rapidly, until in the first quarter of the present century it had succeeded in winding itself through all the departments of the body politic in the United States, and in claiming the sanction of many of the country's most distinguished men. Up to the year 1826, nothing occurred to mar its progress, or to interpose the smallest obstacle to its triumphant success. So great had then become the confidence of the members in its power, as to prompt the loud tone of gratulation in which some of its orators then indulged at their public festivals, and among these none spoke more boldly than Mr. Brainard, in the passage which will be found quoted in the present volume.* He announced that Masonry was exercising its influence in the sacred desk, in the legislative hall, and on the bench of justice; but so little had the public attention been directed to the truth he uttered, that the declaration passed off, and was set down by the uninitiated rather as a flower of rhetoric with which young speakers will sometimes magnify their topic, than as entitled to any particularly serious notice. Neither would these memorable words have been rescued from oblivion, if it had not happened that the very next year after they were uttered

* Page 268.

was destined to furnish a most extraordinary illustration of their significance.

In a small town situated in the western part of the State of New York, an event occurred in the autumn of the year 1826, which roused the suspicions first of the people living in the immediate neighborhood, and afterwards of a very wide circle of persons throughout the United States. A citizen of Batavia suddenly disappeared from his family, without giving the slightest warning. Rumors were immediately circulated that he had run away; but there were circumstances attending the act which favored the idea that personal violence had been resorted to, although the precise authors of it could not be distinctly traced. The name of the citizen who thus vanished as if the earth had opened and swallowed him from sight, was William Morgan. He had been a man of little consideration in the place, in which he had been but a short time resident. Without wealth, for he was compelled to labor for the support of a young wife and two infant children, and without influence of any kind, it seemed as if there could be nothing in the history or the pursuits of the individual to make him a shining mark of persecution, on any account. So unreasonable, if not absurd, did the notion of the forcible abduction of such a man appear, that it was at first met with a cold smile of utter incredulity. Among the floating population of a newly settled country, the single fact of the departure of persons having few ties to bind them to any particular spot, would scarcely cause remark or lead to inquiry. Numbers, when first called to express an opinion in the case of Morgan, at once jumped to the conclusion that he had voluntarily fled to parts unknown. So natural was the inference that even to this day, many who have never taken any trouble to look into the evidence, are impressed with a vague notion that it is

the proper solution of the difficulty. In ordinary circumstances the thing might have passed off as a nine days'
wonder, and in a month's time the name of Morgan might
have been forgotten in Batavia, had it not been for a single
clue which was left behind him, and which, at first followed
up from curiosity, soon excited wonder, and from this led to
astonishment at the nature of the discoveries that ensued.

The single clue which ultimately unwound the tangled
skein of evidence was this. The sole act of Morgan, whilst
dwelling in Batavia, which formed any exception to the
ordinary habits of men in his walk of life, was an undertaking into which he entered, in partnership with another
person, to print and publish a book. This book promised
to contain a true account of certain ceremonies and secret
obligations taken by those who joined the Society of Freemasons. The simple announcement of the intention to
print this work was known to have been received by many
of the persons in the vicinity, acknowledged brethren of
the Order, with signs of the most lively indignation. And
as the thing went on to execution, so many efforts were
made to interrupt and to prevent it, even at the hazard of
much violence, that soon after the disappearance of the
prime mover of the plan, doubts began to spread in the
community, whether there was not some connection, in the
way of cause and effect, between the proposed publication
and that event. Circumstances rapidly confirmed suspicion into belief, and belief into certainty. At first the
attention was concentrated upon the individuals of the
fraternity discovered to have been concerned in the taking
off. It afterward spread itself so far as to embrace the
action of the Lodges of the region in which the deed was
done. But such was the amount of resistance experienced
to efforts made to ferret out the perpetrators and bring them
to justice, that ultimately the whole organization of the

Order became involved in responsibility for the misdeeds
of its members. The opposition made to investigation
only stimulated the passion to investigate. Unexampled
efforts were made to enlist the whole power of the social
system in the pursuit of the kidnappers, which were as
steadily baffled by the superior activity of the Masonic
power. In time, it became plain, that the only effectual
course would be, to go if possible to the root of the evil, and
to attack Masonry in its very citadel of secret obligations.

The labor expended in the endeavor to suppress the
publication of Morgan's book, proved to have been lost.
It came out just at the moment when the disappearance of
its author was most calculated to rouse the public curiosity
to its contents. On examination, it was found to contain
what purported to be the forms of Oaths taken by those who
were admitted to the first three degrees of Masonry—the
Entered Apprentice's, the Fellow Craft's, and the Master
Mason's. If they really were what they pretended to be,
then indeed was supplied a full explanation of the motives
that might have led to Morgan's disappearance. But here
was the first difficulty. Doubts were sedulously spread
of their genuineness. Morgan's want of social character
was used with effect to bring the whole volume into discredit. Neither is it perfectly certain that its revelations
would have been ultimately established as true, had not a
considerable number of the fraternity, stimulated by the
consciousness of the error which they had committed,
voluntarily assembled at Leroy, a town in the neighborhood of Batavia, and then and there, besides attesting the
veracity of Morgan's book, renounced all further connection with the Society. One or two of these persons subsequently made far more extended publications, in which
they opened all the mysteries of the Royal Arch, and of
the Knight Templar's libation, besides exposing in a clear

light the whole complicated organization of the Institution. Upon these disclosures the popular excitement spread over a large part of the northern section of the Union. It crept into the political divisions of the time. A party sprung up almost with the celerity of magic, the end of whose exertions was to be the overthrow of Masonry. It soon carried before it all the power of western New York. It spread into the neighboring States. It made its appearance in legislative assemblies, and there demanded full and earnest investigations, not merely of the circumstances attending the event which originated the excitement, but also of the nature of the obligations which Masons had been in the habit of assuming. Great as the effort to resist this movement, and manifold the devices to escape the searching operation proposed, it was found impossible directly to stem the tide of popular opinion. Masons, who stubbornly adhered to the Order, were yet compelled under oath to give their reluctant testimony to the truth of the disclosures that had been made. The oaths of Masonry and the strange rites practiced simultaneously with the assumption of them, were then found to be in substance what they had been affirmed to be. The vail that hid the mystery was rent in twain, and there stood the idol before the gaze of the multitude, in all the nakedness of its natural deformity.

Strange though it may seem, it is nevertheless equally certain, that the most revolting features of the obligation, the pledges subversive of all moral distinctions, and the penalties for violating those pledges, were not those things which roused the most general popular disapprobation. Here, as often before, the shield of private character, earned by a life and conversation without reproach, was interposed with effect to screen from censure men who protested that when they swore to keep secret the crimes which their brethren might have committed, provided they were revealed to them under the Masonic sign, they did nothing which they deemed inconsistent with their duties as Christians and as members of society. It is the tendency of mankind to mix with all abstract reasoning, however pure and perfect, a great deal of the alloy of human authority, to harden its nature. Multitudes preferred to believe the Masonic oaths and penalties to be ceremonies, childish, ridiculous and unmeaning, rather than to suppose them intrinsically and incurably vicious. They refused to credit the fact that men whom they respected as citizens could have made themselves parties to any promise whatsoever to do acts illegal, unjust and wicked. Rather than go so far, they preferred to throw themselves into a state of resolute unbelief of all that could be said against them. Hence the extraordinary resistance to all projects of examamination, that great wall of brass which the conservative temper of society erects around acknowledged and time-hallowed abuses. Hence the determination to credit the assurances of interested witnesses, who seemed to have a character for veracity to support, rather than by pressing investigation, to undermine the established edifice constructed by the world's opinion.

Neither is there at bottom any want of good sense in this sluggish mode of viewing all movements of reform. Agitation always portends more or less of risk to society, and tends to bring mere authority into contempt. It is therefore not without reason that those who value the security which they enjoy under existing institutions, hesitate at adopting any rule of conduct which may materially diminish it. Such hesitation is visible under all forms of government, but it is no where more marked than in the United States, where the popular nature of the institutions makes the tendency to change at all times imminent. The misfortune attending this natural and pardonable conservative instinct is, that it clings with indiscriminate tenacity to all that has been long established, the evil as well as the good, the abuses that have crept in equally with the useful and the true. It was just so in the case of Masonry. A large number of the most active and respected members of society had allowed themselves to become involved in its obligations, and rather than voluntarily to confess the error they had committed, and to sanction the overthrow of the Institution by a decided act of surrender, they preferred to support it upon the strength of their present character, and upon the combination of themselves and the friends whom they could influence to resist the assaults of a reforming and purifying power. Great as was the strength of this resistance, it could only partially succeed in accomplishing the object at which it aimed. The opposition made to the admission of a palpable moral truth, had its usual and natural effect to stimulate the efforts of those who were pressing it upon the public attention. Admitting in the fullest extent every thing that could be said in behalf of many of the individuals, who as Masons became subjected to the vehemence of the denunciations directed against the fraternity, it was yet a fact not a little startling, that even they should deem themselves so far bound by unlawful obligations as at no time to be ready to signify the smallest disapprobation of their character, not even after the fact was proved how much of evil they had caused. After the disclosure of the Morgan history, it was no longer possible to pretend that the pledges were not actually construed in the sense which the language plainly conveyed. That after admitting the possibility of such a construction, the association which for one moment longer should give it countenance, made itself responsible for all the crime which might become the fruit of it, cannot be denied.

Yet this reasoning did not appear to have the weight to which it was fairly entitled, in deterring the respectable members of the Society from giving it their aid and countenance. De Witt Clinton still remained Grand Master of the Order after he had reason to know the extent to which it had made itself accessory to the Morgan murder. Edward Livingston was not ashamed publicly to declare his acceptance of the same office, although the chain of evidence which traced that crime to the Masonic oath had then been made completely visible to all. When the authority of such names as these was invoked with success to shelter the association from the effect of its own system, it seemed to become an imperative duty on the part of those whose attention had been aroused to the subject, to look beyond the barrier of authority so sedulously erected in order to keep them out, to probe by a searching analytic process the moral elements upon which the Institution claimed to rest, and to concentrate the rays of truth and right reason upon those corrupt principles, which if not effectively counteracted, seemed to threaten the very foundations of justice in the social and moral system of America.

It was the province here marked out which Mr. Adams voluntarily assumed to fill when he addressed to Colonel William L. Stone that series of letters upon the Entered Apprentice's Oath, which will be found to make a part of the present volume. Although this obligation may be considered as constituting the lowest story and least commanding portion of the edifice of Freemasonry, yet he singled it out for examination as the fairest test by which he could try the merits of all that has been built above it. If that first and simple step proved untenable, it followed as a matter of course, that no later or more difficult one could fare a whit better. Of the result of the investigation thus entered into, it is thought that no difference of opinion can now be entertained. No answer worthy of a moment's consideration was ever made. It is confidently believed that none is possible. As a specimen of rigid moral analysis, the letters must ever remain, not simply as evincing the peculiar powers of the author's mind, but also as a standing testimony against the radical vice of the secret Institution against which they were directed.

When the books of Morgan, and Allyn, and Bernard, the admissions of Colonel Stone and of the Rhode Island legislative investigation, had left little of the mysteries of Freemasonry unseen by the public eye, the impressions derived from observation were curious and contradictory. Upon the first hasty and superficial glance, a feeling might arise of surprise that the frivolity of its unmeaning ceremonial, and the ridiculous substitution of its fictions for the sacred history, should not have long ago discredited the thing in the minds of good and sensible men every where. Yet upon a closer and more attentive examination, this first feeling vanishes, and makes way for astonishment at the ingenious contrivance displayed in the construction of the whole machine. A more perfect agent for the devising and execution of conspiracies against church or state could scarcely have been conceived. At the outer door stands the image of secrecy, stimulating the passion of curiosity. And the world which habitually takes the unknown to be sublime, could scarcely avoid inferring that the untold mysteries which were supposed to have been transmitted undivulged to any external ear, from generation to generation, must have in them some secret of power richly worth the knowing. Here was the temptation to enter the portal. But the unlucky wight, like him of the poet's hell, when once admitted within the door, was doomed at the same moment to leave behind him all hope or expectation of retreat. His mouth was immediately sealed by an obligation of secrecy, imposed with all the solemnity that can be borrowed from the use of the forms of religious worship. Nothing was left undone to magnify the effect of the scene upon his imagination. High sounding titles, strange and startling modes of procedure, terrific pledges and imprecations, and last, though not least, the graduation of orders in an ascending scale, which, like mirrors placed in long vistas, had the effect of expanding the apparent range of vision almost to infinitude, were all combined to rescue from ridicule and contempt the moment of discovery of the insignificant secret actually disclosed. Having thus been tempted by curiosity to advance, and being cut off by fear from retreat, there came last of all the appearance of a sufficient infusion of religious and moral, and benevolent profession to furnish an ostensible cause for the construction of a system so ponderous and complicate. The language of the Old Testament, the history as well as the traditions of the Jews, and the resources of imagination, are indiscriminately drawn upon to deck out a progressive series of initiating ceremonies which would otherwise claim no attribute to save them from contempt. Ashamed and afraid to go backwards, the novice suffers his love of the marvellous, his dread of personal hazard, and his hope for more of the beautiful and the true than has yet been doled out to him, to lead him on until he finds himself crawling under the living arch, or committing the folly of the fifth libation. He then too late discovers himself to have been fitting for the condition either of a dupe or of a conspirator. He has plunged himself needlessly into an abyss of obligations, which, if they signify little, prove him to have been a fool; and if, on the contrary, they signify much, prove him ready, at a moment's warning, to make himself a villain.

Such is the impression of the Masonic Institution that must be gathered from all the expositions that have been lately made. Yet, strange though it may seem, there is no reason to doubt that the Society has had great success in enrolling numbers of persons in many countries among its members, and keeping them generally faithful to the obligations which it imposed. This, if no other fact, would be sufficient to relieve the whole machine from the burden of ridicule it might otherwise be made to bear. Perhaps the strongest feature of the association is to be found in the pledge it imposes of mutual assistance in distress. On this account much merit has been claimed to it, and many stories have been circulated of the benefits which individuals have experienced in war, or in perils by sea and land, or in other disasters, by the ability to resort to the grand hailing sign. This argument, which has probably made more Freemasons than any other, would be good in its defence were it not for two objections. One of them is, that the pledge to assist is indiscriminate, making little or no difference between the good or bad nature of the actions to promote which a co-operation may be invoked. The other is, that the engagement implies a duty of preference of one member of society to the disadvantage of another who may be in all respects his superior. It establishes a standard of merit conflicting with that established by the Christian or the social system, either or both of which ought to be of paramount obligation. And this injurious preference is the more dangerous because it may be carried on without the knowledge of the sufferers. The more scrupulously conscientious a citizen may be, who hesitates at taking an oath the nature of which he does not know beforehand, the more likely will he be to be kept down by the artificial advancement of others who may derive their advantage from a cunning use of their more flexible sense of right. That these are not altogether imaginary objections, there is no small amount of actual evidence to prove. There has been a time, when resort to Masonry was regarded as eminently favorable to early success in life ; and there have been men whose rapidity of personal and political advancement it would be difficult to explain by any other cause than this, that they have been generally understood to be bright Masons. Such a preference as is here supposed, can be justifiable only upon the supposition that Masonic merit and social merit rest on the same general foundation ; — a supposition which no person will be able to entertain for a moment after he shall have observed the scales which belong respectively to each.

Another argument which has been effectively resorted to as an aid to Freemasonry, is drawn from it supposed antiquity. To give color to this notion, a very ingenious use has been made of much of the sacred history; but it appears to have no solid foundation whatsoever. Whatever may have been the nature of the associations of Masons who built the gothic edifices of the middle ages, the investigations entered into by those who opposed speculative Freemasonry sufficiently proved that the latter scarcely dates beyond the early part of the last century. The air of traditionary mystery, like the *arugo* on many a pretended coin, has been artificially added to heighten its value to the curious. Yet such has been its effect, that this cause alone has probably contributed very largely to fill up the ranks of the Society. The rapidity of its growth during the period of its legitimate existence, is one of the most surprising circumstances attending its history. Originating in Great Britain somewhere about the beginning of the eigtheenth century, it soon ramified not only in that country, but into France and Germany ; it spread itself into the colonies of North America, and made its way to the confines of distant Asia. Although the seeds of the Institution were early planted in Boston and Charleston, they did not fructify largely until after the period of the Revolution. The original form of Masonry was comprised in what are now called the first three degrees — the Entered Apprentice, Fellow Craft, and Master — but during the first quarter of the present century, so thoroughly had the basis been laid over the entire surface of the United States, that the degrees have been multiplied more than tenfold, and in all directions the materials have been collected for a secret combination of the most formidable character. It was not until the history of Morgan laid open the consequences of the abuse of the system, that the public began to form a conception of the dangerous fanaticism which it was cherishing in its bosom. Even then, the endeavor to apply effective remedies to the evil was met with the most energetic and concerted resistance, and the result of the struggle was by no means a decided victory to the opponents of the Institution. Freemasonry still lives and moves and has a being, even in New York and Massachusetts. And at the seat of the Federal government, Freemasonry at this moment claims and obtains the privilege of laying the corner-stone of the national institution created upon the endowment of James Smithson, for the purpose of increasing and diffusing knowledge among men.

An obvious danger attending all associations of men connected by secret obligations, springs from their susceptibility to abuse in being converted into engines for the overthrow or the control of established governments. So soon was the apprehension of this excited in Europe by Freemasonry, that many of the absolute monarchies took early measures to guard against its spread within their limits. Rome, Naples, Portugal, Spain, and Russia made participation in it a capital offence. Other governments
2

more cautiously confined themselves to efforts to control it by a rigid system of supervision. In Great Britain, the endeavor of government has been to neutralize its power to harm, by entering into it and by placing trustworthy members of the royal family at its head. Yet even with all these precautions and prohibitions, it is believed that in France at the period of the revolution, and in Italy within the present century, much of the insurrectionary spirit of the time was fostered, if not in Masonic Lodges, at least in associations bearing a close affinity to them in all essential particulars. With regard to the United States, there has thus far in their history been very little to justify any of the most serious objections which may be made against Masonry in connection with political affairs. Yet the events which followed the death of Morgan, first opened the public mind to the idea that already a secret influence pervaded all parts of the body politic, with which it was not very safe for an individual to come into conflict. The boast of Brainard, already alluded to, was now brought to mind. It was found to bias, if not to control, the action of officers of justice of every grade, to affect the policy of legislative bodies, and even to paralyze the energy of the executive head. This power, by gaining a greater appearance of magnitude from the mystery with which it was surrounded, was doubtless much exaggerated by the popular fancy during the period of the Morgan excitement; but after making all proper allowances, it is impossible from a fair survey of the evidence to doubt that it was something real, and that it might, in course of time, have established an undisputed control over the affairs of the Union, had not its progress been somewhat roughly broken by the consequences of the violent movement against Morgan, which had its origin in the precipitate but fanatical energy of one division of the Society. And even since the agitation of xix

that day, there is the best reason for believing that throughout the region most affected by it, an organization was made
up after the fashion of Masonic Lodges, the object of which
was directly to stimulate a concerted insurrection against
the governing power of a neighboring country, Canada,
calculated to give rise to a furious contest with a foreign
nation, and to mature plans by which such an attempt could
be most effectually aided by citizens of the United States
in spite of all the national declarations of neutrality and
in defiance of all the fulminations of government at home.

But at the time of Morgan's mysterious disappearance,
the investigations then pursued, imperfect as they were,
and more than once completely baffled for the moment,
brought forth the names of sixty-nine different individuals,
many of them of great respectability of private character,
who had been directly concerned in the outrages attending
his taking off. These sixty-nine persons were not living
within a confined circle. They had their homes scattered
along an extent of country of at least one hundred miles.
That so many men, at so many separate points, should
have acted in perfect concert in such a business as they
were engaged in, would scarcely be believed without com-
pelling the inference of some distinct understanding existing between them. That they should have carried into
effect the most difficult part of their undertaking, a scheme
of the most daring and criminal nature, in the midst of a
large, intelligent and active population, without thereby
incurring the risk of a full conviction of their guilt and the
consequent punishment, would be equally incredible, but
for the light furnished by the phraseology of the Masonic
oath. The several forms of this oath, as shown to have
been habitually administered in the first three degrees, will
be found in the Appendix to the present volume. These,
together with the ceremony attending the Royal Arch and

the Knight Templar's obligation, have been deemed all of
Masonry that is necessary to illustrate the letters of Mr.
Adams. They are believed sufficient to account for the
successful manner in which Morgan was spirited away.
It is not deemed expedient to dwell here upon their nature,
when it will be found fully analyzed in the body of the
present volume. It is enough to point out the fact that
obedience to the Order is the paramount law of association;
that it makes every social, civil and moral duty a matter
of secondary consideration; that it draws few distinctions
between the character of the acts that may be required to
be done, and that it demands fidelity to guilt just the same
as if it were the purest innocence. Every man who takes
a Masonic oath, forbids himself from divulging any criminal act, unless it might be murder or treason, that may be
communicated to him under the seal of the fraternal bond,
even though such concealment were to prove a burden upon
his conscience and a violation of his bounden duty to society and to his God. The best man in the world, put in
this situation, may be compelled to take his election between perjury on the one side and sympathy with crime
on the other. The worst man in the world, put in this
situation, has it in his power to claim that the best shall
degrade his moral sense down to the level of his own, by
hearing from him, without resentment, revelations to which
even listening may be a participation of dishonor.

The facts attending the abduction of Morgan, not elicited
without the most extraordinary difficulty by subsequent investigation, have been so often published far and wide as to
make it superfluous here to repeat them. It may be enough
to state, that from the day when the partnership between
Morgan and David C. Miller, a printer of Batavia, made for
the purpose of publishing the "Illustrations of Masonry,"
was announced, no form of annoyance which could be

expected to deter them from prosecuting their design, was left unattempted. The precise nature of these forms may be better understood, if we class them under general heads, until they took the ultimate shape of aggravated crime.

1. Anonymous denunciation of the man Morgan, as an impostor, in newspapers published at Canandaigua, Batavia, and Black Rock, places at some distance from each other, but all within the limits of the region in which the subsequent acts of violence were committed.

2. Abuse of the forms of law, by the hunting up of small debts or civil offences with which to carry on vexatious suits or prosecutions against the two persons heretofore named.

3. The introduction of a spy into their counsels, and of a traitor to their confidence, employed for the purpose of betraying the manuscripts of the proposed work to the Masonic Lodges, and thus of frustrating the entire scheme.

4. Attempts to surprise the printing office by a concerted night attack of men gathered from various points, assembling at a specific rendezvous, the abode of a high member of the Order, and proceeding in order to the execution of the object, which was the forcible seizure of the manuscripts and the destruction of the press used to print them.

5. Efforts to get possession of the persons of the two offenders, by a resort to the processes of law, through the connivance and co-operation of officers of justice, themselves Masons. These efforts failed in the case of Miller, but they succeeded against Morgan, and were the means by which all the subsequent movements were carried into execution.

6. The employment of an agent secretly to prepare materials for the combustion of the building which contained the printing materials known to be employed in the publication of the book and to set them on fire.

Such were the proceedings which were resorted to at the very onset of this conspiracy, and upon looking at them, it will be seen at a glance that the prosecution of them involved the commission of a variety of moral and social offences, the commission of which *may be fairly included within the literal injunction of the Masonic oath.* Had the matter stopped here, it would have furnished abundance of evidence to establish the dangerous character of a secret Institution, when its interests are deemed to conflict with those of individual citizens or of society at large. But what has thus far been compressed in the six preceding heads, appears as nothing when compared with the startling developments of the remainder of the story.

On Sunday, of all the days in the week, the tenth of September, 1826, the coroner of the county of Ontario, himself Master of the Lodge at Canandaigua, applied to a Masonic justice of the peace of that town for a warrant to apprehend William Morgan, living fifty miles off at Batavia. The offence upon which the application was based was larceny, and the alleged larceny consisted in the neglect of Morgan to return a shirt and cravat that had been borrowed by him in the previous month of May. Armed with this implement of justice, which assumes in this connection the semblance of a dagger rather than of its ordinary attribute a sword, the coroner immediately proceeded in a carriage obtained at the public cost, to pick up at different stations along the road of fifty miles, ten Masonic brethren, including a constable, anxious and willing to share in avenging the insulted majesty of the law. At the tavern of James Ganson, six miles from Batavia, the same place which had been the head-quarters of the night expedition against Miller's printing office, the party stopped for the night. Had that expedition proved successful, it is very probable that this one would have been abandoned. As it was, the failure acted as a stimulus to its further prosecution. Early next morning, five of the Masonic beagles, headed by the Masonic constable, having previously procured a necessary endorsement of their writ to give it effect in the county of Genesee, from a Masonic justice of the peace, proceeded from Ganson's house to Batavia, where they succeeded in seizing and securing the man guilty of the alleged enormity touching the borrowed shirt and cravat. A coach was again employed, the Masonic party lost no time in securing their prey, and at about sunset of the same day with the arrest, that is, Monday, the eleventh day of September, they got back to Canandaigua. The prisoner was immediately taken before the justice who had issued the warrant, the futility of the complaint was established, and Morgan was forthwith discharged. The case affords a striking illustration of the abuse of the remedial process of the law to the more secure commission of an offence against law. Morgan was free, it is true, but he was at a distance of fifty miles from home, alone, and without friends, brought through the country with the stigma resulting from the suspicion of a criminal offence attached to him, and all without expense to the parties engaged in the undertaking, as well as without the smallest hazard of a rescue.

It turned out that the person of whom the shirt and cravat had been originally borrowed, had never sought to instigate a prosecution for the offence. The idea originated in the mind of the Masonic coroner himself. He had executed the plan of using the law to punish an offence of Masonry, to the extent to which it had now been carried. Morgan had been brought within the coil of the serpent, but he was not yet entirely at its mercy. Another abuse of legal forms yet remained to complete the operation. No sooner was the victim landed upon the pavement, exonerated from the charge of being a thief, than he found the same Masonic Grand Master and coroner tapping him on the shoulder, armed with a writ for a debt of two dollars to a tavern keeper of Canandaigua. Resistance was useless. Morgan had neither money nor credit, and for the want of them he was taken to the county jail. The common property and the remedial process of the State was thus once more employed to subserve the vindictive purposes of a secret society.

Twenty-four hours were suffered to pass, whilst the necessary arrangements were maturing to complete the remainder of the terrible drama. On the evening of the succeeding day, being the twelfth of September, the same Grand Master coroner once more made his appearance at the prison. After some little negotiation, Morgan is once more released, by the payment of the debt for which he had been taken. But he is not free. No sooner is he treading the soil of freedom, and perchance dreaming of escaping from all these annoyances, than upon a given signal, a yellow carriage and grey horses are seen by the bright moonlight rolling with extraordinary rapidity toward the jail. A few minutes pass, Morgan has been seized and gagged and bound and thrown into the carriage, which is now seen well filled with men, rolling as rapidly as before, but in a contrary direction. Morgan is now completely in the power of his enemies. The veil of law is now removed. All that remains to be done is to use the arm of flesh. Morgan is now taking his last look of the town of Canandaigua.

It is a fact, that this carriage moved along, night and day, over a hundred miles of well settled country, with fresh horses to draw it supplied at six different places, and with corresponding changes of men to carry on the enterprise, and not the smallest let or impediment was experienced. With but a single exception, every individual concerned in it was a Freemason, bound by the secret tie;

and the exception was immediately initiated by a unanimous vote of the Lodge at Lewiston. It afterwards appeared in evidence, that the Lodge at Buffalo had been called to deliberate upon it, and moreover that the Lodges at Le Roy, Bethany, Covington, and Lockport, as well as the Chapter at Rochester, had all of them consulted upon it. There is no other way to account for the preparation made along the line of the road travelled by the party. Nowhere was there delay, or hesitation, or explanation, or discussion. Every thing went on like clock-work, up to the hour of the evening of the fourteenth of September, when the prisoner was taken from the carriage at Fort Niagara, an unoccupied military post near the mouth of the river of that name, and lodged in the place originally designed for a powder magazine, when the position had been occupied by the troops of the United States. The jurisdiction was now changed from that of the State to that of the federal government, but the power that held the man was one and the same. It was Masonry that opened the gates of the Fort, by controlling the will of the brother who for the time had it intrusted to his charge.

On this same evening, there was appointed to take place at the neighboring town of Lewiston, an installation of a Chapter misnamed Benevolent, at which the arch-conspirator was to be made Grand High Priest, and an opportunity was given to all associates from distant points to come together, and to consult upon what it was best to do next. Here it is, that in spite of the untiring labors of an investigating committee organized for the purpose, and in spite of the entire application of the force of the courts of the country to the eliciting of the truth, the details of the affair which thus far have been clearly exposed, begin to grow dim and shadowy. There is reason to believe that Morgan was carried across the river in a boat at night, and placed at the disposal of a Canadian Lodge at Newark The scruples of one or two brethren, who hesitated at the idea of murder, brought on a refusal to assume the trust. Consultations on this side of the river followed, and messengers were despatched to Rochester for advice. The final determination was, that Morgan must die, to pay the penalty of his violated oath. After this, every thing attending the catastrophe becomes more and more uncertain. It is affirmed that eight Masons met and threw into a hat as many lots, three of which only were marked. Each man then drew a lot, and where it was not a marked lot, he went immediately home. There is reason to believe that the three who remained, were the persons who, on the night of the 19th or 20th of September, took their victim from the fort, where he had been kept for sacrifice, carried him in a boat to the middle of the stream, and, having fastened upon him a heavy weight, precipitated him into eternity.

Such is a condensed statement of this eventful history — a history which in many of its details will vie in interest with any narrative of romance. That such a tragedy *could* be executed in the United States, a country fortified as the people fondly imagine by all known securities to life and liberty; that it could be carried on through a period of ten days, in a populous Christian community, without thought of rescue; that it could enlist as actors so large a number of citizens of good repute, in so many different quarters, as were members of the various Lodges privy to the transaction; and finally, that it could secure the co-operation of the chosen ministers of justice, and even of some set apart to the service of the Deity, one of whom could be found bold enough to invoke the blessing of God upon the contemplated violation of his most solemn law; that it could involve all these possibilities,

was a thing well calculated to rouse the human mind to a
high pitch of wonder, until the problem found its natural
solution in the disclosure of the Masonic oath. Construed
as this obligation was construed, by the members of the
order in western New York, all cause of surprise at the
consequences instantly disappears.

Yet, strange as is this narrative, fearful as is the disclosure of the fanaticism of secret association which could
impel men — holding a respectable rank in society, walk-
ing by the light of modern civilization, acknowledging
the influence of Chistianity over their daily life — to the
commission of outrages so flagrant as were the abduction
and murder of William Morgan, it would not of itself have
sufficed to justify attaching even a suspicion to the entire
Institution of Freemasonry in the United States, or even
to any considerable branch of it existing without the
limits of the region where the events happened. Whatever
might have been the private sentiments entertained of the
danger attending the assumption of secret obligations, the
exact nature of these was at the outset too little understood to sanction the inference that they allowed criminal
enterprises. Extensive as the conspiracy against Morgan
and Miller appeared to be, yet similar things have been
done under the influence of passion, and in open and acknowledged violation of moral and religious duty, in all
stages of the world's progress. It was hence no unreasonable thing to conclude that it might have happened once
more. Censure was to be directed, if anywhere, against
those over-zealous members of the Order who could be
believed to have overstepped the bounds of reason and of
justice, acknowledged as well by the law of the fraternity
as by the higher one of God and of civil society. It was
reserved for events coming somewhat later, to develope
the fact, that in the instance of Morgan, Freemasons, so

far from thinking themselves to be violating, were literally following the injunction which they felt to be laid upon them in their oaths. The law of Masonry was to them more than that of civil government or of the Deity, even when it was known directly to conflict with them. It was the truth of this proposition, slowly and gradually wrested from the lips of adhering members, that turned the current of popular indignation from the guilty individuals towards the Institution itself. It was the proof furnished of this truth, which created the moral power of the political party that soon sprung up in New York and Pennsylvania, and that under the banner of opposition to all secret societies, rallied its tens of thousands in a fierce and vindictive, and at times, even a fanatical persecution of every thing that bore even the semblance of dreaded Freemasonry.

It would be tedious to recapitulate all the particulars of the evidence which ultimately fastened upon the public mind a conviction of the reality of the proposition above named. It may be sufficient to state the manner in which the powerful efforts made to discover the guilty parties and to bring them to justice, were perpetually baffled. The first and most natural impulse operating upon those who united in an endeavor to maintain the law, was to look to the Chief Executive Magistrate of New York for energetic support. The person who held that office at the moment, was a no less distinguished man than the celebrated De Witt Clinton. But he was at the same time a Freemason, and what is more, he was High Priest of the General Grand Chapter of the United States, in other words, the highest officer of the Order. The fact was known throughout the region of western New York, and was unquestionably relied upon as a protection from danger by those who were concerned in the deeds of violence. Indeed it afterwards came out, that what purported to be a letter from him was freely used for the purpose of instigating tne members of the Order to prosecute their schemes. There are many living who yet suspect that the letter was actually genuine; but that suspicion is believed to be unjust to the memory of the late Governor Clinton, who did what he could, as soon as he became apprized of the character of the offence, to bring the guilty to punishment. The fact, however, furnishes an instructive illustration of the great danger attending the existence of secret ties, which may even be suspected to conflict in the mind of a high officer of state with the performance of his public duties. The moral influence of his situation was thus wholly lost upon men who believed, that whatever he might say in public to the contrary, his sympathies were all with them; who supposed that his private obligations to conceal and never to reveal the secrets of his brother Masons, as well as to aid and assist in extricating them from any difficulty in which they might become involved, might be depended upon, at least so far as to shelter them from the legal consequences of their own misdeeds, within the sphere of the Executive influence. Was this an inference wholly unwarranted from the language of the Masonic oath? Let any impartial individual examine its nature, and answer affirmatively if he can. Doubtless De Witt Clinton was wholly innocent of guilt, but his situation was not the less clearly one of conflict between his Masonic and his social and religious duty. Although he may have escaped contamination, another and weaker individual might have made himself accessory to the crime. At all events, it must be conceded, that the situation in which he was thrown, was one not unnaturally the consequence of his assumption of conflicting obligations, and one in which no high civil officer under any government should ever be suffered to stand.

The second manifestation of the force of the Masonic obligation was made visible in the courts of justice, which are established to try persons charged with the commission of offences against human life or liberty. The sheriffs, whose duty it was under the laws of New York to select and summon the grand juries, were, in all the counties in which the deeds of violence against Morgan had been committed, Freemasons. Several of them had themselves been parties to the crime. They did not hesitate to make use of their power as officers of justice to screen the criminals from conviction. The jurors whom they summoned were most of them Masons, some of them participators in the offences into which it became their civil duty to inquire. The consequence may readily be imagined. Money, time and talent were expended in profusion, for the purpose of bringing the perpetrators of the crime complained of to condign punishment; but almost in vain. Some of the suspected persons were found and put upon their trial; but the secret obligation prevailed in the jury box, and uniformly rescued them in the moment of their utmost need. Others vanished from the scene, and eluded pursuit even to the farthest limits of the United States. One man, and probably the most guilty, was tracked to the bosom of a Lodge in the city of New York, by the members of which he was secreted, put on board of a vessel below the harbor, and despatched to a foreign land. Five years were consumed in unavailing efforts to obtain a legal conviction of the various offenders. Nothing that deserves the name of a true verdict followed. Such a history of deeply studied, skilfully combined and successfully executed movements to set at nought the lawfully constituted tribunals of justice, has at no other time been made evident in America. Important witnesses were carried off at the moment when their evidence was indispensable, and placed beyond the jurisdiction of the State; or if present and interrogated, they stood doggedly mute; or else they placed themselves entirely under the guidance of legal advisers employed to protect them from criminating themselves. It was made plain to the most ordinary capacity that the Order was assuming the responsibility of the crime of some of its members. It was exerting itself to throw over the guilty, the protecting garb of the innocent. The obligation of Freemasonry was then the law paramount, and the social system sunk into nothing by the side of it. Even distant Lodges responded favorably to the call made upon them to aid in the defence of the endangered brethren, by actually voting and forwarding sums of money for their relief. And the brief and insignificant period of imprisonment which two or three of them paid as a penalty for comparatively light offences, was spent by them in receiving the sympathy of a martyr's fate. The end of all was, that for the first time Masonry enjoyed its complete triumph. The men who actually participated in the murder have gradually dropped off, until it may be said that not a single individual remains within the United States. But they lived and died secure from every danger of legal punishment. The oath of Masonry came in conflict with the duty to society and to God, and succeeded in setting it aside.

The ends of justice were defeated; but the labors of those indefatigable persons who had striven day and night to promote them, were not altogether thrown away. The materials were collected to show to the world the chain of connection woven by the Masonic obligations between the subordinate Lodges of western New York and the higher authorities in the East. The popular attention was turned to every Masonic movement — not solely in the State in which had been the cause of offence, but in all of the neighboring States. Extraordinary powers to pursue the investigations to its source were demanded of various legislative bodies, and the treatment of these applications elicited the fact that Freemasonry exercised a power almost as great in the deliberative assemblies as in the executive council chamber, or in the jury box of the courts. The opposition to Masonry became gradually more and more intensely political, and in the process took up an aspect of extreme and illiberal vindictiveness towards all who ventured to stay its progress. The other parties were compelled to bend to the force of the blast that was sweeping over them. The revelations made by Morgan, in the book which cost him his life, though at first called an imposture, proved on examination to be strictly true. But they embraced only the first three degrees of Masonry. Other persons, disgusted and indignant at the proceedings of their adhering brethren after the fate of Morgan was known to them, voluntarily came forward and supplied all the remaining forms used in America, and many of those which had been adopted in Europe. A considerable number openly and voluntarily seceded from the Order. A meeting of such persons held at Le Roy, ended, as has been already stated, in a formal renunciation by them of all their obligations. Here and there in other States the example was followed by a few. There were more who silently seceded, having made up their minds never again to visit a Lodge. Yet in spite of all this, in spite of the earnest exhortation addressed to his brethren by Colonel W. L. Stone, in a book written by him to prevail upon them to dissolve the Lodges and Chapters and to abandon Masonry altogether, it must be admitted that the great majority of the Society remained equally unmoved by denunciation, flattery or prayer. Some had the assurance publicly to deny the truth of all the allegations made against

Masonry, and further to affirm that they had never taken
obligations as Masons not compatible with their duties as
citizens. Others — and the most important of these was
Edward Livingston, then uniting with the possession of one
of the chief posts of responsibility in the general government, that of the highest dignity in the Masonic hierarchy,
made vacant by the death of Clinton — deemed it the part
of wisdom to remain sullenly dumb, abstaining from all
controversy, and suffering the excitement against Masons
to blow over and spend itself in vain. In this spirit Mr.
Livingston proceeded to deliver what he called an Address
to the General Grand Royal Arch Chapter of the United
States, upon the occasion of his installation as General
Grand High Priest. He recommended that all attacks
made upon the Order to which they belonged should be
met with dignified silence; as if dignified silence were not
equally a resource for the most atrocious criminal and for
the most unspotted citizen. The charge as against Mr.
Livingston was surely worthy of some little consideration
when connected with the evidence already laid before the
public to sustain it. It was neither more nor less than
this, that he, being Secretary of State of the United States,
one of the confidential advisers of the President, and moreover the reputed author of a strong proclamation issued by
the chief magistrate against those in danger of falling into
treasonable practices by their connection with South Carolina nullification, was yet himself under secret obligations
which required him to conceal the evidence of all the offences denounced in that state paper, provided only that it
should be communicated to him under the seal of Masonic
confidence. Not to answer such a charge as this, implied
rather a doubt of the ability to do so satisfactorily, than a
perfect reliance upon the consciousness of innocence. If
Masonry was free from all the objections raised by its

3

opponents, what more effective step to establish its innocence than a simple statement of the truth? If it was a
valuable institution, worthy of preservation, surely the
effort to sustain it against injurious calumnies was worth
making. Could it be supposed that the unanimous testimony to the alleged character of the oaths, brought by
hundreds of respectable persons who had taken them, but
who now renounce them, was to be discredited by the
merely negative action of adhering Masons, however individually respectable, or however exalted in position? Considering the precise nature of the difficulties by which they
were surrounded, it is clear that no defence could have been
assumed by them, in its character more nugatory. It manifested only the consciousness of wrong, combined with a
dogged resolution never to admit nor to retract it.

The address of Mr. Livingston, such as it was, proved
the inciting cause of the publication of a series of letters
directed by Mr. Adams to him, which will be found to
make a part of the present volume. In these papers the
argument against the Masonic obligation, as the root of
all the crimes committed in the case of Morgan, was
pushed with a force which carried conviction to the minds
of many persons at the time, and which seems even at this
day scarcely to admit of reply. Mr. Livingston himself
made no attempt at rejoinder. This was the part of discretion, for had he done so, there is little reason to doubt
that Mr. Adams would have fulfilled his promise when he
said to him, "Had you ventured to assume the defence
of the Masonic oaths, obligations and penalties — had you
presumed to commit your name to the assertion that they
can by any possibility be reconciled to the laws of morality, of Christianity, or of the land, I should have deemed
it my duty to reply, and to have completed the demonstration before God and man that they *cannot.*"

The opportunity for a complete and overwhelmning victory was thus denied to Mr. Adams by the tacit secession from the field of Mr. Livingston. Yet the effect of his letters was by no means trifling in many States. The moral power of the opponents of Masonry visibly increased, and with it the earnestness of their political hostility to those who practised its rites. It showed itself in the general election of State officers, both in New York and Pennsylvania, and in the nomination of Mr. William Wirt as a candidate at the ensuing election for the presidency of the United States, in opposition to General Jackson, the incumbent, who was found to be a Freemason. Neither was Mr. Adams himself suffered to remain disconnected with the movement of political opinions upon the subject. A large convention of citizens of Massachusetts unanimously called upon him to suffer his name to be used in the canvass for the office of Governor, which took place in that State in the year 1833. Reluctant as he was to enter into the arena, and to sacrifice his preference for the position in the House of Representatives of the United States, which he then occupied, the nature of the appeal made to him overcame all his scruples. The election took place. It terminated in the failure to make choice of any person by the requisite constitutional majority. The power of the party which had for a long time held the control of the government of Massachusetts, and with which Mr. Adams had up to this period co-operated, was broken under the effort to sustain Masonry against him. Had he determined to persevere, it is quite uncertain what might have been the consequences to the position of the Commonwealth. But it was not his wish to press the matter beyond the point which a sense of duty dictated. No sooner was it ascertained by the return of the votes that a continuance of the contest in the Legislature of the State was to be the result of his adherence to his position, than he determined to withdraw his name from the canvass. At the same time that he took this step, he caused to be published an address to the people of the Commonwealth, explaining his views of the connection between Masonry and the politics of the country, and justifying himself from the charges with which he had been most vehemently assailed. With this paper, the last in the present volume, and the close of which is in a strain of eloquence which alone should secure its preservation, Mr. Adams appears to have terminated his public labors in opposition to secret obligations and to Freemasonry. But their effects were soon afterwards made visible, by the adoption of laws prohibiting the administration of extra-judicial oaths, by the voluntary dissolution of many of the subordinate Lodges, and by the tacit secession of a large number of individual members. Indeed, such was the silence preserved for a long time respecting the Institution, that its existence in Massachusetts might almost have been questioned. The purposes for which the organized opposition had been made, seemed so completely answered, that the motives for maintaining it were no longer strongly felt. The current of public affairs soon afterwards took a new turn. Antimasonry gradually disappeared as an agent to effect changes in the political aspect of the States, and the individuals who had associated themselves in the movement, again joined the ordinary party organizations with which they most nearly sympathized.

Thus it happened that Freemasonry, by cowering under the storm, saved itself from the utter prostration which would have followed perseverance in the policy of resistance. Years have passed away, and it again gives symptoms of revivification. A new and kindred Institution has suddenly manifested an extraordinary degree of develope-

ment under the guise of benevolence. What the precise
nature of the obligations may be, which bind great numbers of citizens, mostly young, active men, into this connection, has not yet been fully brought to light. The
objects are stated to be charity and the rendering of mutual aid. If these are all the purposes of the association,
it cannot be otherwise than meritorious. Yet it can scarcely
be maintained that any unlimited pledge of secrecy is essential to the successful execution of them. In a republican form of government, the only real and proper fraternity
is the system of civil society. To that every member is
bound to bow. The obligations which it imposes need no
veil of secrecy to cover them. Illustrated by the law of
love enjoined by the superior authority of the divine command, it marks out with distinctness to each individual the
paramount duty of charity, of benevolence and of mutual
aid and support. There can be, therefore, no good excuse
for resorting to smaller and·narrower spheres for the invi-
dious exercise of such virtues among those who ought to
stand upon a perfectly even footing, when the broad and
general one better answers to every useful and honorable
exertion. The disadvantages attending the formation of
all associations connected by secret obligations, no matter
how harmless may be their appearance, are, first, that if
they have any effect at all, it is injurious to those who do
not choose to join them; secondly, that they substitute a
private pledge of a doubtful nature to a few who have no
moral right to the preference, for a clear and well defined
and entirely proper one given to the many. In all similar
cases, the tendency to introduce objects of exertion in the
smaller circle which conflict with those of society at large,
and which may sometimes even threaten its safety, is obvious. It is the temptation presented to conspiracy which
has made secret associations the objects of denunciation

by the monarchs of Europe. The same thing should at all times render them marks for jealousy and distrust in republican States. They threaten the harmony of the community wherever they are. The pledge of political preference which was rapidly becoming engrafted upon the Masonic Institution in the United States at the time of the Morgan excitement, and which had already produced visible results in many of the smaller towns of New York and New England, by unaccountably exalting some individuals to the depression of neighbors equally worthy, furnishes a good illustration of the mode in which social discord of the bitterest description may be made in the end to spring up. In view of the possibility of this hazard, it would seem as if few could be found, when once made sensible of the difficulty, willing deliberately to give occasion to it.

It is confidently believed that in the materials of the present volume will be found a solemn warning, conveyed by a voice in the feebleness of age still powerful over the sympathy of American citizens, against the formation of secret obligations. As time rolls on its swift career, and as the generation which nursed the infant Republic into strength disappears from the scene, the duty becomes stronger on those who succeed, to heed the counsels which its wisest and most experienced men leave behind them. The arguments of Mr. Adams, although directed against the particular Order of Freemasonry, will yet be found susceptible of broader application, and extending themselves over all societies of which the radical error is, that they shun the light of day. The pride of freemen—living under a system of equal laws, with guarantees of the rights of each individual—should be to sustain the junction of innocence with liberty, the union of an open, honest heart with an efficient and liberal hand. Such a state cannot co-exist with secret obligations. The person who lies under

an engagement which he must not reveal, whatever may
betide, can indeed be innocent and energetic, but he will
not be perfectly frank nor just to all men alike. Occasions may arise in which his fidelity to his private pledges
will come into conflict with his duty to society. Who is
then to decide for him what he must do? On either side
is moral difficulty and mental distress. If he betray his
associates, he spots his heart with violated faith. If he desert his country, he fails in a duty of even higher obligation.
The alternative is too painful to a conscientious spirit ever
knowingly to be hazarded with propriety. That such an
alternative is by no mean impossible, who can doubt after
the cases of Eli Bruce, of De Witt Clinton, and of Edward
Livingston, in the Masonic history of the murder of Morgan? Much as he might regret it, what Freemason was
there in 1826, who did not perceive at a glance that his
pledge to his associates was to conceal the crime and to
shelter the criminal; whilst his duty to State and to Heaven, to disclose the guilt and to denounce the author, was
written with a sunbeam on his heart? And how many
were there, who, instead of judging rightly of the relative
importance of the obligations, actually made themselves
accessories after the fact, by supplying the means of
escape from justice to their unworthy brethren? The
damning evidence of this truth must remain in the minds
of men as long as Masonry shall endure. It may indeed
be that other associations will spring up which may be
free from all the grossly objectionable engagements of that
Institution. But who shall be secure against the intrusion
of evil when the portal stands invitingly open to its admission? Who shall be able to protect himself against the
designs of those of his associates to whom he has given a
secret control over his will? These are questions which
every citizen must answer for himself. It is with the

design that he may have at hand the means of acting
understandingly, that the present volume is put forth.
Young persons, who are especially liable to be carried
away by the fascination that always attends mystery, are
hereby furnished with an opportunity to weigh the arguments of a powerful remonstrant against any secret steps.
May they read, weigh, and deeply ponder the words of
wisdom, and may the effect of them be to preserve them
in the paths of Liberty, of Friendship, and of Faith,* early
marked out by their adviser as the guides of his own career,
unincumbered by obligations which they fear to disclose,
unembarrassed by promises which they know not how
conscientiously to perform!

* Fidem, Libertatem, Amicitiam—the motto abbreviated from that
selected by his father, who found it in Tacitus, in the charge of the
Emperor Galba to Piso, on adopting him. The passage, as it stands
in the original, applicable to the temptations by which great place is
always surrounded, is as follows: "*Fidem, libertatem, amicitiam*, præ-
cipua humani animi bona, *tu* quidem eadem constantia *retinebis:* sed
alii per obsequium imminuent."

MR. ADAMS'S LETTERS

ON THE

MASONIC INSTITUTION.

CONTENTS.

APPENDIX.

LETTERS, &c.

TO A REVIEWER OF SHEPPARD'S DEFENCE OF THE MASONIC INSTITUTION.

The following letter from John Quincy Adams explains the views of his illustrious father and of himself, on the subject of Freemasonry. It was written in reply to a note from our correspondent, who is reviewing Mr. Sheppard's *Defence of the Masonic Institution.* It may be recollected, that Mr. Sheppard claimed the elder Adams as a patron of the Order; and our correspondent took the liberty of addressing Mr. Adams, asking for information on this point. — *Boston Press.*

Quincy, 22 August, 1831.

Sir,—The letter from my father to the Grand Lodge of Massachusetts, which Mr. Sheppard has thought proper to introduce into his address, was a *complimentary* answer to a friendly and patriotic address of the Grand Lodge to him. In it he expressly states that he had never been *initiated* in the Order. He therefore knew nothing of their *secrets,* their *oaths,* nor their *penalties.* Far less had their practical operation been revealed, by the murder of William Morgan. Nor had the hand of the Avenger of blood been arrested for five long years — and probably forever, by the contumacy of witnesses setting justice at defiance in her own sanctuary. Nor had the trial of an accomplice in guilt marked the influence of *one* juror under Masonic oaths upon the verdict of his eleven fellows.

That Mr. Sheppard should resort to a letter from my father, a professedly uninitiated man, to liberate the Masonic Institution from the unrefuted charge of unlawful *oaths*, of horrible and disgusting *penalties*, and *secrets*, the divulging of which has been punished by a murder unsurpassed in human atrocity, is to me passing strange. All that my father knew of Masonry in 1798, was that it was *favorable to the support of civil authority;* and this he *inferred* from the characters of intimate friends of his, and excellent men who had been members of the Society. The inference was surely natural; but he had never seen the civil authority in conflict with Masonry itself. To speak of the Masonic Institution as favorable to the support of civil authority at this day, and in this country, would be a mockery of the common sense and sensibility of mankind.

My father says he had known the love of the fine arts, the delight in hospitality, and the devotion to humanity of the Masonic fraternity. All these qualities no doubt then were, and yet are conspicuous in many members of the Society. They, and qualities of a yet higher order, were not less conspicuous in the Order of the Jesuits. They were conspicuous in many of the Monastic Orders — in the Inquisition itself, whose ministers, in the very act of burning the body of the heretic to death, were always actuated by the tenderest and most humane regard for the salvation of his soul.

The use of my father's name for the purposes to which Mr. Sheppard would now apply it, is an injury to his memory, which I deem it my duty, as far as may be in my power, to redress. You observe, he says he had never been *initiated* in the Masonic Order. And I have more than once heard from his own lips *why* he had never enjoyed that *felicity*.

Mr. Jeremy Gridley, whom he mentions as having been his intimate friend, was Grand Master of the Massachusetts Grand Lodge. He was also the Attorney General of the Crown, when in October, 1758, my father, having finished his law studies, and his school-keeping at Worcester, presented himself — a stranger — poor, friendless, and obscure, to ask of him the favor to present him to the Superior Court of the Province, then sitting at Boston, for admission to the bar. Mr. Gridley, in his own office, examined the youthful aspirant with regard to his professional acquirements; gave him advice truly parental, and dictated by the purest virtue; and then presented him to the Court, with a declaration that he had himself examined him, and could assure their Honors that his legal acquirements were very considerable, and fully worthy of the admission which he solicited.

This kindness of Mr. Gridley was never forgotten by my father; I trust it will never be forgotten by his children. From that day forth, while Mr. Gridley lived, he was the intimate friend, personal and professional, of my father. He died in 1767. My father often resorted to him for friendly counsel, and as he was Grand Master of the Lodge, once asked his advice, whether it was worth his while to become a member of the Society. In the candor of friendship, Mr. Gridley answered him—NO—adding, that by aggregation to the Society a young man might acquire a little artificial support; but that he did not need it, and that there was nothing in the Masonic Institution worthy of his seeking to be associated with it.

So said, at that time, the Grand Master of the Massachusetts Masons, Jeremy Gridley; and such, I have repeatedly heard my father say, was the reason why he never joined the Lodge.

The use of the name of Washington, to give an odor of sanctity to the Institution as it *now* stands exposed to the world, is, in my opinion, as unwarantable as that of my father's name. On the mortal side of human existence, there is no name for which I entertain a veneration more profound than for that of Washington. But he was never called to consider the Masonic Order in the light in which it MUST now be viewed. If he had been, we have a pledge of what his conduct would have been, far more authoritative than the mere fact of his having been a Mason can be in favor of the brotherhood. If you wish to know what that pledge is, please to consult the recently published writings of Thomas Jefferson, vol. 1, from page 416 to 422. and especially the paragraph beginning at the middle of page 418. I would earnestly recommend the perusal and meditation of the whole passage to all virtuous and conscientious Masons, of whom I know there are great numbers. If they wish to draw precepts for their own conduct from the example and principles of Washington, or from the deliberate and anxious opinions and solicitude of Jefferson, they will find in those pages lessons of duty for themselves which they might consider it as presumption in me to offer them. The application of the principles, in a case not identically the same, but in every essential point of argument similar, and in many respects from a weaker to a much stronger basis, I would leave to their own discretion, though first divested of its passions. It is, in my opinion, an unanswerable demonstration of the *duty* of every Mason in the United States at this day.

I never heard, and do not believe, that the Rev. Dr. Bentley ever delivered or published a sermon censuring my father for anything he had ever said upon the subject of Masonry. The electoral vote of Massachusetts in 1801 WAS unanimous for my father.

You are at liberty to make what use of this letter you please; giving notice, if you publish it, that it is an answer to a letter of inquiry received by me.

I am, very respectfully, Sir,

Your obedient servant,

JOHN QUINCY ADAMS.

TO EDWARD INGERSOLL, ESQ., PHILADELPHIA.

[EXTRACT.]

September 21, 1831.

Mr. Chandler has truly informed you that I am a zealous Antimason — to this extent — It is my deliberate opinion, that from the time of the commission of the crimes committed at the kidnapping and murder of William Morgan, it became the solemn and sacred, civic and social duty of every Masonic Lodge in the United States, either to dissolve itself, or to discard forever all administration of oaths and penalties and all injunctions of secrecy of any kind, to its members. I believed it also their duty, though of less imperious obligation, to abolish all their ill-assorted, honorific titles, and childish or ridiculous pageants.

I believed it also a duty sacredly incumbent upon every individual Freemason in the United States, to use all the influence in his power to prevail upon his brethren of the Order to the same end, that is, to the total abolition of the Order, or to its discarding forever all oaths—all penalties—all secrets, and all fantastic titles, exhibitions and ceremonies heretofore used in the institution.

Believing these to be their duties, I did not feel myself called to take an active part in the controversy, which I saw arising in the community concerning them. I took considerable pains to avoid entering into that controversy. I endured from individuals of the fraternity, instigated by the passions of the order, falsehood, by statements in their newspapers, that I was one of their members; *perjury* to affect the presidential election, by an affidavit sworn to before a Masonic magistrate by a Master Mason, that he had sat with me twice at meetings of a Lodge at Pittsfield—insulting, cajoling, threatening, anonymus letters from Masonic sources —abusive slander and vituperation in Masonic newspapers, pamphlets, and even volumes—and other wrongs of which it behooves me not to speak. All these I have endured for a space now of at least four years, without reply, without complaint, never disguising, in the conversation of social intercourse, the opinions above expressed ; never seeking occasion to promulge them ; and declining, time after time, on many occasions and in various forms, to engage in the turmoil of Masonic and Antimasonic warfare. At last an English Shepherd of Masonic sheep at Wiscasset in Maine, has the impudence to vouch in my father, as a witness to the sublime and transcendent virtues of Masonry, and in the same pamphlet casts a due portion of his Masonic filth at me — for what ? — because in a confidential letter, not intended for the public, and published without my consent, I had once written that I should never be a Mason, and because I had twice, by special invitations, been present as a mere spectator at meetings of Antimasons in Boston. Still I should have overlooked Mr. Sheppard and his Masonic virtues with the rest, but that the editor of the Boston Press, undertaking to review his defence of Masonry, wrote to me to inquire what I knew of this pretended panegyric upon Masonry by my father. I then wrote the letter, which you have seen, and which the friendly commentary of Mr. Walsh, to whom you may, if you please, with my compliments, show this letter, attributes to the "*error of the moon.*"

I said, the CRIMES committed at the kidnapping and murder of William Morgan.—Do you know what they were? Were they not —

1. Fraudulent abuse in repeated forms of the process of the law to obtain upon false pretences possession of the person of Morgan.

2. Infamous slander in those false pretences by first arresting him on a charge against him of petty larceny.

3. Previous slander in newspaper advertisements denouncing him as a swindler and impostor, calling upon *brethren* and *companions* particularly to observe, mark and *govern themselves accordingly*, and declaring that the FRATERNITY had amply provided against his evil designs.

4. Conspiracy of Masonic Lodges assembled in great numbers, *per fas et nefas*, by the commission of *any* crime to suppress his book.

5. Arson — by setting fire at night to Miller's printing-office, in which building were eight or ten persons asleep, whose lives were saved only by the early discovery of the projected conflagration.

6. Fraud, deception and treachery, in procuring from Morgan himself a part of his manuscript, which was finally sent by a special messenger to the General *Grand Chapter* of the United States in session at New York.

7. Kidnapping — too successfully practised upon Morgan — attempted upon Miller.

8. False imprisonment and transportation of

Morgan beyond the bounds of the United States into
a foreign territory.

9. A murder, taking nine days in its perpetration
— keeping the wretched and helpless victim throughout the whole of that time in a state of continual
and cruel torture.

Sleep upon this list of peccadilloes, and to-morrow
I will give you upon them a word of comment.

Yours.

JOHN QUINCY ADAMS.

TO EDWARD INGERSOLL, ESQ.

Quincy, September 22, 1831.

DEAR SIR,— I gave you in my last letter a list of
NINE crimes, among the most atrocious that can be
perpetrated by human agency, committed in the
original transactions connected with what has been
by an exceedingly inappropriate euphony called
the *abduction* and murder of William Morgan.—
Abduction is a word of lamb-like innocence compared with the ingredients of wickedness which
composed the crime of his taking off. Language
sinks under the effort to express its complicated
malignity.

These crimes I allege were committed by *the
fraternity*. They were instigated by no impulse of

individual passions — by none of the stimulants to
the ordinary outrages of man upon man — by no
personal animosity — by no purpose of robbery.
They were the crimes of *the Craft*, of which the
guilty agents, by whom they were consummated,
were but the fanatical instruments.

And here I pray you to remark, that I have stated
these crimes interrogatively. I have inquired of
you whether they were *not* the crimes committed in
those transactions; to the end that if you find upon
inquiry that I have set them down incorrectly or
with exaggeration, you may reduce them in number
or in virulence to their just and well-proportioned
standard.

I charge them upon *the Craft*, as *the means* by
which public notice had been given beforehand that
the fraternity had amply provided against his
designs.

In these crimes several hundreds of persons appear to have participated, as principals or accessories
before or after the fact. The measures were taken
not individually, but as results of corporate deliberation in sundry Lodges.

Mr. Miner, one of the most amiable and benevolent of men, has mistaken the terms of the Antimasonic proposition. There are no doubt degrees
of exasperation of different temperature, among the
Antimasons; but I know of none disposed to hold

every individual Mason responsible for the tragedy of Morgan's murder. All know that there are now, as there always have been, Masons among the most respectable and virtuous members of the community. But they belong to a vicious institution, and it is their duty to withdraw from that institution — to abolish it — or to purify it from its vices, oaths, penalties and secrets.

That the institution is vicious might be very conclusively inferred from the effects disclosed in the nine crimes above enumerated, even if their causes were yet secret. But those causes have been divulged. We know that every entered apprentice of Masonry has, hookwinked and with a halter round his neck, administered to him an oath, the words of which he is required to repeat with his lips; never to divulge the secrets of the Order, and binding himself by *"no less a penalty* than to have his throat cut across, his tongue torn out by the roots, and his body buried in the rough sands of the sea at low water mark, where the tide ebbs and flows twice in twenty-four hours." Morgan divulged these secrets, and his fate is the practical commentary upon the penalty.

The oath, the penalty, the secret, and Morgan's corpse at the bottom of Niagara River, where a shrewd brother of the craft "guessed he would publish no more books," are illustrations of each other,

which it would take much sophistry to obscure;
much prevarication to confuse. Mr. Miner has
taken this oath and bound himself by no less than
this penalty. It is wise and prudent in him therefore not to violate the oath, and he would assuredly
not have been the man to execute the penalty upon
Morgan for considering it a dead letter.

But will Mr. Miner tell you that the penalty is,
or that it is not, a dead letter? If it is, surely the
oath is the same — and then it is mere profanity; a
taking of the name of God in vain; odious in proportion to the disgusting solemnity of the form in
which it is administered. If it is not a dead letter,
what is it? Some of the Masonic *Defences* allege
that it is only an imprecation — "under no less a
penalty than *to have my throat cut*" — a mere imprecation! Is it not then a paltering with words in
double senses? A penalty is not an imprecation,
and to have the throat cut across and the tongue torn
out by the roots is not expulsion from a Lodge. The
substance of the defence is, that the penalty is a
brutum fulmen; that there is no authority existing
in, or conferred by the institution to carry it into
execution; and that it is a special *charge* to all
Masons upon their admission, to observe faithfully
the laws of God and of the land. But for every
degree of Masonry there is a separate oath and a
diversified penalty, and in some of the higher

degrees, it includes a promise to carry into effect the punishments of the fraternity. I have heard of the instructions from the owner of a piratical cruiser to his captain, directing him to take, burn, sink or destroy any merchant vessel of any nation that might fall in his way, and to dispose of the people on board of them so as that they might not prove afterwards troublesome; but to be specially careful not to infringe upon the laws of nations or of humanity. This man must have been a Mason of at least the Royal Arch degree.

That the oaths and penalties of Masonry were not understood, by the multitudes of Masons accessory to the commission of the nine crimes enumerated in my list, as mere imprecations, is self-evident. By them they were understood, according to their plain, unambiguous import, as an absolute, unequivocal forfeiture of *life*, and an explicit consent of the person taking the oath, that he should be put to death in the horrid manner described in the terms of the penalty if he should divulge the secrets of the Order. But whether the penalty be, as it purports, a real penalty, or a mere imprecation, will Mr. Miner say that it is a form of words and obligations fit to be administered with a solemn invocation of the name of God to a Christian and a freeman? Cruel and unusual punishments are equally abhorrent to the mild spirit of Christianity, and to the spirit of equal liberty. The infliction of them is expressly prohibited in the Bill of Rights of this Common-wealth, and yet thousands of her citizens have attested the name of God, to subject themselves to death by tortures, which cannibal savages would instinctively shrink from inflicting.

It has therefore been in my opinion, ever since the disclosure of the Morgan-murder crimes, and of the Masonic oaths and penalties by which they were instigated, the indispensable duty of the Ma-sonic Order in the United States, either to dissolve itself, or to discard forever from its constitution and laws all *oaths*, all *penalties*, all *secrets*, and as ridiculous appendages to them, all *mysteries* and *pageants.* Believing this to be the duty of the whole Order, I have deemed it a duty equally indis-pensable of every individual Mason, to use in calm-ness and moderation all his influence with the fraternity to come to one or the other of these results. And I have, since the New York elections of the last autumn, deemed this to be a duty especially and above all incumbent upon Mr. *Clay.* I mean that he should have set a similar example to that of Washington, in endeavoring to prevail upon the Order of the Cincinnati to dissolve themselves, or at least to discard the most exceptionable parts of their constitution in which latter purpose he suc-ceeded. I have not said this to Mr. Clay, because in the estimate of his duties he must be his own counsellor, and I know he has had advice from another quarter, which he has doubtless deliberately weighed; but it brings me to a point upon which I shall ask a few minutes further of your patience, for your friend hereafter.

JOHN QUINCY ADAMS.

TO EDWARD INGERSOLL, ESQ.

Quincy, 23 September, 1831.

DEAR SIR,—From the nature of the Masonic oaths, penalties and secrets, and the construction given to them, not a forced and unnatural one, but conformable to the plain import of their terms, by multitudes of Masons in the western part of New York, the crimes immediately connected with the murder of William Morgan were committed. I charge them therefore upon the Institution; and if Masonry had been until then a perfectly innocent and even useful institution; from the time of the commission of those crimes it would have ceased to be so. From that time, the community acquired the right of calling upon the fraternity to discontinue and renounce at least the administration of oaths, the imposition of all forms of penalties, and all secrets whatever.

A large and increasing portion of the community have made this demand,—a demand just and reasonable in itself, and the more so, as the oaths, penalties and secrets have been divulged not only by Morgan's book, but by the concurring testimony of numerous seceding Masons. The oaths, the penalties and the secrets—whether all disclosed with perfect accuracy or not; whether understood as they were by the murderers of Morgan, or as explained by the defenders of Masonry—are unreasonable, odious, and I believe unlawful. The oaths of all Masons, heretofore admitted, if they ever had any binding force, are dissolved by the fact of the public disclosure of the secrets, which they had bound themselves to keep. Their country calls upon them to disclaim henceforth and forever all secrets, and as incidental to the injunction of them, all oaths and penalties. This reasonable and moderate call has not only been resisted by the great body of Freemasons throughout the United States, but no man, high or low, eminent or obscure, has dared to avow this opinion and unite in this call without being assailed in his reputation, robbed of his good name, insulted, abused and vilified openly and in secret, by individual Masons and by organized Lodges, a body of at least two hundred thousand men, scattered over the whole Union—all active and voting men, linked together by secret ties, for purposes of indefinite extent; bound together by oaths and penalties operating with terrific energy upon the imagination of the human heart, and upon its fears; embracing within the penalty of its laws the President of the United States and his leading competitors; and winding itself round every great political party for support, like poisonous ivy round a sturdy oak, and round every object of its aversion, like the boa-constrictor round its victim. Such in faint and diluted colors is at this time the image of the Masonic Institution in these United States. Commanding despotically a large portion of the public presses — intimidating by its terrors multitudes of others — and amidst all its internal dissensions, uniting with the whole mass of its power against every common adversary, one of the most alarming and pernicious characters in which it now presents itself, is that of its political dominion. You tell me that you are Antimasonic in your opinions and feelings, but are perplexed by the mixture of politics with Antimasonry. But you place herein the effect before the cause. The mixture of politics is with Masonry. It is the misfortune of Mr. Clay to be entangled with Masonry, and I sincerely regret that he has not felt it his duty, as I think it was, to shake off his shackles. His motives I have no doubt were generous, but the effect is that *he* sustains and identifies himself with the Masonic cause. That cause is now

sustained *only* by such artificial and unnatural pillars. Neither Mr. Clay nor you (forgive me for
saying) estimate at its true value the *cause* of Antimasonry. You look chiefly to the motives of its
supporters, and distrust them too much. You ask if
Masonry should be made answerable for the crimes
of a few individual Masons? Should the royal government of Rome have been abolished for the violence committed upon a single woman? Should
the decemvirate have been subverted for the murder
of Virginia by her own father? Should the tribe
of Benjamin have been exterminated for the brutal
abuse of one Levite's concubine? Should the
British nation have gone to war with Spain for the
cutting off by a few Spaniards of one smuggler's
ears? In all those cases and in numberless others
which swarm in human history, the connection
between the crime, and the institution made answerable for it, was infinitely more remote than the
cluster of Morgan-murder crimes is from the vitals
of Masonry. But I have spoken only of the crimes
committed at the time. Look at the government
of the State of New York, struggling in vain from
that time to this — five long years — to bring the
perpetrators of the murder to punishment. See
judges, sheriffs, witnesses, jurors, entangled in the
net of Masonry, and justice prostrated in her own
temple by the touch of her invisible hand.

Several of the *abductors* have indeed been convicted, and among them one sheriff of a county. Three or four upon their own confession of guilt. You say you "have been told by men who care much more for truth than for Masonry, that there is no reason to believe that any Mason has refused to give testimony on account of Masonic obligations." My dear sir, go to the records of the courts. You will find witnesses refusing to testify upon the express ground of Masonic obligations, avowing that they consider those obligations paramount to the laws of the land. You will see them contumacious to the decisions of the court, fined and imprisoned for contempt, suffer the punishment rather than bear the testimony, and instead of expulsion, be refunded, at least in part, for their fines by contributions from the Lodges. I give you names — Isaac Allen, Eli Bruce, Ezekiel Jewett, John Whitney, Orsamus Turner, Erastus Day, Sylvanus Cone, Elisha M. Forbes, Benjamin Enos.

You will find much more. You will find Masonic grand and petit juries, summoned by Masonic sheriffs, eager to sit upon the trials, perverting truth and justice when admitted on the array, and often excluded upon challenge to the favor ; and last of all you will find one of the men, most deeply implicated in the murder, screened from conviction by *one* Mason upon his jury.

"It is not and it cannot come to good.'

That this enormous train of abuses should be sustained by those who have it in abhorrence, and that every individual denouncing it should be hunted down, as if he himself were a pest to society, because Masonry has fastened itself to the skirts both of General Jackson and Mr. Clay, to sink or swim with them, is itself one of the most objectionable properties of the Institution. Clay Masonry has become not only the familiar denomination of a great political party, but of a party which, to put down a high, pure and virtuous manifestation of popular sensibility, takes to its bosom Jacksonism itself. So it was in all the New York elections of last November. So it has been in the elections of the last Massachusetts legislature. Clay Masons gave New York to the Regency to put down the Antimason Granger. Clay Masons made a Jackson man a Senator for our county of Plymouth, over a National Republican, with three hundred more popular votes; because forsooth he was the Antimasonic and his competitor the *Masonic* candidate; and yet I hear Masons complain of proscription and disfranchisement.

I may perhaps publish part of these letters; but without at all implicating you. Show them, if you please, to Mr. Walsh, as the moon-struck visions of your friend.

JOHN QUINCY ADAMS.

TO EDWARD INGERSOLL, ESQ.

Quincy, 22 October, 1831.

DEAR SIR,—One month has elapsed since, in answer to some remarks in a friendly letter from you on the subject of Masonry and its antidote, I gave you with freedom and candor my sentiments concerning them, and a view of the progressive steps by which I had been reluctantly drawn into a public participation in this controversy. I authorized you to show my letters to Mr. Walsh, because having long been with me upon terms of private friendship and of personal confidence, he had denounced me to the public, as a madman (upon this subject) for a letter written and published in vindication of my father's reputation from Masonic slander. I had no expectation of converting Mr. Walsh, though I did hope that this mode of noticing the severity of his censure might awaken a sentiment of kindness in his mind, which either had departed or was slumbering when he consigned me to the jurisdiction of the moon. He since has made me more than amends by his notice of my Eulogy upon Mr. Monroe, and as I have always been a friend of toleration in politics as well as in religion, I must compromise for being considered by him a lunatic upon Masonry and the Hartford Convention, in consideration of an over allowance of merit upon points, on which his opinions concur with mine.

Within that month, events in relation to the Masonic controversy have occurred, of no trifling magnitude. That Mr. Walsh and Mr. Sargeant consider Antimasonry as yet a subject for *scorn*, certainly staggers my faith in the correctness of my own impressions. A very sincere respect for their opinions calls upon me for a severe review of my own, and makes me feel with double force the admonition in your kind letter of the 17th instant to be specially cautious of error and exaggeration in any thing that I may say on this score to the public.

It was indeed under that conviction that I submitted to you *interrogatively*, the list of nine atrocious crimes, committed as I believed in connection with the murder of William Morgan, and which I charged upon the Masonic Institution. If mistaken, either in the number or aggravation of the crimes, or in the *principle* of imputing them to the institution, I was desirous of being corrected by your enlightened judgment and more accurate information. I am, therefore, happy to learn that Mr. Miner will reply to my letters *in full*. But he is the last man in the world, with whom I would willingly have a controversy. I am perfectly willing to publish in his Village Record, that portion of my letters to you, which I shall ultimately conclude to publish at all ; but before that, I wish to have the benefit of your corrections as well in point of fact as of principle, derivable from the inquiries, which at my suggestion you have made. I should also be glad to know, if Mr. Miner, or you yourself, would be willing to have your names introduced in the publication ; you, as the person to whom the letters were addressed; he, as the person referred to in them. In naming him, it did not occur to me that he would see the letters ; but I fully approve of your showing them to him, and also to the other persons whom you have mentioned. From the nature of the controversy, and precisely because Masonic warfare is secret, I have determined to publish nothing against Masonry but under the responsibility of my *name.* I have no right, however, to take the same liberties with the names of others, and shall carefully avoid using them without permission or special justifying reason.

The nomination of Messrs. Wirt and Ellmaker at Baltimore, is one of those prominent events, which have occurred since my letters to you were written. Mr. Miner has sent me a copy of a printed handbill, addressed to the citizens of Chester county, signed by himself and seventeen other Masons, heading a republication of Mr. Wirt's letter to the Convention at Baltimore and declaring their concurrence in every word and sentiment of that letter. But that letter most distinctly declares Mr. Wirt's approbation both of the *end* and the *means* of the Antimasons; the end being the abolition of Freemasonry, and the means the ballot-box against all *adhering* Masons and all neutrals. What part of my charges then does Mr. Miner mean to contest?

The declarations of General Peter B. Porter and W. B. Rochester have also been made public since the date of my letters to you. What is there in my charges, that is not fully sanctioned by them? They unequivocally advise the surrender of the charters. They say Mr. Clay thinks with them. Why has Mr. Clay refused to say so? Delicacy? Has Mr. Clay ever considered it a matter of delicacy for a candidate to give pledges of his opinions upon controverted points of political interest? Does Mr. Clay *scorn* Antimasonry, like Mr. Walsh and Mr. Sargeant? If he does, it is evident General P. B. Porter and W. B. Rochester do not.

I am happy to find *you* do not. Mr. Wirt frankly tells the Baltimore Convention, that until two or three days before they met, he had considered *Antimasonry* as a *farce*, and wondered how such an excitement should have been blown up from what he thought so trifling a cause. He scorned Antimasonry — why? — because he knew nothing of the facts, and believed Masonic misrepresentations.

The moment the facts were disclosed to him, or rather the moment he could bring himself to turn his face to them, the scales fell from his eyes, he approves the *end* of the Antimasons, he approves their *means*. His case is the case of thousands and tens of thousands. Yet Mr. Wirt had sworn to keep the secrets of Masonry upon no less a penalty than the fate of Morgan. He had forgotten the secret, and perhaps the oath. How such a man as Mr. Wirt could ever have taken such an oath, and then forgotten it, is among the inscrutables and unaccountables of human conduct.

The Antimasons of this Commonwealth have nominated Samuel Lathrop for Governor in the place of Mr. Lincoln. They first did me the honor to nominate me, but I declined. Governor Lincoln is my personal friend and I approve of his administration in general. I regretted that they did not nominate him. No answer accepting this nomination has yet appeared from Mr. Lathrop. Mr. Lincoln will at all events be re-elected, for there is not a state in the Union where Masonry is so strong as in this. And the Masons will support Lincoln, though his answer to the Antimasonic Committee is as severe against Masonry as anything I have ever said or written. But there was something in his remarks upon Antimasonry which they took for scorn, though I did not. Their candidate is a man of excellent character, a warm federalist and heretofore *the* federal candidate for Governor.

The State of Vermont is now purely Antimasonic in all its branches, with a Governor, Council and majority of the House of Representatives, elected as Antimasons against both Clay and Jackson Masonry. Vermont is the first State where this victory has been achieved. Yet it was not there that Morgan was murdered.

I shall expect somewhat anxiously your exposition of facts conflicting with my statements. I know Mr. Stone, of the New York Commercial, believes that the kidnappers of Morgan did not at first *intend* to murder him. Perhaps he believes that the arrest of him for petty larceny was not connected with the project to kidnap him. I know too that he dwells much upon the alleged baseness of Morgan's moral character. I set the question of his character aside; but a charge of *theft* against a man for neglecting to return a borrowed shirt — what chance has character against slander like that?

Very respectfully, your friend,

JOHN QUINCY ADAMS.

TO WILLIAM H. SEWARD, ESQ., AUBURN, N. Y.

Quincy, 17 October, 1831.

DEAR SIR,—Your letter from Boston of 15 September was duly received, and not immediately answered, chiefly from a doubt where to address a letter, which would reach you without delay at that time.

The nomination of candidates for the next election of President and Vice President of the United States, by an unanimous vote, relieved me from the only apprehension I had previously entertained, that the Convention at Baltimore would not be able to agree in their choice.

Much now depends, for the cause of Antimasonry, perhaps every thing depends, upon the course pursued by the party in the approaching elections in the State of New York. I learn that in those of Pennsylvania, the present year will indicate rather a falling off from the cause, though no real defection of its supporters. In this Commonwealth the result may be the same. I shall regret this, because the more attentively I have observed the character of the Masonic Institution as it *now* exists in the United States, the more thoroughly I am convinced that it is the greatest political evil with which we are now afflicted.

The Antimasons in this State have concluded to support a candidate against the present Governor, much to my regret. They did me the honor to nominate me, but I felt it my duty to decline the offer. They have nominated Samuel Lathrop, but it is doubted whether he will accept. The opinions of the present Governor are very decidedly against Masonry, and the opposition to him will deter many from joining the Antimasons, who would otherwise have voted with them.

I pray your acceptance of the within Eulogy upon James Monroe, and am,

Very respectfully, dear Sir,
Your obedient servant,
JOHN QUINCY ADAMS.

TO RICHARD RUSH, ESQ., YORK, PENN.

[EXTRACT.]

Quincy, 25 October, 1831.

The Masonic and Antimasonic controversy drags along, deepening — widening — embittering, as it proceeds. In proportion as the popular excitement against Masonry spreads, the Masons close their ranks and rally round their hideous idol. Of the Antimasons, I wish that the discretion and the plain dealing and consistency were equal to the goodness of their cause. I cannot absolutely say they are not, but I do not understand some of their recent movements, and must wait to see their consequences before passing judgment upon them. It has been circulated by some of them here, as it was stated to you, that I had suggested to them the name of Mr. Wirt for their nomination at Baltimore, but it is not so. I much prefer the nomination of Mr. Wirt to that of Mr. McLean, which I fully expected; but of the proceedings at Baltimore, there are rumors circulated by the Masonic party which I hope are without foundation. It is said among other things that the Convention were as equally divided between Mr. Wirt and Mr. McLean as forty-one to thirty-eight, and that it is very doubtful whether the party will sustain the nomination of their Convention. Here, an Antimasonic Convention did me the honor to nominate me for the office of Governor of this Commonwealth, but I felt it my duty to decline the nomination. They then nominated Samuel Lathrop, a very worthy man, but it is said that without declining their nomination, he has answered that he is and will be a warm supporter of Mr. Clay for the Presidency. They have not yet published either my answer or Mr. Lathrop's.

About a month since, Edward Ingersoll made in a letter to me some remarks upon this controversy, in answer to which I wrote him three letters, part of which, 1 informed him I might probably publish. I charged in the form of interrogation *nine* specific atrocious crimes, in the transactions connected with the murder of William Morgan, independent of all the subsequent judicial prevarications, contumacies and perjuries. I charged them not upon all individual Masons, but upon the Masonic Institution, upon its *oaths, penalties,* and *secrets,* and I asked him if my list of crimes was overcharged in number or measure, to reduce them to the standard of truth; and if they were not chargeable upon *Masonry,* to answer the reasons, which I gave him for so considering them. Mr. Ingersoll, who avows himself Antimasonic in principle and feeling, has shown my letters to several persons, and among the rest to our friend Miner, who I understand has undertaken to reply to my letters in full. I learn further that your Grand Lodge or Grand Chapter are about to enter upon the arena and to make a powerful *defence* of Masonry. A principal object of my letters to Ingersoll was to *bring out* the Masons upon the Morgan-murder crimes. Their tactics hitherto have been to smuggle them out of sight. Sheppard's *Defence* speaks of the murder itself as *doubtful,* and styles it a mere *drunken scrape at which Masons were present.* The formal defence of Masonry by the Grand Lodge of Rhode Island, says, they cannot tell whether Morgan was or was not murdered,

for that *they know nothing about it.* So effectually
have they, by their management of the press, kept
those transactions out of view, that thousands and
thousands, like Mr. Wirt, have gone on year after
year scorning and laughing at Antimasonry as a
farce, and thinking Masonry a Sir Roger de Coverly
Club, because they could not *look at the facts.* My
interrogatory specification of an Anti-Parnassus of
crimes, was intended to bring the Masons to an issue
upon the fact and the law, fairly out before the tribunal of the public. I have promised that if I do
publish any part of my letters to Ingersoll, they shall
first appear in Mr. Miner's Village Record. Miner
himself will reply to them, and between him and
me I shall be content to stand alone; but if the
Grand Lodge or Grand Chapter of Pennsylvania
came down upon me, especially during the session
of Congress, I shall want auxiliary force, and hope
you will be in the field again.

Vermont is now completely Antimasonic, because,
from their proximity to the Morgan-murder, the facts
have forced themselves upon the public eye in spite
of all Masonic suppressions. The letters of General
Peter B. Porter and W. B. Rochester give a fore-
boding of the prospects of the New York elections
now at hand. There is danger of a falling off in
this State, owing to the Antimasonic nomination
against Governor Lincoln. Ever faithfully yours,

JOHN QUINCY ADAMS.

TO HIS EXCELLENCY LEVI LINCOLN, GOVERNOR OF
MASSACHUSETTS.

[EXTRACT.]

Washington, 18 December, 1831.

MY DEAR SIR,—I cannot forbear immediately to
acknowledge the receipt of your two kind letters of
the 11th and 12th instants, although a heavy and
quite unexpected burden of occupation, imposed
upon me by the duties of the station in which I fear
I have rashly permitted myself to be placed, will
deprive me of the opportunity of which I *did* propose to avail myself, of communicating with you
upon one topic especially of transcendent interest to
my mind. I mean neither more nor less than the
Institution of Freemasonry in these United States.

The Speaker of the House of Representatives of
the United States has thought proper to appoint me
Chairman of the Committee of Manufactures, a station from which I have in vain endeavored to obtain
a release. It will leave me little time for any thing
else, and particularly not for the review, which it
was my purpose to take, of the Masonic controversy
now in progress in our own and the neighboring
States, and which I believe destined to produce
consequences deeply affecting the interests, the
happiness, and the liberties of our country.

The design must for the present be postponed,
and perhaps my undertaking would, at all events,
have been premature. It is now a little more than
five years since the true character of *Freemasonry*
as existing in this Union, was disclosed to the public eye. It first exploded by the catastrophe of one
of the deepest tragedies that ever was enacted upon
the scene of human being, exploded by a complica-
tion of nine or ten of the most atrocious crimes that
ever were conceived in human hearts or committed
by human hands; crimes committed not by men in
the stations of life to which ignorance is a snare,
intemperance a stimulant, or indigence a temptation; not by men under the instigations of malice or
revenge; but by men in the educated classes of
society; men who had been instructed in the duties
of Christians and citizens; men above the pressure
of want; men, in other respects and independent of
their secret and mystical ties to this Institution, of
fair and respectable lives; men enjoying the confidence of their fellow-citizens and holding offices of
trust committed to them by that confidence.

We see these men, not in the solitary depravity
of a single heart, but after repeated consultation in
Lodges and Chapters, combined, and, for the commission of more than one of the crimes, abusing the
sacred authority of the law, with which they had
been invested for the furtherance and execution of

justice, to the commission of swindling, slander, theft, false imprisonment, man stealing, treachery, arson, transportation of a citizen beyond the limits of his country, and, to close the catalogue, *foul and midnight murder.*

Such was the first disclosure of the *secrets* of Freemasonry,—such was the practical exposition of its laws. The laws themselves were afterwards revealed. It was to prevent the revelation of them that all these crimes were committed, and, by the retributive justice of Providence, it was the very commission of the crimes which brought the laws to light.

It is not then to Freemasonry as a *secret society,* of mysteriously concerted operation and portentous power, of strangely mingled royal and priestly titles with fantastical fooleries of attire and pageantry, of ostentatious devotion and hidden carousals, of charity and of revelry in the proportion of Sir John Falstaff's tavern bill for bread and for sack; it is not to this Society, such as it was before the murder of William Morgan, that I intended to entreat your attention as a citizen, a Christian, a magistrate and a man. Freemasonry as known to the world before the commission of the Morgan-murder crimes, might not be worthy of your attention. From the time when the crimes were committed, and the laws by which they were committed, were revealed, that a citizen of the United States should exist, who can ask himself, "What is this to me?" is as unaccountable as the fascinations of Freemasonry itself.

But the disclosure of the crimes and the disclosure of the laws were not enough — five years has the government of New York been struggling, not as it ought instantly to have done, to strangle this hydra with unnumbered heads, but to execute upon the criminals a feeble and ineffectual justice. Five years in the face of this nation have Masonic sheriffs, jurors and witnesses betrayed their duty to their country and their God, to screen the guilty from punishment; five years have Lodges, Chapters and Encampments aided and abetted in the concealment of the crimes and in the escape of the criminals from justice; while a gang of two hundred thousand Masons, from every nook and corner of the Union, are joining in one concerted yell of persecution! persecution! and certifying and swearing that *they* never took an oath incompatible with their duty to their religion or the laws of the land. "In generalibus latet dolus," was the maxim of the old logicians. The denial of the Royal Arch oath is a miserable prevarication. The Entered Apprentice's oath and penalty is itself a violation of all religion and of the Constitution of our Commonwealth. To say that such an oath is not to affect religion or politics, is to unite impossibilities. It is to take a

firebrand in the hand, by thinking of the frosty
Caucasus. The four Royal Arch Masons who sunk
Morgan's body in the Niagara River, inflicted upon
him the penalty of the Entered Apprentice's oath.
Their names are known probably to every Lodge
in the State of New York, but they cannot be convicted, for none will testify, and the Grand Chapter
at New York, which has the power of expulsion
throughout the State, so far from expelling any one
of the kidnappers or murderers of Morgan, has aided
them with money to support them in prison and to
pay their fines. But I must abridge this letter.
From the combined consideration of these three
elements —

1. The practical disclosure of the character and
laws of Masonry by the Morgan-murder crimes.

2. From the subsequent disclosure of its written
laws, oaths and penalties in literal conformity and
obedience, to which these crimes were committed.

3. From the struggle of five years' duration
between the government of New York to bring
these crimes to punishment, and the successful
Masonic combination to defeat the law of the land
and to screen the guilty from its power.

From these combined considerations there appear
to me to result solemn and sacred duties to every
citizen of the Union, and especially to every citizen
invested with authority. It was therefore that I com-

6

menced this correspondence by the inquiry whether you was acquainted with the facts. They are known to few. I find by your answer, that some of them, not unimportant, are still unknown to you. The extent of the combination, preceding the murder of Morgan, is even now known only to the surviving accomplices in the guilt. Of the four immediate perpetrators of the murder, one may yet reveal the horrid tale, the minute particulars of which are known to many *worthy* brothers of the craft. Much of Masonic participation, both before and after the fact, will probably never be known abroad from the recesses of the Lodge. With these observations I have mingled no reference whatever to the Antimasonic party, their proceedings or their leaders. I look only to their CAUSE; and if that is under bad management, I can only express the hope that it may be more energetically taken into their own hands by the virtuous and the wise.

I am, very respectfully,

Dear Sir,

Your friend and servant,

JOHN QUINCY ADAMS.

TO WILLIAM L. STONE, ESQ.

Washington, 24 December, 1831.

Dear Sir,—The British Acts to Parliament, to
which I referred in our conversation the other evening are two, —

1. Statute **37** George 3d, ch. 123, (19th July,
1797,) making the administration of unlawful oaths
felony, punishable by transportation for seven years.

2. Statute **39** George 3d, ch. 79, for the suppression of seditious societies, (12 July, 1799.)

The fifth, sixth and seventh sections of this last
statute except from its penalties, under very rigorous
restrictions of police, *the Lodges of Freemasons as
they have long been usually held in Great Britain;*
but not Chapters or Encampments. From Profes-
sor Robinson's book and other sources I have been
informed that the Lodges usually held in Great
Britain, never confer beyond the first three degrees
in Masonry, and content themselves with avenging
the murder of Hiram Abiff by those historical per-
sonages Jubela, Jubelo and Jubelum. I sought you
yesterday, immediately after the adjournment of the
House, in the Library of Congress and afterwards at
Gadsby's without success. It was to give you the
above information concerning the British statutes
and to ask the favor of your company to dine with

me to-morrow, Christmas day, at five o'clock. Let me expect you, and believe me your assured friend,

JOHN QUINCY ADAMS.

TO WILLIAM L. STONE, ESQ., NEW YORK.

Washington, 30 June, 1832.

DEAR SIR, — I have received your kind letter and the elegant volume which you have done me the honor of addressing to me on the subject of Masonry and Antimasonry. Anticipating in the course of a few days a release from occupations, which deprive me at this moment of the power of perusing your work with the deep attention which the importance of the subject requires, I shall avail myself of the first hours at my disposal to devote them to that purpose. In the mean time I cherish the hope that the influence of this comprehensive and impartial survey of the Masonic Institutions upon the public mind, will contribute to induce the voluntary abandonment or renunciation of it, which I have long thought and more firmly believe from day to day to be desirable for the peace and quiet of the community.

I am, with great respect and esteem,

Dear Sir,

Your friend and obedient servant,

JOHN QUINCY ADAMS.

TO WILLIAM L. STONE, Esq.

Quincy, 19 August, 1832.

DEAR SIR, — On receiving at Washington the volume of Letters upon Masonry and Antimasonry, which you did me the honor of addressing to me, I wrote you a few lines of acknowledgment, with the assurance of my intention to read with deep attention the work, to the composition and publication of which I felt great satisfaction in believing that I had contributed to give occasion. I have accordingly perused it with the most earnest solicitude, and the result has been not only a confirmed conviction that the Institution of Freemasonry ought in these United States to be totally and forever abolished, but that this event is a consummation devoutly to be wished.

In the three letters which I wrote about a year since to a friend in Philadelphia, and which were submitted to your perusal, I presented in the form of interrogation a list of nine atrocious crimes under the denomination of *Morgan-Murder Crimes*, with the inquiry whether they had not been so committed as in a great degree to have lost the character of individual guilt in their perpetrators and to have assumed that of associate or corporate offences ; as conspiracies, in which numerous bodies of men constituting Lodges, Chapters and Encampments of Freemasons were implicated ;—and inquiring further, whether the commission of those crimes had not been previously instigated by the oaths administered, the obligations imposed, and the penalties imprecated or denounced, in the ordinary forms of the admission of candidates to the numerously graduated hierarchy of Freemasonry.

That these crimes had been committed—that the efficient impulse to the commission of them had been the Masonic oaths, obligations and penalties—and that they were corporate crimes conceived, projected and matured for action in the Masonic deliberative bodies in the western part of the State of New York, I firmly believe from a mass of irresistible evidence, which had been growing into certainty for a series of years. On the other hand, many of the most important facts, both in relation to the commission of the crimes and to the purport of the Masonic oaths and obligations, had been vehemently contested. A considerable number of seceders from Masonry had revealed all the secrets of all the degrees, and all the oaths and obligations and penalties, as established in the Lodges, Chapters and Encampments in all the region round where the murder had been perpetrated. The books of David Bernard and Avery Allyn, both seceding Knight Templars, had been published. Bernard had been

admitted to the ineffable degrees in New York.
Allyn at New Haven in Connecticut. The Rev.
Moses Thatcher and Pliny Merrick had declared
that the Royal Arch oath was in many Lodges in
Rhode Island and Massachusetts administered with
the words "murder and treason not excepted."
That it was so administered in the State of New
York, had been testimony extorted and most reluctantly given upon oath by Royal Arch Masons upon
trials before courts of justice; and yet, adhering
Masons were solemnly declaring that *they* had taken
no such oaths; that *they* acknowledged no obligation
incompatible with the laws of God or of the land ;
that the only penalty ever inflicted was expulsion;
and that *they* did not believe the oaths and obligations were otherwise understood by Masons every
where.

In the controversial conditions of the facts upon
the issue which seemed to have been made up between the adhering and the seceding Masons, I had
preferred stating them to our friend at Philadelphia
in the form of interrogation, rather than to assume
them as granted. He was a Mason, inclining to
Antimasonry, but unwilling to join its political standard. He knew little of what had taken place in the
western counties of the State of New York, and
had been made to disbelieve the most prominent
facts of the tale of horror connected with the fate of

Morgan. I was desirous if possible to keep myself
entirely disentangled from all the politics of Antimasonry, but this was becoming exceedingly difficult. I wished for a more perfect exposition of facts
from a source fully informed; from a person in whose
candor and integrity I could place entire reliance, and
not so connected with either of the parties as to be
under a bias disqualifying to the perception or to
the judiciary faculty. I was well assured that I
should find this in your book, and I have not been
disappointed. The book is marked with integrity
and candor, which not even the fifth libation has
been able to prevent.

There is a lingering attachment to the Institution,
as it had been in better days, like the affection of
a parent, discovering in bitterness of soul the
profligacy of a favorite child, which adds a double
seal of confirmation to the disclosures which you
have had the intrepidity to make and to sustain.
There are many things in the volume, which I do
not see as you do; but the sincerity of your own
conviction of the truth of all that you affirm is apparent in every page. I speak of the intrepidity of
your disclosures, because I have not dissembled to
myself the peculiar position in which you stand towards the Institution, both as a man and as a member
of a responsible profession. I see you as neither an
adhering nor a seceding Mason. I think I perceive

the conflict in your own mind between the obligation of Masonry which you had taken upon you, and
the duties of your profession as the Editor of a
public Journal — duties to the community at large,
which you had resolved never to compromise or to
betray. I think I see that when you took the oaths
of the Entered Apprentice, the Master Mason, the
Royal Arch, and the Knight Templar, you little
imagined the temptations, the trials and the dangers
into which they were to lead you, by their conflict
with your duties as a man, a Christian, and a citizen. You seem scarcely to be aware even now that
the trials through which you are passing originated
there. You are unwilling to acknowledge it to
yourself. But the trials are around you. You have
betrayed no Masonic secret. You have forfeited no
obligations of your own. But you have justly concluded that of what had been divulged by others it
would be absurd to make longer a secret, and dishonest to deny it as false. Yet you are in the midst
of brother Masons, men whom you respect and esteem, who still hold themselves bound by the ties,
which you consider as dissolved, who still tyle the
lodge and swear the candidates upon horrible penalties to keep secrets now as common as the stairs
that mount the capitol. These men look upon you
as an unworthy brother, even if they had not dared
to expel you. How will these men tolerate your

exposure of the contrast between the public proclamation and the secret appropriation of the Grand
Royal Arch Chapter of the State of New York, at
which upwards of *one hundred and ten subordinate
Chapters were represented* in February, 1829, as
detailed in your twenty-first Letter? How will
they endure your confirmation of the essential facts
in Avery Allyn's affidavit, that Richard Howard
had confessed himself the executioner of Morgan?
That he made this confession at an Encampment of
Knights Templars at St. John's Hall, in the city
of New York, under the sealed obligation, and had
then been furnished with money and means to ab-
scond and go to Europe, as related in your twenty-
second Letter? How will they bear the twenty-
fifth Letter? The account of the unblushing grant
of money by the Grand Lodge of the State of New
York to one of the most active conspirators? of the
debates in which you bore a part? and of the appropriation, since which you have never crossed the
threshold of a lodge room? You are still surrounded by members of the Grand Lodge, of the
Grand Chapter, and of the Encampment at St.
John's Hall. And although perhaps you may receive no more letters from Washington like that of
the 25th of February, 1827, there are other modes
of hostility in which we well know that the Masonic
power can make itself felt.

But if the boldness with which you have dared to speak is not without its perils now, neither will it, I trust, be without its remembrance or its recompense hereafter. I believe your letters to be well adapted to promote a great national reform of morals in the abolition of Freemasonry, and the more extensively they are read, the more beneficial will be their effect.

This letter is confidential, and if satisfactory to you may be followed by others suggested by the information contained in your book, and perhaps discussing some of your opinions. The Masonic controversy will form a large chapter in the annals of this Union probably for several years to come. It presents already a prominent feature in the canvass for the Presidential Election, and that is precisely the reason for wishing to meddle as little with it as possible until that question shall have been settled. It will assuredly survive that event, and in all probability will form an essential ingredient in more than one quadrennial choice of President, if more than one we are destined to have. It is my deliberate opinion that the Antimasonic party ought not to subside, or to suspend its exertions, till Freemasonry shall have ceased to exist in this country. The career before them is long and dreary, but not discouraging, the object is single, just and honorable. You have put your hand to the plough. Let it not

be withdrawn. For contributing so largely to the end,
you will deserve to be ranked among the benefactors
of mankind.

1 am, very respectfully, your friend,

JOHN QUINCY ADAMS.

TO WILLIAM L. STONE, ESQ.

Quincy, 25 August, 1832.

DEAR SIR,—In my last letter I observed, with the
freedom and candor which I thought due to you as
the best return I could make for the honor and obligation you had conferred upon me, by addressing to
me your Letters upon Masonry and Antimasonry,
that there were many things in the book which 1 did
not see as you did.

Some further explanation is due from me upon the
subject. The principal objects of your book were
two. First, to vindicate the character of an eminent and illustrious citizen of New York, the late
Governor of the State, De Witt Clinton, from the
opprobrium cast upon him, of having been personally and deeply concerned in the murder of Morgan ;
and, secondly, to prove, by a fair and impartial
statement of the *abuses* to which the Masonic Institutions have been perverted, that they ought to be
voluntarily surrendered and abolished.

These objects were just and laudable. They are
in your volume faithfully perused; nor is there in
the execution of your plan, any thing in the letters
unsuited or redundant. You observe, in the first
letter, that it is no part of your design to write a
vindication of Freemasonry as such,— but to describe Freemasonry as you received, understood and
practiced it yourself, and as it has been received,
understood and practiced by hundreds of virtuous
and intelligent men, with whom you have associated
in the lodge room. To this, the first ten letters are
devoted, and they are, in my estimation, not less
valuable than those which succeed them. But as
Bishop Watson wrote an apology for the Bible, I
trust you will not consider me as intending any dis-
paragement to that part of your work, if I consider
it in the light of an apology for Freemasonry, as received, understood and practiced by yourself and
many others. In that light it is exceedingly well
adapted to its purpose. It is the only rational *plea*
for the Institution that I have seen, since this controversy began; for all the other defences of the
handmaid, which have come to my knowledge, have
smacked too much of the obligation to come to the
aid of a distressed brother, and extricate him from
his difficulties *right or wrong*, to pass for any thing
other than aggravations of the Morgan-murder
crimes.

You have taken all the degrees to, and including that of, the Knight Templar. The oaths, obligations and penalties, as administered to, and understood by you, contained nothing incompatible with your duties to your country and your kind. Whatever there might be in them, apparently incongruous with the prior and paramount duties of the citizen and Christian, was explained and given in charge in such manner as to be made entirely subordinate to them. The obligations, as understood by you, are all auxiliaries to Christian benevolence and patriotism, and so they are undoubtedly understood by great multitudes of Masons, in all parts of the United States. That they are otherwise understood, also, by multitudes of the *worthy* brethren of the craft (worthy according to the *Masonic* meaning of the word,) is apparent in every page of your book.

In your third Letter, p. 23, you allude to an opinion which I once expressed to you in the following terms:—"You, sir, have assured me that the obligations supposed to be administered in conferring the first degree is quite enough in your view, to establish the wicked character of the Institution."

Whether I did make use of terms quite so strong in the freedom of unrestrained conversation, or whether your reference to it is by inference of your own, from words not quite so comprehensive, is not material. The sentiment which I do recollect to have expressed, and which is rooted in my conviction, was, "that the Entered Apprentice's oath, obligation and annexed penalty, was in itself *vicious*—and such as ought never to be administered by man to man." That no explanation of it could take away its essentially immoral character—and that the institution of Freemasonry, requiring absolutely the ad ministration of it to every candidate for admission, necessarily shared in its immorality.

In saying this, I disclaim all intention of censure upon any individual who has ever taken this oath. I consider it according to its own import—stripped of all warrant of authority from the great names of illustrious men who may have taken it.

My objections to it are these :—

First : That it is an extrajudicial oath, and, as such, contrary to the laws of the land.

Secondly : That it is a violation of the precept of Jesus Christ—*Swear not at all.*

Thirdly: That this oath pledges the candidate, in the name of God, that he will always hail, for ever conceal and never reveal any of the *secret arts, parts or points of the mysteries* "*of Freemasonry*, to any person under the canopy of heaven, except it shall be to a true and lawful Mason, or within the body of a just and regular Lodge of such; and not unto him or them until after due trial, strict examination, or by the lawful information of a brother, I shall have found him or them as justly and lawfully entitled to the same as I am myself."

The arts, parts, points and mysteries of Masonry are afterwards, in the oath, denominated the *secrets of the craft.* These are all general and indefinite terms. The candidate, when he takes the oath, is kept in total ignorance of what these *secrets of the craft* consist. *He knows not the nature nor extent of the oath that he takes.* He is sworn to keep secret he *knows not what.* The general assurance that it is not to affect his religion or politics, is the mere word of another man. The assurance that it is not to interfere with any of his duties, is but a mockery, when the administration of the oath itself is a violation of law.

He swears to reveal the secrets of the craft to no person under the canopy of heaven, *except* to a brother Mason, or a Lodge. The single exception expressed, is an exclusion of all others. There is no exception for the authority of law, or for the confession enjoined upon the Catholic brethren by their religion. I use this illustration to show, that the intrinsic import of the oath is incompatible with law, civil and religious.

Now what these secrets of the craft are, to the keeping of which the candidate, thus ignorant of their import, is sworn, is never defined. They are

differently understood by different Masons. The
oaths, obligations and penalties themselves, have,
until very recently, been understood, I believe, universally to form a part of these secrets. Those of
the first three degrees were first revealed by the
publication of Morgan's book; those of the subsequent degrees, to that of the thrice illustrious Order
of the Cross, were divulged by the convention of
the seceding Masons at Le Roy, on the 4th of July,
1828. Those in Morgan's book I understand to be
admitted on all hands to be correct. But with regard to the obligations of the Red Cross Knights,
and the Templars, as disclosed by that convention,
you say that, although you have received those degrees, and assisted in conferring them, you know of
no such obligations in any degrees. Your impression is, that they must have been devised westward
of Albany, and imposed upon candidates without
the sanction of any governing body. You do not
question the correctness of the publication of these
degrees by the convention of seceding Masons.
You are AUTHORIZED TO STATE, that when the forms
of those obligations were received in the city,
measures were taken by the Grand Encampment to
ascertain whether any Encampment under its jurisdiction had, in fact, ever administered any such obligations, and, if so, where and by whom they had
been imposed.

7

It is earnestly to be hoped that the Grand Encampment will sincerely and seriously pursue this inquiry, and make known the result of their researches to the world. In the mean time, observe the inferences to be drawn from this extreme diversity of the terms and import of the obligations as administered in different Lodges, Chapters and Encampments; but *all* under the sanction of this tremendous oath of the Entered Apprentice — all secured by this soul-shackling pledge, given in advance, and in ignorance of what they are to be, and all riveted by the penalty to which I shall next advert.

Fourthly : " All this, I promise and swear — binding myself under no less penalty than that of having my throat cut across from ear to ear, my tongue torn out by its roots, and my body buried in the rough sand of the sea, at low water mark, where the tide ebbs and flows twice in twenty-four hours.

We have been told, over and over again, that this is understood by Masons to be merely an invocation — and the committee of investigation of the Legislature of Rhode Island have gravely told the world that the explanation given by Masons to this *penalty* is, "that I would rather have, or sooner have, my throat cut, than to reveal," &c. It is unfortunate that this explanation is in direct contradiction to the plain and unequivocal import of the words of the oath. The oath incurs the *penalty* for its violation.

The explanation promises fidelity, though at the expense of life. The oath imprecates the death of a traitor, as a *penalty* for treachery. The explanation claims a crown of martyrdom for constancy. If Benedict Arnold had been taken in the act of treason to his country, he would have suffered no less a *penalty* than death,— though not the barbarous and brutal death of the Masonic obligation. When Joseph Warren suffered death on Bunker's Hill, is there an explanatory Mason who dare tell you that he suffered a *penalty?* Yet so it is, that the Masonic oath, and its explanation, confound all moral distinctions to the degree of considering the death of a martyr and the death of a traitor as one and the same thing.

This *explanation* of the penalty annexed to the Entered Apprentice's oath, it must be acknowledged, is not ingenuous — it is not even ingenuous. It is a grand hailing sign of distress; or it is a Masonic murder of the English language.

I say this with the less hesitation, because, in your seventh Letter, containing *your* defence of the Masonic obligations, you have disdained to take this preposterous *explanation* of the Rhode Island Masons. You know too well the import of words. You candidly avow that the oaths and obligations are out of season — out of reason — and ought to be abolished. I will, therefore, forbear to press upon

you the still grosser absurdity of the pretended
Rhode Island explanation, when applied to the
Master Mason's and Royal Arch penalties. The
Master Mason's penalty is to have his body severed
in two in the midst, and divided to the north and
south, his bowels burnt to ashes in the centre, and
the ashes scattered before the four winds of heaven,
*that there might not the least track or trace of remem-
brance remain among men or Masons of so vile and
perjured a wretch, as I should be.* And this according to the Rhode Island explanation, is to be the
consequence of his dying like Hiram Abiff, rather
than betray the Masonic secrets.

My fifth objection is to the horrible *ideas*, of which
the penalty is composed. It is an oath of which a
common cannibal should be ashamed. Even in the
barbarous ages of antiquity, Homer tells you, that
when Achilles dragged the dead body of Hector
round the walls of Troy, it was a dishonest deed
— ἀεικέα μήδετο ἔργα — and Plato severely censures
Homer for even introducing this incident into his
poem. A mangled body, after death, was a thought
disgusting even to heathens. From the very
thoughts, and still more from the lips, of a Christian,
it should be forever excluded, like indelicacy from
the mouth of a female. The Constitution of the
United States, and of Massachusetts, prohibit the
infliction of cruel or unusual punishments, even by

the authority of the law. But no butcher would
mutilate the carcass of a bullock or a swine, as the
Masonic candidate swears consent to the mutilation
of his own, for the breach of an absurd and senseless
secret. I cannot assent to your denomination of
these penalties as idle or unmeaning words. They
are words of too much meaning — of hideous significancy. The Masons are bound for their own honor
to expunge them from their records for ever. Would
that they could be expunged from the language,
dishonored by their introduction into its forms of
speech.

I remain, very respectfully, your friend,

JOHN QUINCY ADAMS.

TO WILLIAM L. STONE, ESQ.

Quincy, 29 August, 1832.

DEAR SIR,—Long, and, I fear, tedious, as you
have found my last letter, I was compelled by a
reluctance at making it longer, to compress the observations in it upon the *intrinsic* nature of the
Masonic *oaths, obligations,* and *penalties,* within a
compass insufficient to disclose my opinion, and the
reasons upon which it is founded.

I had said to you that the institution of Freemasonry was *vicious,* in its first step, the initiation

oath, *obligation* and *penalty* of the Entered Apprentice. To sustain this opinion, I assigned to you five reasons — Because they were,

1. Contrary to the laws of the land — extrajudicially taken and administered.

2. In violation of the *positive* precept of Jesus Christ.

3. A pledge to keep *undefined* secrets, the swearer being ignorant of their nature.

4. A pledge to the penalty of death *for* violation of the oath.

5. A pledge to a *mode* of death, cruel, unusual, unfit for utterance from human lips.

If, in the statement of these five *objections*, upon principles of law, religion and morals, there be any thing unsound, I invite you to point it out. But if you contest either of my positions, I must entreat you not to *travel out of the record*.

I might ask you not to consider it a refutation of either of these reasons, to say that you and all other honest and honorable Masons have never so understood or practiced upon this oath, obligation and penalty. The inquiry is, not what your practice, or that of others has been ; but what *is* the obligation, its oath and its penalty.

I must request of you to give me no *explanation* of this oath, obligation and penalty, directly contrary to their unequivocal import; that you will not

explain *black* by saying that it means *white*, or even
by alleging that you so understand it. I particularly
beg not to be told that honorable, intelligent and
virtuous men, George Washington and Joseph Warren for example, understood that the penalty of death
for treachery meant the death of martyrdom for
fidelity.

I would willingly be spared the necessity of reply-
ing to the averment that the patterns of honor and
virtue whom I have just named, with a long catalogue of such men, *have* taken this oath, and bound
themselves to this obligation, under this penalty.
For I might deem it proper to inquire, whether
the very act of binding such men, by such oath, to
such obligation, under such penalty, is not among
the *sins* of the institution.

I must ask you to suppose that such institution
had never existed — that it were now to be formed,
and that you were one of ten or twenty virtuous and
intelligent men, about to found a charitable and con-
vivial secret association. Suppose a committee of
such a meeting appointed to draw up a constitution
for the society, should report the Entered Apprentice's oath, obligation and penalty, as a form of
initiation for the admission of members. I do not
ask you whether you would vote for the acceptance
of the report ; but what would you think of the
reporters?

I consider this as the true and only test of the inherent and essential character of Masonry, and it was under this conviction, that I told you that the Entered Apprentice's oath was sufficient to settle, in my mind, the immoral character of the institution.

It is, perhaps, too much to ask of you an explicit assent to these positions, because you may consider it an acknowledgment of error. But this is the first and fundamental consideration, from which I draw the conclusion that Masonry *ought* for ever to be abolished. It is wrong — essentially wrong — a seed of evil, which can never produce any good. It may perish in the ground — it may never rise to bear fruit; but whatever fruit it does bear must be rank poison; it can never prove a blessing but by its barrenness.

My objections to this *seminal principle* of Masonry apply, in all their force, to the single obligation, the form of which is given in the Appendix to your volume, (page 3,) where it is stated to have been the only obligation, taken for all three degrees, so late as 1730, when only three degrees of Masonry were known. The oath is in fewer words, but more comprehensive; for the obligation is to keep "*the secrets or secrecy of Masons or Masonry.*" There is indeed a qualification in the promise not to write, print, mark, &c., which seems to keep the obligations within the verge of the law. For the promise is to reveal nothing whereby the secret might be *unlawfully* obtained. The penalty is also death, not for constancy, but for treachery, "so that there shall be no remembrance of me among Masons."

This oath, obligation and penalty, the only one taken in all the degrees of Masonry known but one century ago, is the prolific parent of all the degrees, and all the oaths, obligations and penalties since invented, and of the whole progeny of crimes descended from them. The natural and unavoidable tendency of such an obligation is the multiplication of its kind. This tendency is among the most obvious causes which have led to the interdiction of *all* such oaths and obligations, by the civil, the ecclesiastical and the moral law. The obligation is to keep *undefined* secrets. As they are undefined in the obligation itself, there is nothing in the constitutions of Masonry to define them, or to secure uniformity either of the secrets or of the obligations. Every Lodge may vary the secrets, obligations and penalties ; and, accordingly, they have been so varied, that scarcely any two adhering Masons give the same account of them. Almost the only defence of Masonry, after the publication of the books of David Bernard and Avery Allyn, consisted in efforts to discredit them, by denying that the oaths, obligations and penalties, were truly stated by them. A secret institution in three degrees ; the secret of each degree being withheld from the members of the degrees inferior to it, is a perpetual temptation to the initiated to multiply the secrets and the degrees. Thus it is that the lodges have grown into chapters —the chapters into encampments—the encampments into consistories ; and, so long ago as December, 1802, the Grand Inspectors of the United States of America issued, at Charleston, South Carolina, a circular, announcing the existence and the names of thirty-three degrees of Masonry.

The secrets, to the keeping of which the Entered Apprentice is sworn, are *indefinite.* In genuine Masonry, when revealed to him, he finds them *frivolous.* You acknowledged that your first feeling upon receiving them was disappointment. So must it be with every reflecting, intelligent man; nor is it conceivable that any such Entered Apprentice, on leaving the Lodge after his admission, should fail to have observed, with pain and mortification, the contrast between the awful solemnity of the oath which he has taken, and the extreme insignificance of the secrets revealed to him. Is it to meet this unavoidable impression, that the institution is graduated. The lure of curiosity is still held out, and its attractive power is sinewed, by the very disappointment which the Apprentice has experienced. He takes the degrees of Fellow Craft and Master Mason, and still finds disappointment—still finds himself bound by tremendous oaths to keep trifling and frivolous secrets. The practice of the Institution is deceptive and fraudulent. It holds out to him a promise which it never performs. Its promise is light—its performance is darkness.

But it introduces him to intimate, confidential and exclusive relations, with a select and limited circle of other men—and to the same confidential and exclusive relations, with great multitudes of men, belonging to every civilized nation throughout the globe. The Entered Apprentice's oath is merely an oath of secrecy—but the candidate who takes it, has pledged himself, by his application for admission, to conform to all the ancient established usages and customs of the fraternity. And the charge of the Master, given him upon the Bible, compass and square, presents him with three precious jewels,—a *listening ear*, a *silent tongue*, and a *faithful heart*,— all, of course, exclusively applicable to the *secrets* revealed to him ; and he is told that the listening ear teaches him to listen to the instructions of the Worshipful Master; but more especially to the cries of a worthy distressed brother; and that the faithful heart teaches him to be faithful to the instructions of the Worshipful Master at all times, but more especially to keep and conceal the secrets of Masonry, *and those of a brother*, when given to him in charge as such, that they may remain as secure and inviolable in his (the Entered Apprentice's) breast, as in his (the brother's) own. Two check words are also presented to him, — *truth* and *union*, — the explanation of which concludes that the heart and tongue of Freemasons join in promoting *each other's* welfare, and rejoicing in each other's prosperity.

Thus the essential nature of the Entered Apprentice's oath, preceded by his pledge to conform to all the established usages and customs of the fraternity, and followed by the charge of the Master, is *secret* and *exclusive* favor, assistance and fidelity *to the brotherhood and brothers of the craft.*

Now combine together the disappointment which every intelligent accepted Mason must feel, at the puerility of the secrets revealed to him, compared with the appalling solemnity of the oath exacted from him for the purchase of his lambskin apron, and the secret ties with which he has linked himself with multitudes of other men, exclusively to favor, assist and be faithful to each other, and acknowledge that the temptation to make the secrets more important, and to turn them to better account to the craft, must be irresistible. Judge this system *a priori*, without reference to any of the consequences which it has produced, and say if human ingenuity could invent an engine better suited to conspiracy of any kind. The Entered Apprentice returns from the lodge with his curiosity stimulated, his imagination bewildered, and his reason disappointed. The mixture of religion and morality, blended with falsehood and imposture, which pervade all the ceremonies of initiation, is like arsenic mingled up with balm.

> "Most dangerous
> Is that temptation which doth lead us on
> To sin in loving virtue."

If the candidate has been educated to a sincere and heart-felt reverence for religion and the Bible, and if he exercises his reason, he *knows* that all the tales of Jachin and Boaz, of Solomon's Temple, of Hiram Abiff and Jubela, Jubelo and Jubelum, are impostures — poisons poured into the perennial fountain of truth — traditions exactly resembling those reprobrated by Jesus Christ, as making the word of God of none effect. If, as in this age but too often happens, he enters the lodge a skeptic, the use of the Bible there, if it have any effect upon him, will turn him out a confirmed infidel. The sincere and rational believer in the gospel can find no confirmation of his faith in the unwarrantable uses made of the Holy Scriptures to shed an unction of their sanctity around the fabulous fabric of Freemasonry; while the reprobate miscreant will be taught the uses to which fraud and secrecy may turn the lessons of

piety and virtue, inculcated in the sublimest effusions of divine inspiration. In those Scriptures we
are told, that when "the children of Israel did SE-
CRETLY those things that were not right against the
Lord their God," they became idolaters, and were
carried into captivity. Their cities then were soon
filled with a mongrel race of Babylonians and Assy-
rians, who perverted the word of God with the impostures of paganism; burnt their children in fire,
to the gods of Sepharvaim; and *"feared* the Lord,
and *served* their graven images;"—an emblem of
Freemasonry, far more illustrative of its character
than the tragedy of Hiram Abiff.

The Entered Apprentice's oath is, therefore, in
its own nature, a seminal principle of conspiracy—
and this objection applies to the only oath originally
taken in all the degrees of Freemasonry at its first
institution. The *ostensible* primitive purposes of
Freemasonry were all comprised in *good fellowship.*
But to good fellowship, whether of labor or refreshment, neither secrecy, nor oath, nor penalties are
necessary or congenial. In the original institution
of Freemasonry, there was then an ostensible and
a secret object, and, by the graduation of the Order,
the means were supplied of converting it to any *evil*
purpose of associated power, screened from the danger of detection. Hence all the bitter fruits which
the institution has borne in Germany, in France, in

Mexico, and, lastly, in this our beloved country. Nor could they have failed to be produced in Great Britain, but that, by sharp and biting statutes, they have been confined within the limits of the ostensible object of the brotherhood — good fellowship.

I am, with much respect, dear Sir,

Your friend and servant,

JOHN QUINCY ADAMS.

TO WILLIAM L. STONE, ESQ.

Quincy, 6 September, 1832.

DEAR SIR, — In my two preceding letters you have seen my objections drawn from the fountains of law, religion and morals, against the first step of Freemasonry — the *oath*, with its obligation and penalty, administered to the Entered Apprentice, at his initiation. You will certainly understand that, in this denunciation of the *thing*, it is not my intention to include a charge against any individual who has ever taken the oath — as, on the other hand, I exclude all palliation or justification of it, upon the mere authority of the great names of men by whom it has been taken.

It is a pledge of faith from man to man, solemnized by an appeal to God, and fortified by the express assent of the swearer to undergo the penalty of

death, and mutilation at or after death, for its violation. Such it is in itself, and no explanation can,
without doing violence to the natural connection between thought and language, take away this its
essential and unequivocal import.

The objections are, 1. To the oath; 2. To the
promise; 3. To the penalty.

1. *To the oath*, as a double violation of the law
of the land, and of the law of God. Upon this there
appears, by your seventh Letter, to be very little, if
any, difference of opinion between you and me.
The principles assumed and admitted in the 'introduction to your seventh Letter, are unquestionably
correct with reference to law, to religion and morals;
and it is equally clear that they are all disregarded
in the administration of the Masonic oaths. It is a
vice of the Institution, which no example can justify,
and which no sophistry can extenuate. Your acknowledgment is magnanimous — your argument is
unanswerable.

But if the administration of the oath is, of itself,
a violation of the laws both of God and man, as well
by him who administers as by him who takes it, is
it not a further mockery of both, for the Master, in
the very act of transgressing the laws, and of sub-
orning the candidate to transgress them with him,
to say to him, "This obligation is not intended to
interfere with your duty to yourself, your neighbor,

your country or your God?" Is there not falsehood
and hyprocrisy superadded to the breach of the law,
and profanation of the name of God, in the injunction and explanation itself? He calls upon the candidate to perform an unlawful act; and he tells him,
that it is not to interfere with his religion or politics,
or, with deeper duplicity, that it is to interfere with
none of his civil, moral or religious duties. This
self-contradiction of word and deed is the very essence of all sanguinary religious fanaticism. It is
the very vital spark of the spirit which armed with
daggers the hands of Ravaillac and Balthasar Gi-
rard. Under the excruciating pangs of the torture,
Ravaillac, to his last gasp, protested that he thought
he was serving God by the assassination of a king
who was about to declare war against the pope;
and he signed his name to one of the interrogatories
at his trial — François Ravaillac —

> Que toujours dans mon cœur
> Jesus soit le vainqueur.

> "In my heart, for ever, may
> Jesus hold conquering sway."

If the murder of Henry the Fourth of France had
been concerted in a Masonic lodge room, and the
Master had administered to the perpetrator, as a
part of his oath, the obligation to commit that deed,
he might, with just as much reason and consistency,

8

have assured him that this oath would not interfere with his religion or politics, or with his duty to himself, his neighbor, his country, or his God, as the Master of a Masonic Lodge can now give such an assurance to a candidate for admission, before administering to him the oath of an Entered Apprentice.

2. *To the promise.*

The promise is to keep the secrets of Masonry, and never to reveal them to any human being, not already initiated. I have already objected that this promise is indefinite. The promiser knows not the nature of the secrets which he is sworn to keep; nor are they ever explained to him. In your seventh Letter (p. 71,) you have explicitly stated your own understanding of what the secrets were, and that you have always found your *intelligent* brethren ready to concur in that opinion. Your definition of them is so clear and satisfactory, that, if it were in its very terms so explained by the Master, before administering the oath, *this* objection would be removed.

" The essential secrets of Masonry " (you say) "consisted in nothing more than the signs, grips, passwords and tokens, essential to the preservation of the Society from the inroads of impostors, together with certain symbolical emblems, the technical terms appertaining to which served as a sort of universal language, by which the members of the

fraternity could distinguish each other, in all places
and countries where Lodges were instituted and conducted like those of the United States."

In NOTHING MORE. But no such explanation is
ever given to the candidate for admission, when the
oath is administered to him, or ever afterwards — and
you very candidly admit that this is not the understanding entertained of the secrets of Masonry, by
" the foolish brethren." Now, herein consists my
objection to the promise. It is to keep secret, he
knows not what — he never knows — and this indefiniteness is essential to preserve the graduation
of the order. It is essential to keep alive the *curiosity* of the candidate, who, at each degree that
he attains, is always comforted in his disappointment by the assurance that there is, in the next
degree, a secret worth knowing.

If it be said that the exaction of a promise to
keep a secret must necessarily precede the communication of the secret itself, and that, therefore, no
promiser can know, in advance, what it is that he
pledges himself to keep secret, I reply, that my objection is to the indefiniteness not only of the secret
itself, but of the promise. Jurors in courts of law
are sworn to keep secret the counsels of their fellows
and their own. The juror, to be sure, knows not
what the counsels of his fellows will be, when he
swears to keep them secret, but he knows that they

cannot extend beyond the line of their duty to decide the matter committed to them—and there is nothing indefinite in the obligation from the moment when it becomes binding upon him. The Masonic swearer is ignorant of the extent both of his oath and of his promise—and after his admission, he still is never informed what are the secrets which he has been sworn to keep.

In *your* enumeration of the essential secrets of the Order, you do not include the oaths themselves, as administered to the candidates for admission. These, therefore, are not secrets which any Mason is bound to keep. But has this been the understanding of *intelligent* Masons heretofore? Why, then, have the forms of the oaths never been made public, in the Masonic books published by authority, or without objection from the Order? Why have they become so different in different places? Why, in all the trials which have arisen from the murder of Morgan, and in which evidence of the forms of these oaths, obligations and penalties was essential to the issue, have not authenticated copies of them been produced in court by the Masonic witnesses themselves? In Massachusetts, in Vermont, in Rhode Island, there have been numerous *defences* of Masonry, by individual Masons and Masonic Lodges, very indignantly denying, that *they* ever took or administered the obligations with the words

"murder and treason not excepted," and generally
denying that they were under any obligation contrary to the laws of God, or of their country ; but,
anxious as they have all been to fix the charge of
slander upon Avery Allyn and David Bernard, and
to make the world believe that the forms of Masonic
oaths, obligations and penalties, disclosed in their
books, were fabrications of their own, never used
by any Masonic body—still, in no single instance,
have they ever produced or certified to the oaths,
obligations and penalties as used or administered by
themselves, until the investigation instituted last
winter, by the legislature of Rhode Island, and conducted in a spirit so friendly to Masonry, and so
adverse to Antimasonry, that it could scarcely have
been more so, had every member of the investigating committee but one, been himself an adhering
Mason.   In that investigation, the committee, like
yourself, considered the secrets of Masonry to consist of the signs, grips, passwords and emblematical
figures of speech, and no more—and, with regard
to these, they indulged the brotherhood, by not inquiring into them, by interrogation of adhering
Masons—giving notice that they should take all
these profound mysteries to have been correctly set
forth in the books of Allyn and Bernard, unless
positive testimony to the contrary should be voluntarily offered by adhering Masons.

But the committee did require testimony from the adhering Masons, of the oaths, obligations and penalties,as taken in the Lodges, Chapters and Encampments in Rhode Island, and it was given. The Appendix to the Report of the committee contains this evidence, and authenticates upon full, adhering Masonic authority, the oaths, obligations and penalties, as taken and administered in Rhode Island, of eleven degrees, from the Entered Apprentice to the Royal Master.

It is, therefore, to the *indefiniteness* of the promise in this authenticated obligation of the Entered Apprentice, that I take my first objection — and this indefiniteness is not only intrinsic in the terms of the obligation itself, but is aggravated by the previous pledge of the candidate to conform to the established usages and customs of the order, and by the charge given by the Master who administers the oath, which charge enjoins it upon the candidate as a duty to obey the instructions of the Master of the Lodge, and to keep the secrets of a brother Mason, committed to him as such. The obligation includes also the pledge to keep secret the transactions of the Lodge — without exception.

There are thus, according to the understanding of the Rhode Island Masons, and to yours, *three* distinct classes of secrets, to which every accepted Mason was bound : First, to the secrets of Masonry, consisting only of the signals of communication and tokens of mutual recognition between the members of the fraternity ; secondly, the secrets of brother Masons, communicated as such ; and, thirdly, the transactions in the Lodge. And of these, you and they consider the first class only as essential to the order. But what is the principle of this distinction? None such is found in the oaths themselves, nor in any of the Masonic books, nor in the charges given by the Master to the candidate for admission. Does the promise of secrecy given by the Entered Apprentice extend to the *transactions of the Lodge?* It does not, in the terms of the oath. It does not, by the practice of the Rhode Island Lodges ; for they enjoin this portion of the secrets by their by-laws upon the penalty of *expulsion,* but those same by-laws contain no provision whatever for the violation of the *essential* secrets. In all the oaths and obligations *subsequent* to the degree of the Entered Apprentice, the promise includes the secrets of a brother Mason, communicated as such, but not the transactions of the Lodge, Chapter or Encampment. These are deemed binding only by virtue of the other promise of the candidate, that he will conform to the usages, customs and regulations of the fraternity. But this distinction itself proves that, in Masonic contemplation, the obligation to keep secret the transactions of the Lodge is not the obligation, with oath and penalty, to keep the essential secrets of the craft. For disclosing the transactions of the Lodge, the penalty is expulsion. But the by-laws contain no such penalty for disclosing the secrets of the craft. What is this but a recognition that the penalty for divulging the secrets of the craft is different from the penalty for revealing the transactions of the Lodge?—that it is a crime of much higher order, sanctioned by the oath with its penalty, and for which it would be alike inconsistent and absurd to provide by a by-law or regulation of the Lodge.

My first objection to the *promise* of the Entered Apprentice's obligation is its *indefiniteness*—and this objection extends to all the obligations of the subsequent degrees, and to the institution itself, which is no where limited to any number of degrees, and is thereby rendered a ready engine of conspiracy for any evil purpose.

A second objection to the *promise* is its *universality*. It is to keep the secrets of the craft, and never to reveal them to *any person under the canopy of heaven*. The single exception has no other effect than to exclude all other exceptions. It is confined to initiated brothers and regular Lodges, to whom the Entered Apprentice can, of course, reveal nothing, they being already in possession of secrets which he promises to keep. The promise,

therefore, is never to reveal the secrets of Masonry *to any person under the canopy of heaven.*
I shall pursue this subject in another letter.

JOHN QUINCY ADAMS.

TO WILLIAM L. STONE, ESQ.

Quincy, 10 September, 1832.

DEAR SIR,—The second objection to the *promise* of the Entered Apprentice's obligation is its *universality.* The candidate swears that he will never reveal any of the undefined "arts, parts or points of the mysteries of Freemasonry, *to any person under the canopy of heaven.*" This promise, like the administration of the oath, is, in its terms, contrary to the law of the land. The laws of this, and of every civilized country, make it the duty of every citizen to testify the whole truth of facts, deemed by legislative bodies, or judicial tribunals, material to the issue of the investigation before them. It is also the duty of a good citizen to denounce and *reveal* to the authorities established to execute the laws against criminals, any secret crimes of which he has in any manner acquired the knowledge. Now, there is nothing in the *arts, parts or points of the mysteries of Freemasonry*, which, in the trial of a judicial cause, or in an investigation of a legislative assembly, may not be justly deemed material to the issue before the court or the legislature. Of its materiality, the judges, or the legislators, have the exclusive right to decide. No witness, called before a court of justice, or an authorized committee of a legislature, can refuse to answer any question put to him by the court or the committee, on the ground that *he* deems it immaterial to the trial before them. This principle becomes more glaringly obvious, when applied to the *promise* never to reveal the secrets of a brother Mason, communicated as such, contained in the Master Mason's oath. But the principle is identically the same. The Entered Apprentice promises never to reveal to any person under the canopy of heaven, *that* which the laws of his country *may*, the next day after he makes the promise, make it his duty to reveal to any court of justice before which he may be summoned to appear, or to any committee of the legislature of the State in which he resides, or of the Union. The promise is, therefore, unlawful, by its universality.

You will remember that I am maintaining the position that the obligation, under oath and penalty, administered to and taken by the Entered Apprentice is, *in itself*, essentially vicious. I now state the promise in the words universally admitted to be used in that ceremony. Do you deny that they contain an unlawful promise? Yes, say you, because the candidate is told, by the Master who administers the oath, that "he is expressly to understand that nothing therein contained is to interfere with his political or religious principles, with his duty to God, or the laws of his country." And you, and all honest and worthy Masons, take and administer the oath with this understanding. Well, then, the promise is, in its terms, contrary to the law of the land, but you take and administer it with *tacit* reservation, furnished to you not by the action of your own understanding, but by the previous notification of the Master who administers the oath to you. So, and so only, you say, the terms of the promise are to be construed. But, in the first place, this is not a question of construction, but a question of mental reservation. The words are plain and unequivocal ; but you pronounce them with a reservation, that the promise shall bind you to nothing contrary to law. Now, what possible reason or justification can there be for exacting a promise, under oath, the real meaning of which is totally different from that of the terms in which it is couched? You swear a man to one thing, and you tell him it means another. But, secondly, how far does your exception extend? You say the promise extends only to the essential secrets of Masonry, and to the lawful transactions in the lodges, and to the secrets of Masons, not criminal — the former of which you consider of not the least consequence to the world, but essential for the preservation of the Society. The secrecy of transactions in the lodges you believed to be merely conventional; and the promise of keeping the secrets of a brother Mason are cancelled, when the secret confided to you by him is of a crime committed by himself.

Now, all these exceptions resolve themselves into the tacit reservation, authorized by the declaration of the Master, before administering the oath, that it contains nothing contrary to law. If the oath is taken with that reservation, it applies equally to the promise to keep the *essential* secrets of the Order, and to all the others. And, therefore, a Freemason, summoned before the committee of a legislature, or a court of justice, is bound not less to disclose the grips, signs, due guards and tokens, than he is to divulge the crimes of a brother Mason, known to him.

The simple question I take to be this : I suppose a Freemason to be summoned before a legislative committee or assembly, or judicial tribunal, to testify. Is he or is he not bound to answer any interrogatory put to him by their authority, and which they require of him to answer, respecting *the essential secrets of the craft?* If he is, how can these secrets be kept, and of what avail are all the oaths administered to Masonic candidates, whether with or without penltay? If he is not, then the obligation of the Masonic oath supercedes the obligation of the law of the land. And if the Masonic oath of secrecy is paramount to the law of the land, with regard to the *mysteries of the craft*, where is the principle which *restores* the supremacy of the law, to require the disclosure of Masonic crimes? The Masonic oath makes no discrimination between the secrets—the promise is to keep them all. The declaration of the Master, that there is nothing *unlawful* in the oath, makes no discrimination—it applies to all, or it applies to none.

With this view of the subject, you will perceive that I deem it altogether immaterial to the argument, whether the words "murder and treason not excepted" are or are not included in the Royal Arch Mason's promise of secrecy—whether he promise to espouse the cause of a brother Mason, right or wrong, or not—and whether the words "and they left to my own election" are or are not an innovation in the Master Mason's oath. But when you ask me, as an act of "justice, to believe that, should a brother Mason tell you, as a secret, that he had robbed a store, you would very speedily make the matter public in the police office," I must, while very cheerfully and sincerely believing you, observe, that it would be at the expense of the very explicit import of the Master Mason's oath. By that oath,

the Master Mason promises to keep the secrets of
a brother Master Mason, as secure and inviolable as
if they were in his own breast, "murder and treason
excepted." That is, excepting two specific enumerated crimes. What, then, is the meaning of this
exception? — and why are they excepted? The
naming of them emphatically, leaves all other crimes
included in the *promise*, and *excluded* from the exception. The Master Mason's promise does, therefore, by the plain import of its terms, pledge him to
keep secret the knowledge of any crime committed
by a brother Master Mason, and communicated to
him as a Masonic secret, other than the two specified
by name; and if you should be in the unfortunate
condition of having such a secret communicated to
you, and should give notice of it at the police office,
you would discharge your duty to your country, only
by considering your Masonic promise as null and
void. For here is the dilemma. If the Masonic
promises are *all* made with the tacit reservation that
nothing contrary to law is understood to be included
in them, then the exception of murder and treason
in the Master Mason's oath is not only superfluous,
but deceptive; since it limits to two specific crimes,
the exception already referred to, of all crimes whatsoever; and if the Masonic promises are made without the reserved exception of *all* unlawful things,
then the exception of murder and treason, from the

secrets which the Master Mason pledges himself to keep, leaves all other crimes, as distinctly under the shelter of the promise, as if they had been included in it expressly by name.

3. *To the penalty* — death by torture and mutilation.

I have, in a former letter, exposed the fallacy — I must say, the disgenuous fallacy — of the attempt to defend this part of the Masonic obligation in the late Rhode Island legislative investigation. In the tale of "January and May," when the doting, blind and abused husband, by the miraculous interposition of the king of the fairies, receives instantaneous restoration of sight, to witness his own dishonor, the queen of the fairies, with equal promptitude, suggests to the guilty wife an EXPLANATION. The Masonic brotherhood of Rhode Island are as ready to take a suggestion from the queen of fairies as the youthful and *studious* May. The committee of the Rhode Island legislature was composed of men too intelligent to be duped like the wittol January; yet were they contented to be told, and to believe, that the penalty of death *for* revealing a secret, was identically one and the same thing as the heroic martyrdom of death *rather* than to reveal a secret. All language is a system of logic. All language is a system of morals. All figurative language is translation. The words may say one thing and intend another; but translation must not confound moral distinctions, and irony and dedications are the only figures of speech which are permitted in human intercourse to "wash an Ethiop white."

Your own exposition of this penalty is more candid and more plausible. You consider the words in which the penalty is expressed, as *unmeaning;* because the candidate has been told that the obligation contains nothing contrary to law; and because the society neither possesses nor exercises the power to authorize the execution of the penalty. This, of course, considers the penalty as null and void.

And so, one would think, it *must* be considered by every fair-minded and honorable man. And why, then, do fair-minded and honorable men adhere to this penalty? Is it worthy of fair-minded and honorable men to use words full of sound and fury, signifying nothing? — to use them as the sanction of a promise? — to use them with an appeal to the everlasting God? Are the words so charming in themselves, is the thought conveyed by them to the mind so irresistibly fascinating, that even now twelve hundred fair-minded and honorable men of Massachusetts declare, in the face of their country and of mankind, that they will not renounce the use of them? Oh, say not what fair-minded and honorable men will or will not do! Twelve hundred men of Massachusetts, men of fair and honorable minds, even now, after all the arts, parts and points of the mysteries of Freemasonry have been revealed and published to the world, nay, after the very check-word, transmitted to them for their protection against the intrusion of book-Masons upon their mysteries, had been divulged with all the rest — after all this, twelve hundred Masons of Massachusetts have declared that they will not renounce or abandon the mysteries of Freemasonry; — that they will still continue to hold their meetings, to tyle their lodges, to brandish their drawn swords for the exclusion of cowans and eaves-droppers, and to swear the knave or simpleton who will henceforth submit to take the oath, never to reveal, never to write, print, cut, carve, paint, stain or engrave, secrets known to every one who will take the trouble to read — secrets, in their own estimation, insignificant and puerile — secrets, in the estimation of great multitudes of their fellow-citizens, disgusting and blasphemous;—that they will continue to swear the candidate to this oath of secrecy, under no less a penalty than that of having his throat cut across from ear to ear, his tongue torn out by the roots, and his body buried in the rough sand of the sea, at low water mark, where the tide ebbs and flows twice in twenty-four hours. But that they will take care to explain to him, that this only means he will rather die than reveal to any person under the canopy of heaven these secrets known to all the world; that his oath is not to interfere with his religion or politics, nor with any of his duties to his neighbor, his country, or his God For thus speaks the mystic muse of Masonry :

> And many a holy text around she strews,
> To teach Masonic moralists to die.

Have I proved that the Entered Apprentice's *oath* is a breach of law human and divine? — that its *promise* is undefined, unlawful and nugatory? — that its *penalty* is barbarous, inhuman, murderous in its term, and, in its least obnoxious sense, null and void? If so, my task is done. The first step in Freemasonry is a false step. The Entered Apprentice's obligation is a crime; and, like all vicious usages, should be abolished.

JOHN QUINCY ADAMS.

TO WILLIAM L. STONE, ESQ.

Quincy, 4 September, 1832.

DEAR SIR, — On the 19th ult. I wrote you a letter containing some observations upon the volume of Letters upon Masonry and Antimasonry, which you have done me the honor of addressing to me. It was confidential, and intimated my intention to pursue the subject further hereafter. So far as it is connected with the presidential election now approaching, I abstain from all interference with it. But the abolition of Freemasonry in this Union, is a *cause* which you have made your own, and which I trust you will not abandon.

In the seventh Letter of your volume, in confirmation of the statement that the Masonic obligations are administered in very different phraseology in different places, you refer me to enclosed copies of the obligations of the seven degrees as they were given twenty-five years since in the Lodge and Chapter of an eastern city, you add among other things that these forms were introduced and adopted at Rochester, in the State of New York, when Royal Arch Masonry was introduced there. And you invite my attention to the difference between the Royal Arch obligation as contained in this manuscript and that in Bernard's book.

There is in the volume a reference to the Note B, in the Appendix. But *there* I find only an apology for the omission of this manuscript because it would have swollen the volume to a size beyond your intention.

If it would not give you too much trouble I should be obliged to you for a communication to me of this manuscript, which you can forward by the mail, and which will be returned to you as you may direct.

I am, very respectfully, dear Sir,

Your friend and servant,

JOHN QUINCY ADAMS.

TO HIS EXCELLENCY LEVI LINCOLN, GOVERNOR OF
MASSACHUSETTS.

[EXTRACT.]

Washington, 1 February, 1832.

DEAR SIR,—My Antimasonry has cooled down a
little while objects less important but more urgent
absorb my time and attention; but it has not been
extinguished by the mental reservations of the
twelve hundred certifiers to their own integrity,
which I never thought of impeaching, nor has it been
remarkably edified by the *ostensible* investigation of
the committee of the Rhode Island Legislature, or
its results. I share in no spirit of Antimasonic *proscription*, if such there be; but if I had any right of
person or property pending in a court of justice
with an Entered Apprentice or a Knight Templar
for my adversary, I should much disincline to see any
man sworn upon my jury, who had been present at
the murder and resuscitation of Hiram Abiff, and still
more to any one who should have crawled upon all-
fours under the living arch. In other words, I do
hold as disqualified for an impartial juror, at least
between a Mason and an Antimason, any man who
has taken the Masonic oaths and adheres to them,
not excepting the twelve hundred certifiers themselves. With regard to church fellowship I am not

prepared to speak so particularly. I am in church communion with several of the twelve hundred, and have perfect confidence in their integrity. But I would challenge them as jurors, between me and the Master Mason who made oath that he had been twice present with me at a Lodge in Pittsfield; or between me and the Master Mason who had the impudence to vouch in my father as a patron of Masonry.

I have said that I share in no Antimasonic proscriptions, if such there be; and I repeat the assurance, that so far from approving or countenancing their nomination of any candidate in opposition to you, I did unequivocally disapprove of that measure, and as far as I could dissuade them from it. I am happy to give you this assurance, nor will I press further for the name of him who attempted to induce in your mind a different belief. I have no doubt he was acting under Masonic law as faithfully as the brethren of the Royal Arch, who Morganized the bottom of Niagara river. — *Agnosco fratrem.*

JOHN QUINCY ADAMS.

TO ALEXANDER H. EVERETT, ESQ., BOSTON.

[EXTRACT.]

Quincy, 18 August, 1832.

WITH respect to conciliating the Antimasons in this Commonwealth, though it is rather late for the National Republicans to begin, it may be better late than never. I most sincerely and heartily wish that they would. The National Republicans of this Commonwealth have not understood, they do not and I fear *will not* understand, the state of the Antimasonic question. About a year ago the Grand Lodge of Rhode Island published a formal *defence of Masonry,* in which they said they could not tell whether Morgan had been murdered or not, for *they knew nothing about it.* I have read a declaration published on the last day of the last year, signed by twelve hundred Masons of this our own State, who speak of a high excitement, which *had been* in the public mind, carried to it " by the *partial and inflammatory* representations of *certain offences* committed by *a few misguided members* of the Masonic Institution in a sister State." The National Republicans of Massachusetts know nothing about *these certain offences;* but they have for two years past taken most especial care to turn out of office every Antimason upon whom they could lay their hands, all the while bitterly complaining of the persecuting and proscriptive spirit of political Antimasonry.

The cause of Antimasonry must and will survive the next Presidential election. And if the National Republicans of Massachusetts really wish for the co-operation of Antimasons, I have no doubt they can obtain it. Whether they can agree upon a ticket for the Presidential election now so near at hand, is doubtful in my mind, but I take it for granted that for this time the National Republicans can carry their elections without them. The Masonic declaration of last winter, to which I have alluded, considers the Antimasonic excitement as having subsided, and they certainly did appear to have lost ground in this State, and at least to have gained none in the States of New York and Pennsylvania. There is now an apparent union of the two parties in New York, but whether it will be cordial or successful is very problematical. The National Republicans there are more sanguine than the Antimasons, and there are wounds between them not easily to be healed. You know how it is here.

Upon the subject of Antimasonry I have not suffered myself to be excited, although there has been no lack of provocations. But I *do* know something about the *Masonic murder* of Morgan, and the clusters of crimes perpetrated for the suppression of his book. I know something also of the laws, oaths, obligations and penalties of Masonry, and I have not been unobservant of their practical effect, from murder under the sealed obligation, down to the prevarication of pretending that to have the throat cut from ear to ear *means* expulsion from the Lodge. If the Masonic controversy were now raging in Cochin-China, and the name of Hiram Abiff had never been heard upon this continent, the subject would be worthy of investigation, as a philosophical inquiry into the mysteries of human nature. I have endeavored to consider it as a question upon the first principles of morals. I have sought for the facts from the Masonic as well as from the Antimasonic side, and have read Henry Brown, as well as Avery Allen and David Bernard. Col. Stone's Letters, which you have doubtless seen, were addressed to me, in consequence of inquiries which I had addressed to a brother Mason of his in Philadelphia, which were communicated to him. Stone is a Knight Templar, and as you know, a very ardent National Republican. His Masonic spirit lingers with him through his whole book, but he is an honest man; unperverted, even by the fifth libation; and a bold one, or he never would have dared to proclaim the truths contained in those Letters. I ask your particular attention to the Letters from twenty-one to twenty-five inclusive, and to the forty-eighth, and I wish you would recommend the perusal of them to those of your National Republican friends, who are accessible to reason upon this subject. I abstain purposely from any public manifestation of opinion upon this topic, to avoid all appearance of interfering with the approaching Presidential election.

Faithfully your friend,

JOHN QUINCY ADAMS.

TO RICHARD RUSH, ESQ., YORK, PENNSYLVANIA.

Quincy, 30 August, 1832.

MY DEAR SIR, — Since my letter of the third instant, I have not had the pleasure of hearing from you. In the interval I have been solicited with some urgency, on one hand by the National Republicans, and on the other hand by the Antimasons of this Commonwealth, to repair to their respective standards, which are not here the same. There is yet some obscurity with regard to the result of the compromise, said to have taken place in New York and Pennsylvania; and there is no prospect of an agreement between them here.

Of this I have had the opportunity to satisfy myself, and it has confirmed my conviction of the propriety of my abstaining from interference with the elections. I have therefore declined attending as a delegate at the Antimasonic State Convention, to be held at Worcester on the 5th of next month, to make nominations for the offices of Governor and Lieutenant Governor of the Commonwealth, and of an Electoral ticket for the choice of President and Vice President of the United States.

But while refraining from all agency in the approaching elections, I am, as a true and faithful *Anti-Mason, in search* of light. Now there are three modes of lighting a lamp, with which I am almost equally familiar. One at noon-day, with a burning-glass, by the radiance of the sun. One in times of clouds and darkness, with flint, steel, tinder and a match; and one either by night or day, in sunshine or in shade, kindled at the light of another lamp. In the analogy between the worlds of matter and of mind, electioneering seems to me to light the lamp by the collision of flint and steel. But I, reserving that process for use when the others fail, or cannot be applied, content myself for the present with lighting my lamp by the flame of another, or by the concentrated illumination from the source of light.

I have, therefore, since my return home, read with close and critical attention the volume of Letters addressed to me by Col. Stone. This book was, if not composed, at least addressed to me in consequence of those letters, which about this time last year I wrote Edward Ingersoll, and which he then communicated to Mr. Stone. They contained a specification of nine crimes, atrocious as any that can be committed by man, with *inquiries* whether they had not been committed in the transactions connected with the murder of Morgan, and whether the organized Institution of Freemasonry, its corporate bodies of Lodges, Chapters and Encampments, were not accessory to all these crimes, before or after the fact.

Mr. Stone's book is the answer to these inquiries. He is, against the Institution, the best of witnesses. He has taken ten degrees of Masonry; and is, in Masonic language, a worthy Sir Knight Templar. He has never renounced nor ever formally seceded from the Institution. Long after the murder of Morgan he believed that no Masonic *Lodge* had in any manner polluted itself with the guilt of his blood. But as the editor of a respectable journal, he did not suffer his Masonic obligations to control his moral duties. He disdained to justify, to connive at, or to suppress, the commission of crimes. His journal did give to the public, statements of the facts as they became authenticated, and this soon brought him into collision with numbers of adhering Masons, and with the *Grand Lodge* of the State of New York. Then after a sharp altercation and bitter reproaches for his admission into the columns of his newspaper of *truth* against *Masonic murder;* and after an ineffectual struggle to save the Grand Lodge from the turpitude of an appropriation of money for the benefit of the Western sufferers, he withdrew; and says he has never set his foot in a lodge-room from that day.

Col. Stone, I have said, is the best of witnesses against Masonry, for he is an upright, intelligent, and most *unwilling* witness. He testifies under the shackles of all his Masonic obligations, and with the knowledge that he is incurring the vindictive and unforgiving resentment of the craft. This is the destiny of every non-adhering Mason, and it places him in a position of no trifling or inconsiderable peril. His testimony confirms, far beyond any anticipation that I had formed, the extent to which the Lodges, Chapters and Encampments of the State of New York are implicated in the Morgan-murder crimes. It demonstrates beyond all possibility of reply, not only that the nine crimes specified in my letters to Edward Ingersoll, have been committed, but that Lodges, Chapters and Encampments have been accessory to every one of them, before or after the fact. It proves also that the crimes committed were more numerous than my specifications, and that several others should be added to the list. As you have Stone's book, I refer you to the Letters from twenty-one to twenty-five inclusive, and **to**

Letter forty-eight, and will ask at your leisure for
your thoughts on the *facts* there disclosed.

With a view to the ultimate object of Antimasonry, *the abolition of Freemasonry in these
United States*, it appears to me to be an important
point gained, if we produce on the public mind a
full conviction that those crimes have been committed, and that *Masonry* is responsible for them.

The honest adhering Masons turn away their
eyes from the facts, and urge the people to do the
same. The reason of this is that they cannot look
at the facts, and defend the Institution ; but they
give thereby an immense advantage in the controversy to their adversaries. For as argument must
be founded upon facts, he who has most perfect
possession of facts, must have the firmest foundation
for argument.

But after establishing the facts, first of the crimes
committed, and secondly of the participation of
many organized Masonic bodies in them, there is
another point of view, to which it seems to me
advisable to call the attention of the public to
induce them to look at the institution *a priori*, to
examine and analyze it, as it is in its nature. In a
conversation with Col. Stone, after he had proposed
to address the Letters to me, but before he had
begun the work, he was pleading, as he does in his
book, for the Institution as *he* had known and

shared in it, and denied that he had ever taken the
oath with the words "*murder and treason not excepted.*" I said to him that the first step of Masonry
was a stumbling block to me. That the Entered
Apprentice's oath was vicious, and infected the
whole Institution. He has stated this observation
of mine in his book, in terms I think rather stronger
than those that I used. I have therefore written
him two letters, with a full development of the sentiment which I did express to him, and of the
reasons upon which it is founded. I have not written them for the purpose of present publication ;
and I enclose them to you, before transmitting
them to him, and will be grateful to you for any
remarks that may occur to you upon the perusal of
them ; after which I will ask you to return them to
me. You will perceive that a concentration of
legal, religious and moral objection against the very
first act of initiation to Masonry, is in truth laying
the corner stone to the edifice of Antimasonry.
This part of the system seems to me not to have
been sufficiently canvassed. The adhering and
seceding Masons have been disputing about single items in the Master Mason's, Royal Arch, and
Templar's obligations, which are differently administered in different Lodges, Chapters and Encampments ; while the vital question seems to me to be
in the Entered Apprentice's oath, obligation and

penalty. The chemist who detects arsenic in a cup of coffee, may inquire, for curiosity, whether it was mingled up with the powder of the berry, or poured into the boiling kettle ; a motive of more intense interest to those who repair with the pitcher to the fountain, should be, to examine whether the poison has not been deposited there.

You will estimate the confidence which I repose in your candor as well as in your judgment, when I add, that in submitting the enclosed letters to your examination, I have not forgotten that you, like Washington and Warren, had once taken the Entered Apprentice's oath yourself.

Accept the assurance of

my respect and affection.

JOHN QUINCY ADAMS.

TO BENJAMIN COWELL, ESQ., PROVIDENCE, R. I.

Washington, 28 November, 1832.

Sir,—Your letter of the 22d instant, enclosing your address before the Antimasonic convention, holden at Providence on the 2d instant, proposes a question of considerable difficulty — namely, by what means the Institution of Freemasonry, with all its exceptionable properties, may be put down.

I answer, by the voluntary dissolution of the

society, or by its extinction by the forbearance of others to contract its obligations.

I have hoped that the virtuous and intelligent members of the order, upon finding that all their secrets have been revealed and made public; upon perceiving the numerous atrocious crimes connected with the murder of Morgan, and to which their oaths, obligations and penalties have given rise; and upon discovering the general obloquy into which the Institution was gradually sinking, would frankly have abandoned it, of their own accord. This expectation has not been fully realized. But great numbers of Masons have ceased to frequent the Lodges — numbers of Lodges and Chapters have suffered their charters to expire; and I believe the instances are now few in which they swear a man upon the penalty of having his throat cut from ear to ear, to keep secret from every human being, what every human being who will read the books of David Bernard and Avery Allyn, knows as well as the brightest Masons of the land — still, the majority of Masons do adhere to the craft, and refuse to give up their idol. The only way to deal with them is, to bring to bear upon them public opinion; and that mode of treatment has been pursued with regard to the disease, with considerable and encouraging success.

I concur with you in the opinion that the admin-

istration of Masonic oaths, obligations and penalties
ought to be prohibited by statutes of the State legislatures, with penalties annexed to them, not of cutting throats from ear to ear, nor of cutting the body
in two by the middle, nor of opening the left breast
and tearing out the heart and vitals, nor of smiting
off the skull to serve as a cup for the fifth libation ;
but with good, wholesome penalties of fine and imprisonment, adequate to their purpose of deterring
every Master, Grand Master, Grand King, or other
dignitary of the sublime and ineffable degrees, from
ever more polluting his lips with the execrable for-
mularies, which have at length been dragged into
light. Most cordially would I, were I a member of
any State legislature in the Union, give my voice
and vote for the enactment of such monitory statutes.
But this cannot be effected, so long as Masonry controls the majorities in the State legislatures; that is,
so long as the people continue to elect, as members
of the State legislatures, adhering Freemasons—or
men who are neither Masons nor Antimasons ; or,
what you call *moral* Antimasons ; men who disapprove Masonry, but are afraid of incurring Masonic
vengeance, by raising a finger or uttering a word
against it—men whose virtue consists in neutrality
between right and wrong ; and who are willing to
believe that to refuse their votes to a man, because
he is an adhering Freemason, is *persecution.* So

long as the people continue to constitute majorities of their State legislatures of such men as these, so long will it be idle to expect any statutory enactment against Masonic oaths, obligations and penalties.

It is, therefore, the duty of pure and disinterested Antimasonry to operate, as well as it can, upon public opinion ; and one of the most effective modes of thus operating is the ballot box. It is just and proper, that every individual, honestly believing that the Masonic Institution is an enormous nuisance in the community, which, if not voluntarily relinquished, ought to be broken down by the arm of the law, should resolve that he will vote for individuals, as members of the State legislatures, entertaining, upon this subject, the same opinions as himself, and for none other. If this resolution be just and proper for each individual separately, it is equally so for as many individuals collectively as can agree upon the principle. Far from being obnoxious to the charge of persecution, it is, perhaps, the mildest of all possible forms of operating upon public opinion — by public opinion itself. It is thus that the Antimasons have acted ; first in the State of New York, where the Morgan-murder has fastened upon the hand of Masonry a spot of blood, like that which the dream of Macbeth's wife paints upon hers, and which all the perfumes of Arabia can never sweeten ; and subsequently in other States, including that of Rhode

Island. Thus far, the principle of political Anti-masonry has my hearty approbation ; and in the diversity of opinion which still unhappily prevails on this question, it is a satisfaction to me that the dictate of my judgment coincides with that of a large majority of the inhabitants of my native town, my friends and neighbors, and of a highly respectable portion, if not a majority, of the constituents whom I have the honor of representing in the Congress of the United States.

With regard to the political course of the Anti-masons in Rhode Island, I am not a competent judge. To the *cause* of Antimasonry, I consider the legislative investigation of the last winter as having essentially contributed. It has substantially settled the question what the *oaths*, *obligations* and *penalties* of Freemasonry ARE. It has cut short all quibbling equivocation, and attempts to blast the credit of Avery Allyn and David Bernard. It has given us those oaths, obligations and penalties in their naked deformity. It has dragged the struggling savage into day, and has shown us the last writhings of his Protean form, in the impudent pretension that the death of a traitor, in Masonic language, means the death of a martyr. To the conclusions of the majority of the committee of investigation — namely, that it is the indispensable duty of the Masons to dissolve their fraternity, I respond, Amen and amen;

though, when I read their report, and observe the process by which they reach them, I cannot forbear an exclamation of astonishment at the novel process of induction, by which their conclusion slaps the face of all their premises.

I hope and trust that the Freemasons of Rhode Island will ultimately follow the advice of the committee of investigation, which so magnanimously waived the legislative right of exacting testimony to their secrets, and thus suffered the law of the land to cower before the law of Masonic secrecy. I thank the committee for having peremptorily exacted the real oaths, obligations and penalties, as taken and administered in Rhode Island, and consider the result as having settled, in the mind of every reasonable and independent man, their nature and their character.

Respectfully, Sir,

Your servant and fellow-citizen,

JOHN QUINCY ADAMS.

TO JAMES MOORHEAD, ESQ., MERCER, PENN.

Washington, 23 December, 1832.

SIR,—Mr. Banks, the worthy representative of your district, delivered to me your friendly letter of the 26th of last month. I have, since the commencenment of the session of Congress, regularly received the numbers of the Mercer Luminary, and have observed with pleasure the zeal and assiduity with which it disseminates the light of Antimasonry. To that cause I am devoted, because I believe it to be the cause of pure morals and of truth. Until the murder of Morgan, I had very little knowledge of the Institution of Freemasonry, except as an occasional witness of its childish pageantry, and the mock solemnity of its processions. These I believed to be harmless, and I gave willing credit to their boastful professions of benevolence and charity. Very soon after the Morgan catastrophe, however, the Masonic *obligations* were diclosed to me in the escape of Col. William King, from the pursuit of justice, in the territory of Arkansas. I saw their operation, without being able to punish the offender or even judicially to authenticate the offence. King escaped by the connivance of Masonic obligations paramount to the laws of the land. He re-appeared afterwards upon the theatre of his guilt; and as you know, died suddenly, on the disclosing of facts which he had flattered himself were hidden from every person under the canopy of heaven, without the pale of Masonic oaths and penalties. Other evidences of the practical effect of Masonic obligations soon revealed themselves to me in the forms of *secret slander* and perjury. But of the multitude of atrocious crimes committed, first in the conspiracy which terminated in the murder of Morgan, and for five years afterwards in baffling and defeating the laws of the State in their efforts to bring the murderers to justice, I had a very imperfect idea till the publication of Col. Stone's book.

There remained yet, not any reasonable doubt, but some deficiency of evidence, with regard to the essential, inherent, and indelible viciousness of the Masonic obligations, in the solemn protestations of the adhering Masons, that those obligations were falsely represented in the books of Bernard and Avery Allyn; in the bold asseverations that no such oaths, obligations and penalties existed; and in reiterated declarations, couched in delusive generalities, that *they* had never taken any oath or obligation inconsistent with their duties to their country or their religion; but always without disclosing what *were* the terms of those which they had taken. The investigation by a committee of the Legislature of Rhode Island, finally brought out the obligations of ten degrees, as avowed to be practiced in the Lodges, Chapters and Encampments of that State. It exposed them in their hideous deformity, and took from the defenders of Masonry their last refuge of prevarication.

It was to show them in their naked nature,

divested of all sophisticated explanations, and all mental equivocations, that I wrote the four letters on the Entered Apprentice's oath, which you have republished in the Luminary. I am happy that they have met your approbation,

I am, with much respect,

Your friend and fellow-citizen,

JOHN QUINCY ADAMS.

TO EDWARD LIVINGSTON, ESQ.

Washington, 10 April, 1833.

SIR,—In the National Intelligencer, of the 22d of April, 1830, there appears an address, there said to have been delivered by you, to the General Royal Arch Chapter of the United States, upon your installation to the high Masonic official dignity of their General Grand High Priest.

In that address, after a feeling and elegant acknowledgment of the grateful emotions which you experienced on being apprized of the unexpected and unsolicited distinction which had been conferred upon you by your election to that office, and a pathetic allusion to that period of life when all worldly honors fade into the "sear and yellow leaf," you assign as your reason for accepting the dignity and the charge of presiding over an association in whose labors you had "for many years retired from any participation," that your refusal might have been "ascribed to an unmanly fear of encountering the clamor raised against *our Institution*, [of Free-masonry,] or to a consciousness, that the vile and absurd accusations against it were well founded. Either of these suspicions (you added) would have injured not my character only, but that of the whole fraternity."

You further assigned an additional motive for overcoming the reluctance suggested by the consciousness that your long retirement had rendered you less fit to fill the station than many others, equally well qualified in other respects; and this motive was your confidence in the Masonic skill and excellent character of the worthy companion who was, at the same solemnity, installed with you as your Deputy General Grand High Priest.

After these ceremonial preliminaries, you proceed as follows : — " Companions and Brethren! For the first time in the history of our country, persecution has raised itself against our honorable fraternity It does not, indeed, as in other countries, incarcerate our bodies, strain them on the wheel, or consume them in the flames of the Inquisition; but its attacks are, to an honorable mind, as unjustifiable. It assails our reputation with the blackest calumnies; strives, by the most absurd inventions, to deprive us of the confidence of our fellow-citizens; belies the principles our order, and represents us as bound to each other by obligations subversive of civil order, and hostile to religion."

Mr. LIVINGSTON,—In moulding this personified image of persecution, did it never occur to you that the foul and midnight hag, who justly bears that name, is never to herself more deliciously occupied than in charging *persecution* upon others? In those Holy Scriptures, which it is your official duty to read and expound to your companions and brethren of the Royal Arch, it is related, that when your predecessor in the high priesthood, Ananias, commanded that Paul should be smitten on the mouth, the apostle of the Gentiles turned upon him and said, "God shall smite thee, thou whited wall; for sittest thou to judge me after the law, and commandest me to be smitten, contrary to the law?" I will not imitate this exclamation of Paul, for which he himself apologized, when informed that it was the high priest to whom he spoke—but I will ask you, sir, to reconsider this charge of persecution, imputed by you, in the face of the world, not indeed to any individual by name, but to a numerous and respectable class of your fellow-citizens in nine or ten States of the Union—to all that class of citizens known in the community by the denomination of Antimasons. I am one of them myself. As respects

myself I know, as regards the whole party I firmly
believe, that in the above passage of your address,
you did them great injustice. In charging them
with calumny, you calumniated them yourself. In
accusing them of persecution, you are yourself the
persecutor.

I will not say that on your part this persecution
and calumny were wilful. You had for many years
retired from any participation in the labors of the
craft. If this fact is not very pregnant of evidence,
that, in your estimation, the labors of the craft were,
when you participated in them, of a high order of
public usefulness or private beneficence, it excul-
pates you at least from all participation in labors of
evil. You did not know what new labors had, most
especially in your own native State of New York,
and extensively elsewhere, been engrafted upon the
old stock. You did not know the additions which
had been, in many Lodges and Chapters, made to the
whole graduation of your oaths. The tree had not
borne all its fruits. The Morgan tragedy had been
enacted, and more than three years of impunity had,
in evasion or defiance of the laws of nature, of justice, and of the land, sheltered the guilt of its perpetrators; but you did not know, nor was there
mortal out of the pale of your penalties who did
know, the catalogue of *Masonic* crimes which had
been committed in affiliated connection with that

Masonic murder — you know them not to this day. Multitudes of them are, and will ever remain, secreted under the seal of the fifth libation, and under the obligation to conceal from every person under the canopy of heaven, the secrets of a WORTHY brother — murder and treason not excepted, or excepted at the option of the swearer. More than a year after your address was delivered, the Grand Lodge of Rhode Island published a defence of Masonry against those same charges, which they, like you, pronounced persecutions and calumnies. Yet, even then, they said that whether Morgan had been murdered or not, they could not tell — *for they knew nothing about it.* They knew nothing about it! They knew nothing about the facts proved in the judicial tribunals of New York, not only by clouds of witnesses, but by the confessions and pleas of guilty of several among the conspirators themselves. The Grand Lodge of Rhode Island, one and all, knew nothing about all this, and yet they published a defence of Masonry, and pronounced persecution and calumny, the denunciations of virtuous indignation against those very judicially authenticated facts, about which they declared that *they knew nothing.*

Sir, your address to your Royal Arch companions had more of candor or more of discretion. You advised them that calumnies so absurd as those

uttered against you (the Masons) were best met by
dignified silence! And yet you did not meet them
by dignified silence; you pronounced them from
your exalted seat of General Grand High Priest of
the Order, black and absurd calumnies, and you
attributed them all to persecution.

But if I am bound to acknowledge the candor
and discretion of your advice to your brethren to
meet the charges against their Institution with
dignified silence, I cannot offer an equal tribute of
commendation to your consistency, when after all
your bitter complaints of calumny and persecution,
you urge them to "be just, and reflect how much
cause for excitement has been given, by the out-
rageous abduction of a citizen dragged from his
family and friends, in the midst of a populous State,
followed up, *most probably*, by the perpetration of a
most atrocious murder."

You then remind them that

"It was natural, from all the circumstances of
this most extraordinary and savage act, to believe
that it was committed by Masons."

Sir, was it not committed by Masons?

"It was in human nature, *unenlightened and
prejudiced* human nature, to impute the cause of
the offence to some secret tenet of the fraternity,
and to involve them in the criminality of their guilty
members."

Why the words *unenlightened and prejudiced?*
Was not some secret tenet of the fraternity the
cause of the offence? That tenet of the fraternity,
secret at the time of the murder of Morgan, is
secret now no longer. For the mere intention to
reveal it, Morgan paid the penalty of his Entered
Apprentice's oath — his book revealed it after his
death. Its revelation was authenticated on the 4th
of July, 1828, by the testimony, not of unenlightened and prejudiced human nature, but of the Le
Roy Convention of seceding Masons — men who
themselves had taken these oaths, and declared
themselves subject to the penalties which had been
inflicted by Masonic hands upon Morgan.

"It was natural that ambitious men should keep
up the excitement, and direct it against political
adversaries for their own elevation."

Perhaps it was. You, Mr. Livingston, are versed
in the ways of ambition and of ambitious men.
You know their propensity to keep up excitements,
and to direct them against political adversaries for
their own elevation. You must know, you cannot
but know, that Masonry has been used by ambitious men for the same purposes. You must know
that in many of the New York Lodges, the promise
to promote a brother's political advancement, was
one of the recent additions to the Masonic obligations. You may and ought to know, that wherever

the spirit of Antimasonry has arisen, one of the first discoveries made by it has been, that wherever a Lodge or Chapter has existed, at least three-fourths of all the elective offices in the place were held by worthy brethren and companions of the craft, chosen by men, multitudes of whom knew not themselves the influence under which their votes were cast. You know, too, that the charge of ambitious and selfish motives is one of the most vulgar, and most hacknied imputations of all ambitious rivals and competitors against one another. In condescending to use it yourself against the Antimasons, you certainly gave no additional dignity to it ; — and as a defence of the Institution against Antimasonry, you might with advantage to yourself have remembered your advice to your brethren, and preferred to such a shield, the armor of dignified silence.

"And it was quite natural that men should be found simple enough not to see through their views, credulous enough to believe their absurd tales, or sufficiently unprincipled to propagate them, knowing them to be false."

This again may be true. Of simple, of credulous, and of unprincipled men, there are always numbers in every community, and they are the natural instruments of politicians of more ambition than principle. But, in this respect, as in many

115

others, Antimasonry is and has been more sinned against than sinning. Simple and credulous men have, for example, been told by the General Grand High Priest of the General Royal Arch Chapter of the United States, that the charges against the Masonic Institution, of having had some secret tenet, which was the cause of the murder of Morgan, were black and absurd calumnies, invented by persecution, and which none but fools and cullies could believe, and none but knaves would propagate. Simple and credulous men may believe these assertions of the General Grand High Priest, because they are made by him, and because his character gives them the weight of authority. To simple and credulous men, the highest of all evidence is the authority of great names, and accordingly your own most plausible answer to the Antimasonic charges against your institution, is an appeal to the great and good men who have belonged and still belong to it.

But, sir, this is not sound reasoning to influence the minds of other than simple and credulous men. The question, permit me to say, upon the issue which I am about to take with you, is not WHO— but WHAT—not *who* have bound themselves by the Masonic oaths, obligations, and penalties ; but *what* these oaths, obligations and penalties are. *What* is their nature? and *what* have been their fruits?

Now, sir, I do aver, that "the cause of the offence"—that is the murder of William Morgan, and of a multitude of other crimes indissolubly connected with it, was a secret tenet of the fraternity—secret then, but no longer secret now. It consisted in the obligation and penalty of the *Entered Apprentice's oath.* It was the secret tenet of *initiation* to the Masonic Institution.

This, sir, is the issue which I, an Antimason, tender to you, the General Grand High Priest of the General Royal Arch Chapter of the United States. I call upon you, sir, in that capacity, to sustain the charge of persecution and calumny, made by you in your address to your brethren and companions, upon your installation, against the whole body of Antimasons in the United States, and to sustain the Institution over which you preside, against the charges which you pronounce persecuting and calumnious.

But this, sir, is not my whole, or my ultimate purpose. I do conscientiously and sincerely believe, that the Order of Freemasonry, if not the greatest, is one of the greatest moral and political evils, under which this Union is now laboring. I further believe that the primary and efficient cause of all this evil, is that same rite of *initiation;* for as all the oaths, obligations and penalties of the subsequent degrees are but variations, expansions and aggravations of that primitive vice, let that be once abolished, and all the rest must fall with it ; knock away the underpinning, and the whole scaffolding must come to the ground.

With this address, I have the honor of submitting to you a pamphlet containing four letters on the *Entered Apprentice's oath.* You will perceive, sir, that they arraign that act of initiation upon five distinct charges—as contrary to the laws of religion, to the laws of morality, to the laws of the land.

Those letters have been now more than six months published. Their existence has not been noticed by any of the newspapers of the country under Masonic influence ; but they have been very extensively circulated in pamphlets, and numerous editions of them have been issued in several of the States of the Union. They have of course attracted much of that benevolence and charity, in the construction of motive, for which the Masonic Order is so conspicuous, upon the head of their author;—but no attempt has to my knowledge been made to answer them. They were first published in the Commercial Advertiser of New York, and addressed to its editor, Col. William L. Stone, known to you as a distinguished companion of your Order, in the degree of a Knight Templar.

I have expected that some show of defence against the charges in those letters would have been made. The charges are grave—they are specific—they are made under the responsibility of my name. And now, sir, as no individual brother or companion of the craft has been willing to undertake its defence, I call upon you, as the General Grand High Priest of the Order in these United States, to undertake it. I call upon you the more freely, because, if the charges are true, there is a debt of justice and of reparation due from you to all the Antimasons of the United States. The charges are in part the same with those which you have pronounced absurd, calumnious, and persecuting. If, upon examination, you find them TRUE, I expect from your candor an acknowledgment of your error ; from your magnanimity, a retractation of your charges against the Antimasons.

I expect more. If, upon a fair examination of these charges against the *Entered Apprentice's oath, obligation and penalty*, you should find yourself unable to defend them before the tribunal of public opinion—if you should, by the natural rectitude and intelligence of your *enlightened and unprejudiced* mind, come to the conclusion that the first initiatory rite of Freemasonry is in its own nature vicious, immoral, and unlawful—that no mental reservation can excuse it—that no explanation can change its nature—that no plea of nullity can purify the attainder of its bloody purport—then, sir, I expect that,

as the General Grand High Priest of the Order, you
will immediately advise its abolition, or at least
recommend that it should never more be administered. I ask not merely of the Grand High Priest
of Masonry, but of the profound and eloquent and
humane legislator of the criminal code for Louisiana;
I ask of him the abolition forever of that brutal penalty of death by torture and mutilation, for the disclosure of senseless secrets — or rather, now, of
secrets proclaimed from every housetop of the land.
I say to you, in the language of the Roman orator,
in the sentiment of a heart congenial with your own,
"Hanc domesticam crudelitatem tollite ex civitate ;
hanc pati nolite diutius in hac republica versari ;
quæ non modo id habet in se mali, quod civem
atrocissime sustulit, verum etiam hominibus lenissi-
mis ademit misericordiam. Nam cum omnibus horis
aliquid atrociter fieri videmus, aut audimus ; etiam
qui natura mitissimi sumus, assiduitate molestiarum
sensum omnem humanitatis ex animis amittimus."*

I propose to address you upon this subject again.

* Banish from our borders, suffer no longer to prey upon our vitals,
this *home-bred* cruelty among a people hitherto renowned for the merciful treatment of their *foreign* foes. Its greatest evil is not this most
atrocious murder of a free citizen, but that it extinguishes the very
sentiment of compassion in the mildest hearts. For when our eyes
and ears are hourly tortured with the sight and recital of deeds of
horror, they cease even in the tenderest natures to sympathise with
human calamity, *and the very sense of humanity is obliterated from our
souls.*

There is in the pamphlet herewitn enclosed a fifth letter addressed to Benjamin Cowell, of Rhode Island, containing my opinion in favor, to a certain extent, of what has been called political Antimasonry. As this principle has had, and must continue to have, a powerful influence upon the policy and upon the history of this Union, it will not be unworthy of your consideration in your other capacity of Secretary of State of these United States. I shall endeavor to prove to your conviction that your exhortation to the brethren and companions of your Order throughout the Union, but *under your jurisdiction, not to be tempted to the slightest interference in political parties,* has been and must be unavailing and nugatory — that so long as you adhere to the administration of the Entered Apprentice's oath, your Lodges and Chapters must and will be political caucuses, and that Masonry will be the signal for political proscription to one party, as Antimasonry has been and will be to the other.

I am, very respectfully, Sir

Your fellow-citizen,

JOHN QUINCY ADAMS.

TO EDWARD LIVINGSTON, ESQ.

Philadelphia, 15 April, 1833.

SIR,—In a former letter, I stated to you the motives and purposes by which I was induced to address you, as the presiding officer of the Masonic Order in the United States, through the medium of the press. They were,

1. To defend the Antimasons of the United States from severe and unjust imputations and charges against them, preferred by you in your address to the brethren and companions of the Society upon your installation in your high Masonic dignity.

2. To make, distinctly, specifically, and under the responsibility of my name, the charge against the Institution of Freemasonry, which you in that address had pronounced a vile and absurd calumny, instigated by a spirit of persecution, unjustifiable as arbitrary imprisonment or the tortures of the inquisition; namely, that "the cause of the offence," that is, of the murder of William Morgan, and of a multitude of other crimes connected with it, was a secret tenet of the Masonic fraternity; consisting in the Entered Apprentice's oath, obligation and penalty — the first rite of initiation in the Masonic order.

3. To transmit to you four letters upon that
Entered Apprentice's oath, obligation and penalty,
published by me in November last, and intended to
prove that this first rite of initiation to the Order of
Freemasonry, is, — in its naked nature, divested of
mental reservation, stripped of the authority of
great names, and disarmed of the shield of fraudulent explanation, — vicious, contrary to the laws of
God, to the laws of humanity, to the laws of the
land.

4. To call upon you, as the head and chief of the
whole Masonic brotherhood of the United States,
to sustain your charges against the Antimasons — to
vindicate the purity, the humanity, the lawfulness
of the Entered Apprentice's oath, obligation and
penalty — or to advise and recommend to the companions and brethren under your jurisdiction, ITS
ABOLITION.

This last, sir, was my principal and ultimate
object in addressing you — the *abolition* of that dis-
graceful initiatory act, which continues the vital
essence of Freemasonry.

I intended and intend no disrespect to you.
Admiring your talents, concurring in many of your
political opinions, and believing that in the discharge of your official duties in the service of the
one, confederated North American people, you have
at a critical moment of their Union, contributed

much to its preservation, by dashing from their lips the deadly but Circæan cup of nullification and secession, my confidence in your character has been strengthened. Giving you the credit of bold resist-ance to dangerous political errors, and of intrepidity in the honorable undertaking of redeeming others from the same, I have been encouraged to hope that you will discern the pure and well-deserved honor which will assuredly await your name in after ages, if you shall avail yourself of that summit of Masonic dignity which you have attained, by pre-vailing upon the whole association to discard forever the use and administration of those horrible invo-cations of the name of a merciful God, as the witness to promises of secrecy to things no longer secret to any one, under penalties of death in every variety of form which a fury could devise, or a demon could consummate.

One of those oaths — that of the Royal Arch Companion — it is your* special province, as the

---

* It appears from Allyn's Ritual that it is not the High Priest, but the Principal Sojourner of a Royal Arch Chapter, who administers the oath and obligation to the *Team* of candidates whom he leads by their halter to the altar. But the High Priest gravely declares to them that an old chest which he receives, *with great surprise*, from the Principal Sojourner, is *the ark of the covenant of God.* He takes out of this chest an old book, which upon beginning to read, he finds to be "the book of the Law," long lost, but now found, and he solemnly declares to the candidates, that " *the world is indebted to Masonry for the preser-vation of this sacred volume.*" How edifying must this solemnity be to the ministers of the Gospel who take part in it !

Grand High Priest of the Order, to administer to
every Most Excellent Master, who, not satisfied
with this superlative excellence, still pushes forward
in search of more light — it is the seventh of that
series of blasphemies, or of calls upon the name of
God in vain, by which the Masonic aspirant pur-
chases the floods of light which pour upon him
from every successive degree. It is in this degree
that you turn that scene of awful solemnity, the
calling of Moses by God himself in the burning
bush, into a theatrical representation, and actually
make your candidate take off his shoes, declaring
the place on which he stands to be holy ground.
This representation I know is emblematical, and is
explained by you to your candidate so to be. The
solemnities of admission to the Royal Arch are
deeply impressive, and therefore the more exceptionable by their mixture in the same ceremonies
with childish fables and gross impostures. You
commence with a fervent prayer to God — you open
the Royal Arch Chapter, and read to the three candidates for admission (for so many you must have)
a great part of the 139th Psalm. You interrogate
them, and bid them travel three successive times;
and on their return you read portions of the 141st,
142d and 143d Psalms. You then order them to
be conducted to the altar, and there you administer
to them the Royal Arch oath. This is the oath,

which, in many of the Chapters of the State of
New York, pledges the candidate to conceal the
secrets of a Royal Arch companion, communicated
to him as such — murder and treason not excepted.
It pledges him also to assist a brother companion to
extricate him from his difficulties, whether he be
right or wrong. In other Chapters the engagements are less onerous. They vary in almost every
Chapter. In an authenic copy of the manuscripts
mentioned by Col. Stone in his Letters on Masonry
and Antimasonry, one of the promises of this
degree is to support, protect and defend a Royal
Arch Mason, *even with the sword if necessity requires.* But in whatever form the oath is administered, its promises, whether more or less comprehensive or exceptionable, are all made with invocation of the name of God; and all under no less
penalty than to have the swearer's skull smitten off,
and his brains exposed to the scorching heat of the
sun. This, sir, is the penalty under which you
require of the candidate for the Royal Arch degree
to swear, that he will keep all the secrets of the
Order and of its companions and brethren, and that
he will perform the other obligations appertaining
to that degree. You deliberately pronounce, word
by word, causing the candidate to repeat them after
you, the words of this oath, promise and penalty,
closing with the adjuration, So help me God, and

keep me steadfast to this my oath of a Royal Arch Mason. And before he can be qualified to take upon himself this obligation, he must have had six similar oaths administered to him, and have pledged himself to them, so help him God, under no less penalties than,

1. To have his throat cut across from ear to ear, his tongue torn out by the roots and buried, (his tongue or his body,) buried in the rough sands of the sea, where the tide ebbs and flows twice in twenty-four hours.

2. To have his left side cut open, his heart torn out by the roots, and cast away to be devoured by vultures.

3. To have his body severed in two by the midst, his bowels burnt to ashes, and scattered to the winds.

The three succeeding penalties are of the same character, equally cruel and inhuman.

All these penalties William Morgan had incurred by writing the secrets and mysteries of the craft for publication. If it were possible to concentrate upon one human being the torture of them all, the agonies of that mortal would not be more prolonged or more excruciating than was the punishment inflicted upon William Morgan. He was seized by Masonic ruffians at noonday, hurried away from a dependent wife and infant children, by a warrant

upon a false charge of larceny, taken out at thirty
miles distant from his abode — taken out upon the
day hallowed to the worship of God; he was carried into another county, and discharged as innocent
the moment he was brought to trial. Then forthwith arrested again for a debt of two dollars,
imprisoned for two days, though he offered his coat
in payment of the debt; finally discharged again in
the darkness of night, by an impostor under the
guise of friendship, and, immediately upon issuing
from prison, seized again, under cover of the night,
by concerted signals, between the man-stealers of the
Lodge and of the Chapter — gagged to stifle his cries
for aid, forced into a coach, and transported, by
changes of horses and carriages prepared at every
change beforehand for his reception, one hundred
and fifty miles, there lodged in solitary confinement,
within the walls of an old abandoned fortress, there
detained five days and nights, under perpetual
threats of instant death, subject to uninterrupted
indignity and abuse — denied the light of heaven in
his cell, denied the use of a Bible, for which he
earnestly entreated, and finally, at dead of night,
transported by four Royal Arch companions of the
avenging craft, to the wide channel of the Niagara
river, and there sunk to the bottom of that river.
Nine days were occupied in the execution of this
Masonic sentence. At least three hundred worthy

brethren and companions of the Order were engaged as principals or accessories in the guilt of this cluster of crimes — and *this*, Mr. Livingston, is "the offence," the "CAUSE" of which I aver to be the *then* secret tenet of the fraternity, the oath, the obligation and penalty of initiation to the mysteries of the craft.

I attribute them all to the Entered Apprentice's oath, because I consider that as the cause and parent of all the oaths, obligations and penalties of all the subsequent degrees. My ultimate object in these addresses being to obtain, through your influence and recommendation, the voluntary relinquishment by the fraternity, in this Union, of these oaths and penalties, I have been desirous of narrowing down the controversy to its simplest point. I ask of you, and through you, I petition of the General Grand Royal Arch Chapter of the United States, to abolish the Royal Arch oath and penalty — to require of all the Chapters under your jurisdiction to cease from administering that and all other oaths tainted with the penalty of death, forever; and this I trust and believe will induce the Lodges to follow the example of the Chapters, and abolish their oaths and penalties too, forever.

And when I charge the Entered Apprentice's oath as the cause of the offence — that is, of the kidnapping and murder of William Morgan — I only meet and repel your charge against the Antimasons, as persecutors and calumniators of your fraternity, because they impute that offence to that cause. But this is not *all* the offence of which I impeach the Masonic penalties as the cause. The abduction and murder of Morgan are but two of a multitude of crimes, connected with that series of transactions of which they formed a part, *all* of which I impute to the same cause. There were crimes committed against Morgan before his abduction and murder — crimes of equal atrocity, committed against his associate Miller — crimes committed *after* the murder of Morgan, to shield, and screen, and protect, and aid and abet, its perpetrators — crimes committed by Masonic sheriffs in returning juries — crimes committed by Masonic witnesses, some in standing obstinately mute, and others in refusing to give the testimony required of them by the laws of the land — crimes committed by Masonic jurors in returning false, or in refusing to return true verdicts. All these I charge to the same cause; and not the least among them is a false and calumnious imputation upon the character and good name of your own immediate predecessor, in the office of General Grand High Priest of the Grand Royal Arch Chapter of the United States, and then Governor of the State of New York — an imputation which embittered the last days of his life. It must be known to you that one of the principal conspirators against Morgan gave out among his associates, to stimulate their faltering courage to the deed of horror, that he had a letter from the General Grand High Priest, declaring that the Morgan manuscripts must be suppressed, even at the cost of blood; that such a letter, purporting to be from Governor Clinton, was exhibited, and that he, the Governor of the State of New York, eminent and distinguished as he had long been, was reduced to the humiliating necessity of directing that an action of slander should be commenced to vindicate his character before a judicial tribunal, where Masonic witnesses have since been sentenced to imprisonment for refusing to testify to the truth. To refute this calumny upon Governor Clinton, was one of the honorable motives of Colonel Stone, for the publication of his Letters upon Masonry and Antimasonry. He has in my judgment done it effectually; but he has admitted and shown that it was a calumny strictly Masonic; a natural and congenial deduction from the same oaths, obligations and penalties which sunk Morgan in the waters of the Niagara.

In the address to your companions and brethren, at your installation, which has been the occasion of these letters to you, it was said that it would be not more unjust and absurd to impute to the Christian religion all the crimes which have been committed in its name, than it is to charge the Institution of Freemasonry with the outrages of a few misguided and infatuated members of the craft. This argument is familiar to all the defenders of Freemasonry, and has an appearance of plausibility; but it is fallacious. All the crimes committed in the name and under color of the Christian religion, have been perpetrated under false or erroneous constructions of its precepts. There is nothing in the Christian religion to warrant them. But whenever and wherever those false and erroneous constructions have been detected and exposed, they have been exploded. This is precisely the object of the Antimasons at this time, with regard to the errors and vices of the Masonic Institution. They are to the Order of Freemasonry what the Protestant reformers were to the Christian religion. Perhaps an analogy still more accurate may present itself to your mind between the letters of Blaise Pascal upon the morals of the order of Jesuits, and those which I have now the honor of addressing to you upon the morals of Masonry. The tenets which in the name of the Christian religion have drenched the world in blood, were spurious; they formed no part of the religion itself. The tenets of the order of Jesuits, detected and exposed by Pascal, were not universally held by the members of that institution — they formed no part of the constitution of the

society, and were disclaimed by its brightest orna-
ments. The order of Jesuits was a religious community. The whole system of their establishment
was founded upon the precepts of Christ. They
read the Bible as assiduously, and with devotion as
profound and sincere, as animates the Grand High
Priest of the Royal Arch, upon the admission of a
triad of candidates to that Masonic degree. And
yet the order of Jesuits has been abolished by the
head of the Catholic church himself, for holding
tenets and adopting practices inconsistent with good
morals.

But the vices of the Masonic Institution are not
false and erroneous constructions of precepts ill
understood and susceptible of different meanings.
They are vices inherent in the Institution itself, and
not corruptions foisted upon it. Cruel and barbarous as was the penalty inflicted upon Morgan, it
was no more than he had at least seven times
sworn to endure for violation of his Masonic oaths.
His murderers, those of them who survive, are still
WORTHY brethren, and companions of the craft.
Not one of them has ever been expelled from Lodge,
Chapter or Encampment. They have been, on the
contrary, cheered with the sympathies and relieved
from the funds of the Grand Lodge and Grand
Chapter of New York. You perceive, then, that
whatever analogy there may be between the crimes

committed by the corruptions of the Christian religion, and those resulting from Masonry, the inferences to be drawn from it all speak trumpet-tongued for the abolition of the Masonic oaths and penalties.

In concluding this letter, I am bound to make my acknowledgments for a poetical parody of its predecessor, which I have seen in the newspaper called the Globe, and by which I see that you are disposed to treat the subject with pleasantry. Well, sir, so be it. The Globe is generally considered as your POLITICAL organ. In that country which it is said you are about to visit, you may, perhaps, at your hours of leisure and recreation, occasionally frequent the first dramatic theatre in the world, and there be entertained with exhibitions, not of Moses in the burning bush, but of some of the masterpieces of the human mind, in the form of comedies of Moliere. You may chance to see, among the rest, a personage upon the stage, speaking to his servant, and about to give him an order, when the servant interrupts him by the inquiry, whether he is speaking to his *coachman* or to his *cook.* A similar question occurs to me with regard to your poet laureate. Is it one of your charioteers of the department of state, or a scullion of the kitchen? In either event, I commend this epistle to the inspiration of his muse — and as for you, sir,

when the time for seriousness shall return, and you
shall incline to justify yourself from the charge of
unjust accusation against multitudes of your fellow-
citizens, or to vindicate from still more serious
charges, the oaths, obligations and penalties, which
it is among your official Masonic functions to administer—when you shall return to the grave and
solemn and religious character of the General Grand
High Priest, I shall hope to hear from you, in verse
or prose, in the Globe or the Intelligencer, at your
option, but in your own person, and with the signa-
ture of your name.

 I am, in the meantime,

 Very respectfully, your fellow-citizen,

 JOHN QUINCY ADAMS.

TO EDWARD LIVINGSTON, ESQ.

Quincy, 1 May, 1833.

Sir,— The Entered Apprentice's oath, obligation
and penalty, upon which I undertook to animadvert,
in the four letters to Col. William L. Stone, a copy
of which was transmitted to you, with the first of
these letters to yourself, was in the terms of that
obligation as furnished by the officers of the Grand
Lodge of Rhode Island themselves, to the committee

of the Legislature of that State, appointed to investigate the charges against the Institution which had been made since the murder of Morgan, and which they and you pronounce calumnious. The obligations themselves had never been authenticated by the authority of adhering Masons, until they were produced by the officers of the Grand Lodge and Grand Chapter, at the peremptory requisition of the legislative committee. They were generally considered by Masons as constituting essential parts of the mysteries of the craft, and included strictly within the promise never to write, print, cut, carve, paint, stain or engrave them. In the practice of the Chapters and Lodges, the oaths are all administered by rote, and pass by tradition alone. This is of course the cause of the differences in the phraseology of the oaths as administered by different persons. It is one of the great inherent vices of the Institution. It affords constant opportunity and frequent temptation to every Chapter and Lodge to make additions to the promises pledged by the recipient of each degree.

The manuscript obligations furnished by the Grand Chapter and Grand Lodge of Rhode Island were drawn up and reduced to writing for the occasion. The Grand Lodge had previously published a *defence* of Masonry, stoutly denying that there was any thing in the Masonic obligations contrary to religion, morals, or the laws of the land; but carefully abstaining from any statement of what they were. They had used that notable device of explaining the penalty of death *for* revealing the secrets of the craft, or of any of its members, as meaning only a promise to suffer death *rather* than reveal them. They had expounded and explained and denied the several parts and parcels of the Masonic obligations, till they had made them all as innocent as their lambskin aprons. They had especially denied, with abundance of indignation, that *they* had ever administered or taken the oath to conceal the secrets of a brother Mason — " murder and treason not excepted." These words, or others equivalent to them, are stated, in Elder Bernard's Light on Masonry, and in Avery Allyn's Ritual, to form a part of the Royal Arch obligation. They are certified as such by the convention of seceding Masons, held at Le Roy, on the 4th of July, 1828, twenty-three of whom had taken this oath; and they have since been attested by adhering Masons, upon trials before judicial tribunals in the State of New York. They are not in the Royal Arch obligation reported by the Grand Chapter of Rhode Island; but in the Master Mason's obligation, reported by the Grand Lodge. Among the promises of admission to that degree are the following words, — " That I will keep a brother's secrets as my own, when committed to me in charge as such, murder and treason excepted." This, of course, is a pledge of immunity, for all other crimes, but it does except murder and treason. So said the Grand Lodge of Rhode Island. Yet even in that State, Nathan Whiting, an attorney and counsellor at law, who had taken the degree in the Lodge at East Greenwich, and had been Master of that Lodge, testified that in the Master's degree, after "murder and treason excepted," the usual form was to add "AND THAT AT MY OPTION"— and what the difference is between that, and "murder and treason not excepted," I leave as a problem in morals for Masonic casuists to solve.

In the seventh of Col. Stone's Letters upon Masonry, page 66, referring to the disagreement in the phraseology of the obligations, as given in different places, he makes mention of a manuscript then in his possession, containing copies of the obligations of the several degrees, as they were given twenty years before in the Lodge and Chapter of an eastern city—copied from the manuscript of a distinguished gentleman who had been Master of the Lodge and High Priest of the Chapter. The forms, says Col. Stone, are the same that were used in that city for a long series of years; and when Royal Arch Masonry was introduced *into Rochester, in the State of New York, these forms,*

*from these identical papers, were then and there intro-
duced and adopted.*

There is at this passage a reference to a note in
the Appendix, stating it to have been the original
intention of Col. Stone to insert all the obligations
contained in that manuscript, in his text ; but that
he was compelled to suppress them from the unfore-
seen extent of his work. He observes that neither
of the obligations in the first three degrees, in
those manuscripts, is more than half as long as
those disclosed by Morgan, and in common use.
He further adds that these manuscripts give a more
sensible and intelligible, and a less exceptionable
account of the seven degrees of Masonry, than any
other work he had seen ; and he concludes by
observing that *when Morgan was at Rochester, these
papers were there, and already written to his hands.*

It is to be regretted that Col. Stone did not
adhere to his first intention of publishing these obligations, or rather that he did not insert the whole
manuscript in his Appendix. I have obtained it
from him, and annex hereto the three obligations,
as there recorded, of the Entered Apprentice, the
Fellow-Craft, and the Master Mason.* It will be
found upon examination, that although truly represented by him as perhaps not more than half so

* The obligations here referred to, will be found in the Appendix to
this volume.

long as the same obligations in Morgan's and Bernard's books, they lose nothing of pith and moment by the retrenchment of words. They were the forms used at Rochester, and no other Masonic Institution in the State was more deeply implicated in the tragedy of Morgan's kidnapping and murder, than that same Chapter at Rochester. Now, in the Entered Apprentice's oath of this manuscript, the promise is expressly and explicitly to keep and conceal the secrets of Masons as well as Masonry. The penalty is the same as that reported by the Grand Lodge of Rhode Island, but in the lecture to the candidate on his admission there is in the manuscript an *explanation* of the meaning of the *penalty*, which not only utterly falsifies the explanation of the Rhode Island Masons, so strangely accepted and countenanced by the majority report of the legislative investigating committee, but proves that the murderers of Morgan understood but too well the real character of the obligation.

In this Entered Apprentice's Lecture, the candidate, after going through the forms of admission, is examined by the Master, upon interrogatories with regard to the meaning of all the ceremonies through which he has passed. Upon giving the account of his admission at the door, the following, word for word, are the questions put to him by the Master, and his answers :—

Q. "What did you next hear?"

A. "One from within, saying with an audible voice, Let him enter."

Q. "How did you enter?"

A. "Upon the point of a sword, spear, or other warlike instrument, presented to my naked left breast, accompanied with this expression — Do you feel?"

Q. "Your answer?"

A. "I do."

Q. "What was next said?"

A. " Let this be a prick to your conscience, a shield to your faith, AND INSTANT DEATH IN CASE YOU REVOLT."

Yes, sir, this is the explanation given to the Entered Apprentice, at the time of his admission to the degrees, of the penalty under which he binds himself by his oath — this was the formula used in *Connecticut* more than twenty-five years since, and thence introduced into Rochester, in the State of New York. Who shall say that the murderers of Morgan misunderstood the import of the Entered Apprentice's obligation?

And in this same manuscript of the forms of admission used at Rochester, the following, word for word, are clauses of the Master Mason's obligation : —

"I furthermore promise and swear, that I will attend a brother barefoot, if necessity requires, to warn him of approaching danger ; that on my knees I will remember him in my prayers ; that I will take him by the right hand and support him with the left, in all his just and lawful undertakings ; that I will keep his secrets as safely deposited in my breast, as they are in his own, *treason and murder only excepted*, AND THOSE AT MY OPTION ; — that I will obey all true signs, tokens and summonses, sent me by the hand of a Master Mason, or from the door of a just and regular Master Mason's Lodge, if within the length of my cable-tow."

This was the form of admission to the Master Mason's degree, at Rochester, when the Chapter at Rochester decided that Morgan had incurred the penalties of his obligations, and sent out their signs, tokens and summonses accordingly.

These were the oaths which every Master Mason admitted at the Lodge in Rochester, had taken. All this he had "most solemnly and sincerely promised and sworn with a full and hearty resolution to perform the same without any evasion, equivocation or mental reservation — under no less penalty than to have his body cut across, his bowels taken out and burnt to ashes, and those ashes scattered to the four winds of heaven ; to have his body dissected into four equal parts, and those parts hung on the cardinal points of the compass, there to hang and remain as a terror to all those who shall presume to violate the sacred obligation of a Master Mason."

Col. Stone, in his seventh Letter, page 67, says,

that in his apprehension the words, "*and they left to my own election*," are an innovation, and that he has not been accustomed to hear the obligation so conferred. The words in his own manuscript are, "and those at my option ; " fewer words, but bearing the same meaning. They were no innovation at Rochester.

The only words in this obligation which need any explanation, are the words *cable-tow*, and they are always so explained as to give them a definite meaning. The rest are all as explicit as language can make them, and they are taken with a broad and total disclaimer of all evasion, equivocation or mental reservation. So they were taken at Rochester, and so they are recorded in the old manuscript of Col. Stone.

You are a classical scholar, sir, and you doubtless remember the humorous remark of Cicero, in his dialogue on the nature of the gods ; that he could not conceive how one Roman Haruspex could look another in the face without laughing. I find it equally difficult to conceive how you, performing the functions of a Master of a Lodge, as among the duties of a Grand High Priest you may be required to do — how can you look in the face of a man after administering to him such an oath as this, without shuddering. But we have not yet done with the old manuscript of Col. Stone.

After the ceremonies of admisson to the degree
of Master Mason are completed, and the recipient
has been invested in his new dignity, he is conducted to the Master of the Lodge in the East, there to
hear from him the history of the degree. There,
sir, with equal regard for historical truth, and reverence for the Holy Scriptures, you mingle up the
building of Solomon's Temple, as recorded in the
Bible, with the murder of Hiram Abiff by three
Tyrian Fellow Craft, Jubela, Jubelo and Jubelum,
as preserved in the chronicles of Masonic mystery.
You relate them all as solemn truth of equal authen-
ticity, and in the manuscript now before me, the
story goes that after the murder of Hiram Abiff
was consummated, King Solomon was informed of
the conspiracy, and ordered the roll to be called,
when the three ruffians were missing. Search
"was made after them, and they were found by
their dolorous moans, in a cave. Oh, said Jubela,
that my throat had been cut across, &c. [repeating
the whole penalty of the Entered Apprentice's obli-
gation] before I had been accessory to the death of
so good a Master. Oh, said Jubelo, that my heart
had been torn out, &c. [repeating the whole penalty
of the Fellow Craft's obligation] before I had been
accessory to the death of our Master. Oh, said Jubelum, that my body were cut across, my bowels
taken out and burnt to ashes, &c. [repeating the

whole penalty of the Master Mason's obligation] before I had been the death of our Master Hiram Abiff. They were then taken, and sent to Hiram, King of Tyre, who executed on them the several sentences they had invoked upon themselves," WHICH HAVE EVER SINCE REMAINED "THE STANDING PENALTIES IN THE THREE FIRST DEGREES IN MASONRY."

This, sir, is the history of the Master Mason's degree, which was delivered by the Master of the Lodge at Rochester to every individual received as a Master Mason. This was the explanation given to him of the obligation assumed by him, immediately after the administration of the oath. This is in substance the explanation which you, the reporter of a criminal code to the Legislature of Louisiana, must give to every Master Mason whom you receive, of the penalty of the oath which you administer to him in the name of the ever living God — without evasion — without equivocation — without mental reservation.

And will you say, sir, as the Grand Lodge of Rhode Island have said, that these penalties mean no more than that the swearer, who invokes them upon himself, will *rather* die like Hiram Abiff, than reveal the secrets of Masonry? Is it Hiram Abiff in this story who pays the *penalty* of violated vows? Is it Hiram Abiff who invokes these penalties upon himself? The Entered Apprentice, the Fellow

Craft, and the Master Mason, invoke upon themselves the penalties of their respective degrees. The Entered Apprentice is told that he enters the Lodge on the point of a naked sword pricking his breast, to remind him of INSTANT DEATH IN CASE OF REVOLT; and the Master Mason is told that the penalties *executed* upon Jubela, Jubelo and Jubelum, have ever since remained *the standing penalties in the three first degrees of Masonry.*

And now, sir, what are we to think of High Priests, and Royal Arch Chapters, and Grand Masters, and Grand Lodges, who after taking and *administering* in secret these oaths, with these penalties, for a long series of years, when their real character has been proclaimed by the voice of midnight murder from the waters of Niagara in tones to which the thunders of her cataract are but as a whisper — when their unequivocal import has been divulged, to the amazement and disgust and horror of all pure, unsophisticated minds; what are we to think of High Priests, and Grand Kings, and most illustrious Knights of the Cross, who face it out in defiance of the common sense and common feeling of mankind, that there is nothing in these oaths and penalties inconsistent with the duties of those who take and administer them to their country or their God? The manuscript from which I now give to the world the three obligations of the Entered Apprentice, of the Fellow Craft, and of the Master Mason, is upon the testimony of Col. Stone, a Knight Templar and a man of unimpeached integrity, *Masonry in its most mitigated and least exceptionable form* — it was the Masonry of Connecticut more than twenty-five years since and for many years before — it was the Masonry of Rochester at the time of the murder of Morgan.

I have yet more to say to you, sir, on this subject, nor shall I be discouraged from continuing to address you upon it by your observance of a "dignified silence." If my letters are not read by you, there are those by whom they will be read, I trust, not without effect. If the presses under your jurisdiction, Masonic or political, refuse their columns to the discussion of Masonic morals, when the Grand High Priest of Masonry is the Secretary of State of the Union, it may serve to illustrate the subserviency of the periodical press to Masonry — but your address to your companions and brethren at your installation as the Grand High Priest of the Royal Arch of this Union, is not the perishable effusion of a day. It is a state paper for history, and for biography — for the present age and for the next — it shall not be lost to posterity — it shall stand as a beacon to future time — the admiration, or at least the wonder of other generations.

JOHN QUINCY ADAMS.

TO EDWARD LIVINGSTON, ESQ.

Quincy, 23 May, 1833.

SIR, — The position which I have undertaken to prove, beyond all possibility of rational denial, is, that the "cause of the offence," that is, of the murder of William Morgan, and of a multitude of other crimes associated with and subsequent to that act, was the oath of initiation to the Masonic institution, with its appended penalty.

Had Morgan ever taken any other oath than that of the Entered Apprentice, he would, after *writing* his Illustrations of Masonry, have been liable to the penalty which he suffered — even before they should be published. Like Jubela, Jubelo and Jubelum, he had invoked the penalty upon himself; he suffered nothing more than the penalty which he had been assured had been executed upon them; nothing more than what he had been warned had been the standing penalties of Freemasonry from the time of the building of Solomon's Temple.

All the obligations are assumed, with invocation of the penalty of *death*, upon him who takes the oath of admission to each of the several degrees; pronounced with his own lips, and with a solemn appeal to God, disclaiming all evasion, all equivocation, all mental reservation.

Such is the law of Masonry.

Shall I cite to you, sir, from your able and eloquent report to the Legislature of Louisiana, the powerful argument against the infliction of death upon *any* criminal for the commission of *any* crime whatsoever? The whole argument is well worthy to be read and studied, by every person conversant with the administration or enactment of criminal law, and of the deep consideration, especially of the brethren and companions of the craft. But the introduction to it is so peculiarly appropriate to the purpose of these addresses to you, that I take the liberty of presenting it to you in your own words.

" I approached the inquiry into the nature and effect of this punishment (of death) with the awe becoming a man who felt most deeply his liability to err, and the necessity of forming a correct opinion on a point so interesting to the justice of the country, the life of its citizens, and the character of its laws. I strove to clear my understanding from all prejudices which education or early impressions might have created, and to produce a frame of mind fitted for the investigation of truth and the impartial examination of the arguments on this great question. For this purpose I not only consulted such writers on the subject as were within my reach, but endeavored to procure a knowledge of the practical effect of this punishment on different crimes in the several countries where it is inflicted. In my situation, however, I could draw but a limited advantage from either of these sources; very few books on penal law, even those most commonly referred to, are to be found in the scanty collections of this place, and my failure in procuring information from the other States, is more to be regretted on this than any other topic on which it was requested. With these inadequate means, but after the best use that my faculties would enable me to make of them; after long reflection, and not until I had canvassed every argument that could suggest itself to my mind, I came to the conclusion, THAT THE PUNISHMENT OF DEATH SHOULD FIND NO PLACE IN THE CODE WHICH YOU HAVE DIRECTED ME TO PRESENT."

Now, sir, I ask of you, as the Grand High Priest of the General Grand Royal Arch Chapter of the United States, to make to the Chapters and Lodges, to the companions and brethren under your jurisdiction, that same recommendation to abolish the penalty of death, which with such deep and affecting solemnity you did make, in reporting a code of criminal law to the Legislature of Louisiana. The argument of which I have here given only the introductory paragraph embraces a very large portion, nearly one half, of your report on the criminal code. In the system reported with it, murder, and joining
13

an insurrection of slaves, are made punishable with hard labor for life. At the close of this letter, I annex several other extracts,* as well from the report, as from the preamble to the penal code reported with it, indicative not only of your deliberate and solemn opinions, adverse to the punishment of death in all cases whatsoever, but of the abhorrence which you must feel at heart, for those brutal mutilations of the body, which constitute the penalties of *every* Masonic obligation.

It is not, Mr. Livingston, for the poor purpose of bringing against you a charge of inconsistency before the tribunal of public opinion, that I address these letters to you, and call earnestly upon you to make this recommendation. I would, if possible, speak to your heart. I would say, you have recommended, you have urged by appeals to the best feelings of our nature, to the supreme legislative authority of your State, the total abolition of the penalty of death — the reformation of every thing cruel, indecorous or vindictive in her code of criminal law. You are at the head in these United States of a private association of immense power — co-extensive with the civilized world — knit together by ties of strong prevailment even when *secret*, scarcely less efficacious when divulged. When

---

* These extracts are inserted in the Appendix to this volume.

secret, they were riveted by pledges to the penalty of death and multilation in a multitude of forms, given in the name of God, and varnished with an imposture of sanctity, by being mingled up with the most solemn testimonials of Holy Writ. Even now, when your secrets are divulged, when your obligations and penalties have been exposed in their naked and undeniable nature, when you *dare not* attempt to vindicate or defend them, when the attempts of your brethren to explain them have been proved fraudulent and delusive, when your only resource of apology for using them is that they are null and void — words utterly without meaning, yet you still persevere in adhering to them as the ancient landmarks of the Order. Ask yourself, sir, not whether this is *consistent* with your report and criminal code for Louisiana; but whether it is worthy of your character — of your stand in the face of your country and of mankind; of your reputation in after time; and if it is not and cannot be, why should you not take the occasion of the high dignity which in this association you have attained, to propose and to promote its reformation? to divest it of that, which, so long as it continues, can never cease to shed disgrace upon the whole Order; of that which cannot even be repeated without shame?

You have taken no public notice of these letters

in your own name, nor have I been particularly solicitous that you should. Had you ventured to assume the defence of the Masonic oaths, obligations and penalties — had you *presumed* to commit your name to the assertion that they can by any possibility be reconciled to the laws of morality, of Christianity, or of the land, I should have deemed it my duty to reply, and to have completed the demonstration before God and man that they *cannot*. Of the multitude of defences of Masonry, which have been obtruded upon the public since this controversy arose, not one has dared to look these obligations in the face, and assert their innocence. Abuse upon the Antimasons for denouncing them — impudent denials of their import, so long as a remnant of the ragged veil of secrecy rent by the seceders, could yet be drawn over their nakedness — false and fraudulent *explanations* of their meaning when disclosed beyond all possibility of denial, and mystical and mystified declarations of inflexible adherence to them under the name of the *ancient landmarks* of the Institution — these have been the last resources, the forlorn hopes of the Masonic obligations.

And this inflexible adherence to these *ancient landmarks* is again recommended to the Chapters and Lodges under your jurisdiction by the General Royal Arch Chapter of the United States, of which

you are the High Priest, at their triennial meeting
in Baltimore last November. At that meeting you
were re-elected to the dignity which you had held
from the time of your address to the companions
and brethren of the Order at your installation in
April, 1830. A letter from you was read at that
meeting, apologizing for your absence from it, and
perhaps for the better accommodation of the Grand
High Priest, that meeting was adjourned to be held
again in November, 1835, at the city of Washington.

There is a point of view in which I believe this
subject to be deeply interesting to the people of
this Union, upon which I have hitherto said nothing,
and upon which I do not wish to enlarge. The
President of the United States is a brother of the
craft, bound by its oaths, obligations and penalties,
to the exclusive favors, be they more or less, of
which they give the mutual pledge. That in the
troubles and difficulties which within the last seven
years have befallen the craft, they have availed
themselves of his name, and authority, and influence to sustain their drooping fortunes, as far as
has been in their power, has been matter of public
notoriety. A sense of propriety has restrained him
from joining in their processions, as he has been
importunately urged by invitations to do, but he has
not withheld from them his support. It is not my

intention to comment upon the operation of the
Masonic obligations, upon the two most recent
elections to the Presidency of the United States, or
upon the official conduct of the President himself in
relation to the Institution or its members. But
whoever will impartially reflect upon the import of
the Masonic obligations, and upon the public history
of the United States for the last ten years, must
come to the conclusion, that no President of the
United States ought ever to be shackled by such
obligations, or under the self-assumed burden of
such penalties. They establish between him and
all the members of the Institution, and between
him and the Institution itself, relations not only
different from, but utterly incompatible with those
in which his station places him with the whole community. That the President of the United States
is not at this moment an impartial person in the
question between Masonry and Antimasonry, nor
between Masons and Antimasons, has been fully
authenticated, by something more than the effusions
of your scullions in the Globe. He is not impartial.
How can he be impartial after trammelling himself
with promises, such as those which are now unequivocally authenticated before the world?

And you, Mr. Livingston, Secretary of State of
the United States, are at the same time Grand
High Priest of the General Grand Royal Arch

Chapter of the United States ; and all the **Royal**
Arch Chapters of all the States of this Union are
under the jurisdiction of that over which you preside. Are you impartial in the question between
Masonry and Antimasonry? Are you, or can you
be impartial in any question which can arise
between Masons and Antimasons? You commenced your official duties as Grand High Priest,
by a sweeping denunciation of all the Antimasons in
the Union. The Antimasons were then a great
political party. They are so still. You brought
against them, what I have proved to be, a most
unjust accusation. Are you impartial between
them and their adversaries? Has human nature
changed its properties since one of them was by
a profound observer said to be, to *hate* those whom
you have injured, "odisse quem læseris?" How
far distant from such a denunciation of Antimasonry
as that with which you gratified your companions
and brethren at your installation, is the dismission
for Antimasonry of an officer of the United States,
dependent on you for his place? Is it as far
as the department of state from the general post
office? In all the trials before the judicial courts of
the State of New York, to which the abduction and
murder of Morgan has given rise, the efficacy of the
Masonic obligations upon sheriffs, jurors and witnesses to warp them from their duty to their country

has been lamentably proved — what security can the country possess that they will not operate in the same manner upon a Secretary of State, or a President of the United States? Were the Masonic obligations equivocal in their character, were they even susceptible of the explanations which have been attempted to be given of them, the undeniable fact, that they have been understood and acted upon according to their literal import, by great multitudes of Masons, to the total prostration of their duties to the laws of their country, would be a conclusive reason for abolishing them altogether. For if the obligations are of a nature to be differently understood by different persons, their consistency or inconsistency with the laws of the land, must depend upon the individual characters of those who have assumed them. Bound by the same oaths, some of the witnesses and jurors on the Masonic trials in New York have given their testimony and true verdicts, while others have obstinately refused their testimony to facts within their knowledge, and denied their assent to verdicts upon the clearest proof. It has been judicially decided in the States of New York and of Rhode Island that a person under Masonic obligations, must be set aside as disqualified to serve upon a jury in cases where one of the parties is a Mason, and the other is not From the letter of his obligations he cannot be

impartial, and although some Masons may understand them otherwise, neither the court, nor the
party whose rights and interests are staked upon
the trial, can have any assurance that the trial will
be fair. The same uncertainty must rest upon the
administration of executive officers. If the President of the United States, and the Secretary of
State, are bound by solemn oaths, and under horrible
penalties to befriend and favor one class of individuals in the community more than another, the purposes for which those offices are instituted must be
frustrated ; a privileged order is palmed upon the
community, more corrupting, more pernicious than
the titles of nobility which our constitutions expressly prohibit, because its privileges are dispensed
and enjoined under an avowed pledge of inviolable
secrecy. In many of the New York Chapters, the
promise to promote the *political* preferment of a
brother of the craft, over others equally qualified,
was one of the Royal Arch obligations to which the
companion was sworn upon the penalty of death.
How far such an obligation would influence the
official conduct of a President of the United States,
it is impossible to say; but not more impossible than
for that officer to fulfil the obligations of such a
promise and to perform his duties with impartiality.

At the time when you delivered the Address upon
your installation as Grand High Priest of the Gen-

eral Grand Chapter, Antimasonry had already existed upwards of three years. It was an extensive
political party, although then in a great measure
confined within the limits of the State of New York.
You denounced it in no measured terms. Had the
charges which you openly brought against it been
true, every individual within the scope of your denunciation must have been an unworthy citizen and
a dishonest man. Such has been the tone of all the
defences and defenders of Masonry, from that day to
this. If the Masonic obligations were understood in
all ordinary times not to interfere with the religion
or the politics of individuals, how can it be possible
to preserve this nominal exception when Masonry
itself has become the most prominent object of political dissension? As a political party, the Antimasons of the United States are, at this day, probably more numerous than the Masons. In several
of the States, the most important elections turn upon
that point alone. The Antimasons openly avow the
principle of voting for no other than Antimasonic
candidates. How is it possible for the Masons to
preserve themselves from the political bias, prompt-
ing them to repeal Antimasonry? They have in fact
no such equanimity. They never fail to bring forward a candidate of their own when possible ; and
when they find it impracticable, they unite with any
party, whatever may be their aversion to it, and

however obnoxious its politics, to exclude the Antimason.

In your letter to the General Grand Royal Arch Chapter of the United States, of the 26th of November, 1832, apologizing to them for not attending at their meeting, then about to be held at Baltimore, you said thus—"You know (notwithstanding the allegations of our enemies) that the duties we owe to our country are paramount to the obligations of Masonry, or to the indulgence of fraternal feelings." Now, sir, my appeal is to the very principle here asserted by yourself. I aver that your duty to your country is violated by the administration of the Masonic oaths and obligations under penalties of death, invoked in the name of God — penalties multiplied beyond those of the most sanguinary code that ever disgraced human legislation, and for offences which the supreme law of the State cannot recognize as the most trifling of misdemeanors.

At that triennial meeting of the General Grand Royal Arch Chapter of the United States, a committee was appointed "to take into consideration the present situation of our [the Masonic] Institution, and recommend such things and measures as they in their wisdom may consider expedient and necessary."

The report of that committee, and the resolutions proposed by them, and adopted by the General

Grand Chapter of the United States, were the immediate occasion of these letters to you. This circumstance may account, in part, for what appears to have surprised some of your friends — that I should *now* hold you accountable for an address delivered so long since as April, 1830. That was your declaration of war against the Antimasons. In November, 1832, you still proclaimed them to be *your enemies*, and the General Grand Royal Arch Chapter, in full triennial meeting, repeated with renewed and aggravated denunciations, all your erroneous charges against them. Upon that report, and upon the resolutions with which it closed, I shall in my next letter submit to the consideration of the public some observations.

JOHN QUINCY ADAMS.

TO EDWARD LIVINGSTON, ESQ.

Quincy, 12 June, 1833.

SIR, — From the official published report of the proceedings of the General Grand Royal Arch Chapter of the United States, at their triennial meeting at Baltimore, last November, it appears that a communication was made to that meeting from the M. E. Nathan R. Haswell, G. H. P. (meaning Grand High Priest) of the Grand Chap-

ter of Vermont, together with accompanying documents, and that this communication and the accompanying documents were referred to a committee
which is denominated one of the most important
committees then appointed, and they were instructed to take into consideration the present situation
of the Masonic Institution, and to recommend such
things and measures, as they in their wisdom might
consider expedient and necessary.

The first remark that invites attention here, is, that
this meeting was composed of individuals all belonging to different States of this Union, some of
them occupying stations of power and dignity in
their several States. The chairman of the committee to whom this communication was referred, and
who made the report upon which I am to comment,
is a member of the executive council of the Commonwealth of Massachusetts, elected from a county
exceedingly divided upon the questions between
Masonry and Antimasonry — elected at the same
time another was excluded from the same office, who
though an ardent National Republican, and a sufferer
by proscription from office by the present national
administration, was discarded for a slight real or
suspected taint of Antimasonry.

Here then is a member of the council of the State
of Massachusetts, elected expressly in opposition to
the Antimasonic party of the county of Bristol in

that State, representing the Grand Royal Arch
Chapter of Massachusetts, at a general convention
of all the Royal Arch Chapters of the United States,
to which is referred a communication and documents
from the Grand Royal Arch Chapter of Vermont.

That the report of a committee of which this gentleman was the chairman, should be marked with
strong resentment against the Antimasons of Vermont, was to be expected. Political Antimasonry
has been more successful in Vermont than in the
county of Bristol in Massachusetts.

The report, therefore, states that it appears from
the appeal published by the Masons in Vermont in
1829, that various presses have been established in
that State as vehicles of slander and malignity
against the adherents of Masonry.

This is precisely a repetition of the language of
your address at your installation in April, 1830. It
is certainly not a correct representation of facts, and
it contains itself a slanderous imputation upon a
majority of the people of the State of Vermont.

Now, sir, for a far more rational and accurate
history of Antimasonry as it existed in the State of
Vermont in the years 1829 and '30, I refer you to a
pamphlet entitled "Masonic Penalties," published
in August, 1830, by William Slade, now a member
elect of the House of Representatives of the United
States from that State.

In this pamphlet you will see that Mr. Slade commenced the publication of his essays on the Masonic penalties, on the 7th of April, 1830, a very few days before your installation and the delivery of your address. You have probably never seen those essays, for it appears to be one of the maxims of Masonry, while denouncing as slander, malignity and persecution, every impeachment of the institution, to "*know nothing about*" the real serious charges against it. It is therefore highly probable that you know nothing about Mr. Slade's essays on Masonic penalties. And I take it for granted that the committee of the General Grand Royal Arch Chapter of the United States, who reported this bitter denunciation against the Antimasons of Vermont, knew no more about it than you do. I will hazard a conjecture that among the *documents* transmitted by the Grand High Priest of the Grand Royal Arch Chapter of Vermont, and upon which the committee made their report, it would be a vain search to look for Mr. Slade's essays upon the Masonic Penalties. "Dignified silence" was the rule to be observed with regard to them — and yet, sir, attempts were made to answer them. It is so far from being true that presses were set up in Vermont as vehicles of slander and malignity *against* the adherents of Masonry, that the editor of the Vermont American, who began the publication of Mr. Slade's essays, suspended them after the third number, under the terror of Masonic vengeance; and Mr. Slade was compelled to publish the remaining numbers in an extra sheet. Yet the columns of the Vermont American, when closed against Mr. Slade, were opened to the defenders of Masonry, and two writers, under the signatures of "Common Sense of the Old School," and of "Senex," vainly attempted to refute the unanswerable arguments of his first three numbers. Mr. Slade replied, but was obliged to resort to the pages of a *free press*, one of those defamed by the report of the committee of the General Grand Royal Arch Chapter of the United States. Mr. Slade published in a pamphlet, under the responsibility of his name, his own essays, and those of his adversaries; and this procedure was in the same spirit of fairness and candor, which marked his whole management of the controversy. I recommend to you the serious and attentive perusal of the pamphlet; for if it should serve no other purpose than to preserve you and the General Grand Royal Arch Chapter of the United States from the reiteration of insult and slander upon the people of a highly respectable State of this Union, it will have a just claim to your grateful acknowledgments — insult and slander upon the people of Vermont, who by their votes at the last Presidential election, as well as by their suffrages at two succeeding elections for the executive officers and the State Legislature, have signally vindicated the cause of Antimasonry. To this result it is obvious that Mr. Slade's essays upon the Masonic penalties, did in an eminent degree contribute. It was impossible that they should fail to produce their effect upon the minds of an intelligent and virtuous people. These essays carry with them internal and irresistible evidence in refutation of the charge against the Antimasonic presses of Vermont, proffered by the committe of the General Grand Royal Arch Chapter of the United States. The essays on the Masonic penalties are not less remarkable for their moderation, delicacy and tenderness to the adherents of Masonry, than for the close and pressing cogency of their arguments against the Institution. They charge not the adherents of Masonry, but Masonry itself, with the murder of Morgan, and all its execrable progeny of crimes.

The report of the committee proceeds to state, that the members of the Grand Lodge of Vermont, and other Masons in the State, to the number of nearly two hundred, published in 1829, an appeal declaring that *they* as Masons had been charged —

1. With being accessory to the abduction of William Morgan.

2. With shielding Masons from just punishment for crimes they might have committed.

3. With exercising a Masonic influence over legislative, executive and judiciary branches of the government.

14

4. With tampering with juries.

5. With exerting an improper influence for the political preferment of the brotherhood.

6. With various blasphemous practices.

7. With causing the death of a distinguished Mason.

8. With sanctioning principles at variance with religion and virtue.

9. With the assumption of a power to judge individual Masons by laws known only to the fraternity, and to inflict punishments corporeally, even unto the pains of death.

Of each and all of these charges they affirm in the most solemn manner, that they were entirely guiltless.

Now the error which pervades the whole of this declaration consists in this : that the individual Masons who volunteer this plea of not guilty, apply gratuitously to themselves the charges which the Antimasons bring against the Institution to which they belong, and to its initiatory obligations and solemnities. The charges are against the plain unequivocal import of the *laws* of Masonry. The charges are that those laws do in their own nature lead to and instigate the commission of all those crimes, and that they *have* led to and instigated the perpetration of them. Two hundred Masons of Vermont declare themselves guiltless of all these charges. There are perhaps two thousand Masons in the State — suppose the two hundred appellants to be not guilty; that surely no more proves the innocence than it does the guilt of the remaining eighteen hundred. Had the Masons of Vermont been desirous of making up a *real* issue between themselves and the Antimasons, they should have said, We have been charged with administering and taking oaths and obligations, with multiplied penalties of death, which lead into the temptation of all those crimes, and which have led to the commission of them, and we have been urged to abolish these oaths, obligations and penalties.

There is another error in this statement of the charges against themselves, to which the appellants pleaded not guilty, evidently suited to evade the real question at issue. Their charges are couched in general and indefinite terms, prepared for the purpose of meeting them with positive denial, by the mental reservation of their own misconstructions. They say, for example, that they have been charged with various blasphemous practices. Now what do they mean by blasphemous practices? Blasphemy, by the common law, and by some of the statutes of the States, is an indictable crime — and it is defined by Blackstone to be the denial of the being or providence of God ; or contumelious reproaches of our Saviour, Christ; or profane scoffing at the Holy Scripture, or exposing it to contempt and ridicule.

Now, sir, if before the disclosures of William Morgan, at the ceremonies of initiation to the several degrees of Masonry, the Grand High Priests of Royal Arch Chapters, and the Masters of Lodges, instead of consciously hiding their heads in secrecy; if you, sir, as the Sovereign Master, or Most Excellent Prelate of an Encampment, as the Grand High Priest or Principal Sojourner of a Chapter, or as the Master of a Lodge, had exhibited in public the theatrical representations of the murder of Hiram Abiff, of Moses and the God of heaven in the burning bush, and of drinking the fifth libation from a human skull, with an invocation by the drinker of all the sins of him whose skull formed that cup, upon his own head; if in the presence of your fellow-citizens, you had uttered, as equally grave and solemn truth, a narrative compounded one half of quotations from holy writ, and the other half of the senseless and brutal mummeries of Masonry, would you have been surprised, if the next morning a grand jury of your country had presented you for blasphemy? Could you have imagined any thing more calculated to bring reproach and contempt and ridicule upon the name of God and upon the Holy Scriptures? If any one of the ministers of God whom you allure into the bosom of a charitable institution, by admitting them gratuitously to its promises and its rewards, should tell his people from the pulpit, that Hiram Abiff, the widow's son, was Master of a Lodge of Masons, at the building of Solomon's Temple; that he was murdered by three Fellow Crafts, named Jubela, Jubelo and Jubelum; that those three Fellow Crafts had suffered the penalties which they had invoked upon themselves, and that ever since that time those same penalties had been the standing penalties in the three first degrees of Masonry, would there be one hearer of that minister of Christ beyond the reach of the cable-tow, but would pronounce him guilty of provoking contempt and ridicule upon the Scriptures?

Why, sir, if the pastor of a Christian church should bind up Gulliver's Travels between the Old and New Testament of his Bible, and read indiscriminately from the whole, the gospel, epistle, or collect of the day, what opinion would his auditory form of his piety or his morals? And yet there is much of truth, and much of moral instruction in Gulliver's Travels. Far, far more of wisdom in the philosophers of the flying island of Lagado, than in the bungling metamorphosis of Hiram, the Tyrian brass-founder at the building of Solomon's Temple, into a Master Mason, or in the "butcheries which would disgust a savage" executed upon the three Tyrian Fellow Crafts, and which you require of the candidates for admission to the three first degrees, to invoke upon themselves.

These are the practices which some of the ardent and zealous Antimasons of Vermont may possibly have qualified as blasphemous. I am not willing to consider them as such. That very secrecy under which they are performed, and which otherwise constitutes one of the most powerful objections to the Institution, may perhaps relieve it from the charge of blasphemy. The intention is not to provoke contempt and ridicule upon the Scriptures, although the effect of them, as dramatic fictions, must often be to produce it. When John Milton published his Paradise Lost, Andrew Marvell declared that he for some time misdoubted his intent,

> That he would ruin
> The sacred truths to fable and old soug—

And he adds —

> Or if a work so infinite be spanned,
> Jealous I was that some less skilful hand,
> Might hence presume the whole creation's day,
> To change in scenes, *and show it in a play.*

That which the penetrating sagacity and sincere piety of Andrew Marvell apprehended as an evil which might result even from the sublime strains of the Paradise Lost, is precisely what the contrivers of

the Masonic mysteries have effected. They have
travestied the awful and miraculous supernatural
communications of the ineffable Jehovah to his favored people, into stage plays. That Word, which
in the beginning was with God, and was God; that
abstract, incorporeal, essential and ever-living existence; that eternal presence without past, without
future time; that BEING, without beginning of days
or end of years, declared to Moses under the name
of I AM THAT I AM ; the mountebank juggle-
ries of Masonry turn into a farce. A companion of
the Royal Arch personates Almighty God, and declares himself the Being of all eternity — I AM
THAT I AM. Your intention in the performance
of this ceremony is to strike the imagination of the
candidate with terror and amazement. I acquit the
fraternity, therefore, of blasphemy. But I cannot
acquit them of extreme indiscretion, and inexcusable
abuse of the Holy Scriptures. The sealed obligation, the drinking of wine from a human skull, is a
ceremony not less objectionable. This you know,
sir, is the scene, in which the candidate takes the
skull in his hand and says, "As the sins of the whole
world were laid upon the head of our Saviour, so
may the sins of the person whose skull this once
was, be heaped upon my head in addition to my
own ; and may they appear in judgment against me,
both here and hereafter, should I violate any

obligation in Masonry or the orders of knighthood which I have heretofore taken, take at this time, or may be hereafter instructed in ; so help me God," — and he drinks the wine from the skull.

And is not this enough? No. The Knight Templar takes an oath containing many promises — binding himself under no less penalty than to have his head struck off and placed on the highest spire in Christendom, should he knowingly or willingly violate any part of his solemn obligation of a Knight Templar.

Mr. Livingston, is this a fitting obligation for a *Christian man* to take or to administer? Can you, can any man be surprised if some of the Antimasons of Vermont have mistaken it for blasphemy? When the Masons of Vermont, or when the Grand Encampment of the United States shall feel sufficient confidence in their own integrity to meet the real charges against the Institution face to face, let them not resort to the refuge of secrecy, as a hunted ostrich hides his head in the sand — let them frankly acknowledge the dramatic exhibition of the burning bush, and the mystical cup of the fifth libation, and give their definition of blasphemy from which these practices shall be pure.

And these remarks apply equally to the declarations of the Masons in Connecticut, and of the twelve hundred in Massachusetts. The report of the com-

mittee of the General Grand Royal Arch Chapter
says, that these declarations were made with apparent sincerity of heart, that they *denied* the
charges against them, [the Masons,] "and universally cast themselves and their cause upon the good
sense of the country, for a calm, dispassionate and
enlightened verdict."

And here the report of the committee rested the
statement respecting the condition of Masonry in
Vermont, Connecticut and Massachusetts. The
meeting of the General Grand Royal Arch Chapter
was held at the close of November, 1832. The
committee was raised to report upon the *present*
condition of Masonry—and they report a declaration
of two hundred Masons in Vermont in 1829, and a
declaration of twelve hundred Masons of Massachusetts in 1831.

Mr. Slade's essays upon the Masonic penalties
were published in Vermont in 1830, a year after the
appeal of the two hundred Masons. The charters
of incorporation of the Masonic Lodges in Vermont
were revoked by the Legislature of that State in
1831. An Antimasonic Governor and Council, and
Antimasonic Electors of President and Vice-Presi-
dent of the United States, were elected in 1831 and
1832 — the last within one month before the meeting of the General Grand Royal Arch Chapter of the
United States. These were all significant indica-

tions of the verdict passed by the people of Vermont upon the appeal of the two hundred Masons of 1829. But upon all these, the committee of the Grand Royal Arch Chapter of the United States observe a "dignified silence." Like the Rhode Island Grand Lodge, with regard to the kidnapping and murder of Morgan by Royal Arch Masons, *they knew nothing about it.*

The declaration of the twelve hundred Masons of Massachusetts was published in December, 1831. In September, 1832, less than three months before the meeting of the General Grand Royal Arch Chapter of the United States, a State Antimasonic Convention was held at Worcester, at which an address was adopted, containing a counter declaration to that of the twelve hundred. A committee of that Convention tendered to the Grand Lodge and Grand Chapter, an issue, upon thirty-eight specific allegations against the Masonic Institution, to be tried, in any form best adapted to establish truth and expose imposition. And what was the answer of the twelve hundred Masons, who had made the declaration? "Dignified silence." What was the answer of the Grand Lodge and Grand Chapter of Massachusetts? "Dignified silence." And what the report of the committee of the Grand Royal Arch Chapter of the United States, on the [then] PRESENT condition of the Masonic Institution? "Dignified silence."

The twelve hundred Masons of Massachusetts, like the two hundred Masons of Vermont, make a statement of charges which they can safely deny — assume them as the charges of the Antimasons against them, deny them, and then put themselves upon the country. When the Antimasons tender them a direct issue, upon specific charges, equally serious and explicit, the twelve hundred — the Grand Lodge — the Grand Chapter — all *stand mute*, and the report of the committee of the General Grand Royal Arch Chapter of the United States, upon the PRESENT condition of the Masonic Institution, goes back one, two and three years to tell of the declarations of Masons in Massachusetts and in Vermont. But as to any Antimasonic refutation of those declarations, the committee *knew nothing about it.*

The report of the committee of the General Grand Royal Arch Chapter of the United States was therefore an incorrect representation of the state of the Masonic Institution, so far as concerned the States of Massachusetts and Vermont, nor was it more accurate in its reference to the state of Masonry in Rhode Island.

JOHN QUINCY ADAMS.

TO EDWARD LIVINGSTON, ESQ.

Quincy, 23 July, 1833.

SIR,— You have seen in my last letter, the statement made by the committee of the General Grand
Royal Arch Chapter of the United States, at their
meeting in November last, of the then PRESENT
CONDITION of the Masonic Institution, in the States
of Vermont, Massachusetts and Connecticut. You
have seen that to exhibit this *present condition* of
the craft, the report of the committee travelled
backward in the race of time, one, two and three
years, to the declarations of their own innocence, by
certain Masons of those States — the exclamation of
Macbeth to Banquo — "*Thou canst not say* I *did it!*"
But that upon the more recent events — the revoca-
tion of the Masonic charters in Vermont, the successive issues of the popular elections in that State
and the thirty-eight specific charges against Masonry
tendered by the committee of the Antimasonic Convention at Worcester, to the presiding officers of the
Grand Royal Arch Chapter of Massachusetts and of
the Grand Lodge ; upon all this, the committee of
the General Grand Royal Arch Chapter of the
United States observed a profound and "dignified
silence." And yet, sir, that issue of thirty-eight
charges had been tendered on the 11th of Septem-

ber, 1832 — nearly nine months after the declaration of the twelve hundred Masons of Massachusetts, and less than three months before the meeting of the General Grand Royal Arch Chapter of the United States at Baltimore.

Now, sir, was not the presiding officer of the Grand Chapter of Royal Arch Masons of Massachusetts, to whom this issue was tendered, the identical chairman of the committee of the General Grand Royal Arch Chapter of the United States, which made this report on the then *present condition* of Masonry in the United States? And if he was, upon what principle admissible in a narrative of realities, could a report upon the PRESENT CONDITION of Masonry in the United States, go back *three years* for declarations of Masonic innocence, and overlook or totally suppress the recent and actually present charges of Masonic guilt, which must have been yet sounding in the ears of the chairman of the General Grand Royal Arch Chapter who made the report? Is not the chronology of Masonry as peculiar to itself as its logic?

The committee upon the present condition of Masonry in the United States proceeded further to report, that from certain documents which had been *for a long time* before the public, it appeared that very different measures in relation to the subject had been adopted in the State of Rhode Island ; and so the committee reporting upon the *present* condition of the Institution, chose to resort only to documents which had been a long time before the public. They say,

That in Rhode Island, "a memorial emanating from an Antimasonic Convention, held in December, 1830, charging the Grand Lodge and other Masonic bodies with violations of the constitution and the laws of the land, was formally presented to the Legislature of the State, and the Grand Lodge, in reviewing that memorial, challenged the strictest scrutiny, and offered the greatest facilities to an investigation of all their concerns;" but that "it seems, however, that after the most laborious and patient investigation of the subjects referred to in the memorial by an able and impartial committee, the Lodges were sustained by the Legislature of the State, and were VIRTUALLY and triumphantly acquitted from all the charges which had been brought against them."

And who would imagine that within two months after this representation of the present condition of Masonry in Rhode Island, the Legislature of that State did, by unanimous assent in both houses, enact a law, prohibiting the administration of all extra-judicial and of course of all Masonic oaths, upon no less penalties than a fine of one hundred dollars for the first offence, and political disfranchisement for the second? This was the first result of that investigation, which the committee of the General Grand Royal Arch Chapter consider as having issued so triumphantly for the Lodges and Chapters of Rhode Island.

They pronounce the investigating committee of the Rhode Island Legislature "able and impartial." Of their ability no question will be made; but where did the reporter of the Grand Royal Arch Chapter of the United States find the evidence of their impartiality? Was it in the report of the majority, or in that of the minority of the investigating committee? Was it in the exclusion by the majority of the committee, of the very memorialists who had brought the charges against Masonry before the Legislature, from all participation in the investigation? Was it in the bargain made by the chairman of the committee with the Masonic dignitaries of the State, that if they would give their obligations, they should not be questioned about their secrets? — a bargain made without the knowledge or consent of at least one member of the committee. A bargain to which the Masonic authorities held the committee of the Legislature so strictly, that they repeatedly refused to answer questions most pertinent to the investigation, appealing to the chairman himself for the performance of his promise, that they should not be required to disclose any of their secrets. Is that the impartiality of a legislative investigation of charges of crimination?—first to exclude those who make the charges, from all participation in the process of inquiry—and then to contract with the parties accused, that they shall be privileged to refuse answering upon every thing which they choose to keep secret. This was the course of proceeding of this impartial committee.

You are too well acquainted with the prevailing politics in the Legislature of Rhode Island, at the time when this committee was appointed, not to know, that the main object of its appointment was to put down Antimasonry in Rhode Island. The resolution for appointing it was prepared by the chairman, but was offered by another member. In urging the passage of the resolution, both these persons indulged themselves in bitter invectives against the Antimasons, and the report of the majority of the committee carries upon every page the most conclusive internal evidence that the purpose for which the committee was raised, was to screen the Masonic Institution and brotherhood from the investigation which had been demanded by the Antimasonic memorial, and to substitute in its place a colorable examination, upon which the Masons should answer just so much as should suit themselves, and fall back upon their obligations of secrecy whenever they should think a disclosure adverse to their interests.

The proceedings of the majority of the committee were conformable to the principles with which they entered upon the performance of the service assigned to them. The examination was so conducted that the Masonic witnesses answered just so far as they thought proper, and when a question was put, which from very shame they loathed to answer, they appealed to their agreement with the chairman, and set the inquiry at defiance.

The committee stated in their report that, aware of the scruples of the Masonic witnesses about disclosing their Masonic secrets, which they had promised not to disclose, they "resolved unanimously that they would require the Masons to communicate to them fully, their Masonic oaths or obligations, and to answer all questions which should be asked respecting them — those obligations not being considered as part of their secrets" — but "as to their signs, and tokens, and words, contrived to enable Masons, and none others, to enter Lodges and to distinguish one another from those not Masons, *a majority* of the committee believed that the public *would have no curiosity about them,* and that it would not be a profitable or creditable employment for the committee to *endeavor to pry into them.*"

Admirable impartiality ! Unlawful and immoral *secret* rites and ceremonies, was the first and foremost of all the charges against Masonry, from the
15

sinking of their victim in the waters of the Niagara river. The supreme legislative authority of the State are called upon to investigate the subject. They appoint a committee for that purpose. The committee, possessed of the whole authority of the State to command testimony and elicit the whole truth — begin by excluding the accusers from all participation in the inquiry, and then bargain with the accused to ask no questions about their secrets, if they will but divulge what they themselves consider as no secret at all.

I do not propose to follow the majority of the committee through the mazes of their most extraordinary report. The report of Mr. Sprague, the member of the committee whose views differed from those of his colleagues, and the authentic report of their proceedings by Benjamin F. Hallett and George Turner, have shown in full relief the meaning of the word *impartiality*, as exemplified by the committee and their chairman who drew up their report. And yet, so far was the committee entitled to the praise of impartiality, that they came unanimously to the conclusion that the Institution of Freemasonry *ought to be abolished*, and the report concludes with an earnest and eloquent exhortation to the Masonic fraternity to abandon it.

Is it not very remarkable that the report to the General Grand Royal Arch Chapter of the United

States, upon the *present* condition of Masonry, which so highly approves this report of the Rhode Island investigating committee, takes not the slightest notice of this their opinion and exhortation? The Grand Royal Arch report affirms that upon the report of the Rhode Island investigating committee, "the *Lodges were* SUSTAINED by the Legislature of the State." *Sustained!* This "able and impartial" committee say,

"It cannot be doubted that the Lodges and Chapters in that part of the State [of New York] had it fully in their power to have detected and brought to justice many of the criminals concerned in the abduction of Morgan, if not those concerned in his murder. And yet we do not find that they have expelled a single member, or made any manner of inquiry about them. Can it be denied that by such conduct those Lodges and Chapters have implicated themselves in the *guilt of those transactions* and made themselves responsible for it? And not they alone are implicated. *The higher Masonic authorities, to whom they are subordinate and accountable, are equally implicated and responsible.*"

The higher authorities, to whom the Chapters in that part of the State of New York are subordinate and accountable, are the Grand Chapter of the State, and the General Grand Royal Arch Chapter of the United States. Yes, sir, in this passage of the Rhode Island "able and impartial" investigating committee's report, the very Chapter of which you are the High Priest, the General Grand Royal Arch Chapter of the United States, is implicitly charged with being implicated and responsible for the guilt of the murder of Morgan. How comes it, sir, that the committee of the General Grand Royal Arch Chapter of the United States, reporting upon the present condition of Masonry, and expressly referring to this report of the investigating legislative committee of Rhode Island, should have overlooked entirely this charge against the Grand Royal Arch Chapter of the United States itself? How dared that committee to affirm that, as the result of that investigation, the Lodges were sustained by the Legislature of the State? The report of the Rhode Island investigating committee expressly charges the Grand Chapter of New York, and the General Grand Royal Arch Chapter of the United States, with being implicated in and responsible for the murder of Morgan, and the atrocious transactions connected with it, and the report of the General Grand Royal Arch Chapter of the United States, calls this a triumphant acquittal of the Lodges of Rhode Island.

Permit me, sir, to present to your consideration two more extracts, from the same report of the majority of the Rhode Island investigating committee : —

" The old forms of the oaths, which are still adhered to, are extremely improper. It is true that the construction which the Masons put upon them in this State [Rhode Island] renders them harmless, but that is by no means the natural construction of the language itself. The oaths taken by themselves, without being corrected and controlled by the addresses and charges, are, according to the terms of them, clearly criminal. And can it be proper to take obligations, the different parts of which are in direct collision with and contradiction to each other, and yet the whole to be sworn to?

" But it is an insurmountable objection to those oaths, that they are liable to a construction which renders them in the highest degree criminal and dangerous; and that such a construction has actually been put upon them by Masons, and has been productive of the most dreadful consequences."

The following is the concluding sentence of the report : —

" This committee cannot but come to the conclusion that the Masons owe it to the community, to themselves, and to sound principles, now to discontinue the Masonic Institutions.

To what a desperate extremity must the committee of the General Grand Royal Arch Chapter of the United States have been reduced for matter to report upon the present condition of Masonry, when they

were willing to accept and represent this as a triumph-
al aquittal of the Rhode Island Lodges and Chapters!

Yet this was a report of a committee so partial
to the Masonic fraternity, that, invested with the
entire legislative power to investigate their Institution, they did in fact abdicate their legitimate rights
and powers, by a bargain with the Masons, to screen
them from the exposure of their most odious ceremonies. They accepted and countenanced a fraudulent explanation, and pretended construction of the
penalties of the Masonic oaths. Fraudulent, as
every Master Mason must know, who at his reception is told that the penalties are, and have been
from the building of Solomon's Temple, the same
penalties which were *executed* upon the murderers
of Hiram Abiff.

The allegation by the Rhode Island committee,
that they considered it an unprofitable employment
to be prying into Masonic secrets, would be more
plausible, if those secrets consisted only of the
"signs, and tokens, and words, contrived to enable
Masons, and none others, to enter Lodges, and to
distinguish one another from those not Masons;"
but how is the fact? The tokens and passwords
are, to be sure, of the character described by Sir
Tobey Belch, in Shakspeare's Twelfth Night, "most
excellent, sense-*less*." But the *signs* are explanatory
of the true meaning of the penalties, and when

the committee compelled the Masons to give the
words of their obligations, was it not an incongruous
scruple of delicacy, to draw the vail over the coinci-
dent signs which give to those words their most
energetic significancy?

Under the exceedingly accommodating indulgence
of the investigating committee, the Knights Templars of Rhode Island were permitted to skulk from
all testimony relating to the fifth libation, denominated in Masonic language the *sealed obligation.*
How the committee, consistently with their own
rule, could release the witnesses from testifying to
that *pious* solemnity, it is not easy to see. The
oath of the Knight Templar has, like the rest, a
penalty, which is, having the swearer's skull smitten
off and suspended to "rest high on spires," as the
Masonic minstrels deliciously sing; and that oath
and penalty the Rhode Island Knights did give according to contract with the committee. But the
fifth libation is an obligation of higher order. The
temporal penalties of cruel death, and barbarous
mutilation, are not sufficient to bind the conscience
of the Knight Templar. In the fifth libation, he
invokes eternal punishment upon his immortal soul.
He calls upon God, his Creator, to visit upon him at
the judgment day, not only his own sins, but all the
sins of his fellow-mortal man, from whose skull he
quaffs the cup of abomination and of mystery.

The most remarkable scene in the investigation of the Rhode Island committee, was that in which William Wilkinson, a Knight Templar, and a man of most respectable character, was examined with reference to this sealed obligation, the fifth libation. The words always uttered before drinking the wine from the skull, were read to him from Allyn's Ritual, page 250, and he was asked whether they were administered to him on taking the Knight Templar's obligation. He answered, "These words made no part of the OBLIGATION which was administered to me on taking the Knight Templar's degree."

From this answer an unlearned and uninitiated person would naturally conclude that these words form no part of the ceremony of initiation to the Knight Templar's degree, and it is from denials of precisely the same character as this, that the great mass of adhering Masons, ministers of the holy gospel included, have. labored to blast the credit of Allyn's and Bernard's books; but Mr. Wilkinson's denial hinged upon the word *obligation* only. There is, as I have remarked, another *obligation* administered to the Knight Templar, on taking his degree, and that obligation was among those furnished to the committee. That was the obligation which Mr. Wilkinson had in his mental contemplation, when he denied that the words of the sealed obligation were part of THE obligation administered to him. Had the examination rested there, well might the committee of the Grand Royal Arch Chapter of the United States have boasted of the *triumphant* acquittal of the Rhode Island Masons. But here the examination did not rest. Mr. Wilkinson was asked whether these said words were used in *any* ceremony of initiation to the Knight Templar's degree? His answer was, " In regard to the secrets or ceremonies of this, or any other degrees in Masonry, I neither affirm or deny any thing." Upon this there was some altercation between the witness and the chairman of the committee, who very justly considered this as an obligation which the Masons were bound to give, but instead of exercising the authority vested in the committee by the Legislature, and exacting an answer, he argued with the witness to persuade him to answer, and finished by *submitting* to his refusal. This was indeed the triumph of Masonry; not the triumph of acquitted innocence, but the triumph of sturdy contumacy, setting at defiance the legislative authority of the State.

That Mr. Wilkinson should be ashamed to acknowledge that he had ever pronounced, with an appeal to God, such words as those, and accompanied them with such an action, is creditable to his sense of discrimination between right and wrong. The sealed obligation is not one of those signs, grips, tokens or passwords, by which the Masonic

fraternity discern the *genuine* from the *spurious* impostor. It is one of the obligations of the craft,
which the committee had determined to require, and
which the Rhode Island Masons were bound by the
terms of their agreement with the chairman of the
committee to give. The fifth libation, therefore —
the potation from the skull of "Old Simon," and
the invocation of all the sins, heinous and deadly as
they may be, of another man, upon the head of the
self-devoted Knight Templar, are yet, so far as
adhering Masonic acknowledgment is concerned,
"undivulged crimes — unwhipped of justice." Mr.
Wilkinson did not venture to deny that the words
of the sealed obligation were precisely those recorded in Allyn's Ritual — he neither affirmed nor
denied. The full, adhering Masonic authentication
of the sealed obligation, is reserved for the investigation of a committee more resolute and less com-
promising with the transcendent sovereignty of
Fremasonry than the Rhode Island committee was
found to be. A more searching investigation of the
laws of the Masonic empire will be required to discover in all its *loveliness*, that feature of its code.
In the Rhode Island investigations another witness,
a minister of the gospel, upon being asked if he
had drank wine from a human skull, answered, —
"I do not know that it can affect the interests of
any one whether I drank wine out of a skull, a tin

cup or a bason." A third witness declined answering the question.

In the 251st page of Allyn's Ritual — the very next page after that which discloses the formula used in drinking the fifth libation, there is the following note : —

"The sealed obligation is referred to by Templars, in confidential communications relative to matters of vast importance, when other Masonic obligations seem insufficient to secure secrecy, silence and safety. Such for instance was the murder of William Morgan, which was communicated from one Templar to another, under the pledge and upon this sealed obligation. The attentive ear receives the sound from the instructive tongue; and the mysteries of Freemasonry were safely lodged in the repository of faithful breasts — until it was communicated in St. John's Hall, New York, in an Encampment of Knights Templars, March 10, 1828."

To this fact, Mr. Allyn made oath before a magistrate in the city of New York, and that it was so communicated to him at an Encampment of Knights Templars. Of the pains that have been taken to discredit Allyn's testimony, it is not necessary for me to speak; but in the twenty-second of Col. Stone's Letters, page 238, there is a frank and full acknowledgment by him, himself a Knight Templar, that after having long totally disbelieved the statement, he did finally satisfy himself that it was substantially true.

With the thoughts that crowd upon me in recurring to this proof of the power and practices of Masonry, I will not now trouble you or the public. The Legislature of Rhode Island, after such an investigation even as this, prohibited the administration of all extra-judicial oaths. How their committee could submit to the suppression of Masonic testimony to the sealed obligation is not easily explained. But the agonies of the Knights Templars at the very call upon them to testify to the sealed obligation, are eloquent commentaries upon the note in the 251st page of Allyn's Ritual, and upon the candid acknowledgment in Col. Stone's twenty-second Letter.

And so, sir, the murder of William Morgan was, by one of its perpetrators, regularly communicated to an Encampment of Knights Templars in the city of New York, in March, 1828, and those Knights Templars (Col. Stone, who certifies to the fact, knows not who they are — he thinks them unworthy, but in the vocabulary of the handmaid they are worthy Masons) assisted this murderer, and furnished him with the means of escaping from the retribution of public justice and the laws of the land!

And yet, this was entirely conformable to the laws of Masonry. It interfered in no respect with the religion or politics of any one Knight Templar of the Encampment! It was a memorable exemplification of the promise to assist a worthy brother in extricating him from difficulty, whether he is right or wrong. It was most sincerely explanatory of the obligation to conceal the secrets of a worthy brother, murder and treason not excepted, or excepted at the option of the Sir Knight himself—and it did not even exact of the illustrious brotherhood that they should go barefoot to apprize this "western sufferer" of the danger with which he was threatened ; and these transactions all occurred before the revelation of the obligations of the higher degrees of Masonry by the Le Roy convention of seceders, on the 4th July, 1828. Of these facts, thus notorious, thus abominable, thus undeniable, why have the Legislature, why has the executive of the State of New York, why have the grand juries of the city never been informed? Why have the General Grand Encampment of the United States observed upon these acts of men under their jurisdiction, a dignified silence? Why, but because they have resolved to adhere, and have recommended to the brotherhood under their jurisdiction to adhere, to the *ancient landmarks* of the Institution?

Mr. Livingston, I shall here close the series of letters which I have addressed to you as the head and most conspicuous member of the Masonic fraternity in these United States — holding at the same time offices of high dignity, power and influence in the government of the Union. The General Grand Royal Arch Chapter of the United States, of which you are the Grand High Priest, did, at their triennial meeting at Baltimore last November, highly commend certain Chapters and Lodges which had changed, most essentially changed, their own nature, by substituting the study of the useful arts and sciences, for the miserable fooleries of their pageantry, and did earnestly recommend to all the Chapters under their jurisdiction, the same excellent reformation and transformation. It was that recommendation which suggested to me the idea of calling upon you to accomplish a revolution still more useful and commendable — the abolition of all the execrable oaths, obligations and penalties, which, until they shall be utterly abolished, are, and must be, an indelible disgrace to the Institution. If you have power to convert your Lodges into lyceums and your Chapters and Encampments into schools of science, you cannot lack the power of redeeming the Institution from the infamy of lawless oaths, of barbarous obligations, of brutal penalties — with that infamy your Institution is now polluted, as it is with the blood of William Morgan, nor can the "labor" or "refreshment" of all the Royal Arch Chapters on the globe wash it out.

It is in your power, sir, to remove this stumbling-block and this foolishness from the Institution over which you preside, forever. Look to the seventh chapter of the First Book of Kings, and you will find that Hiram of Tyre, the widow's son, who worked at the building of the Temple of Solomon, was not a Mason — but "cunning to work all works in brass." Whether this fitted him the better for the selection of the first contrivers of your Order, as the founder of the craft, is a problem for your learned and especially for your clerical antiquarians to solve ; but the fact that he was a workman in brass, and that the two pillars in the porch of the temple, Jachin and Boaz, were not works of Masonry but of *brass*, stamps with gross imposture the whole history of the Institution. In like manner every pretension of the Order to historical connection with any portion of the Holy Scriptures, is imposture, and must be known so to be to every intelligent minister of the gospel, who takes upon himself your obligations.

The existence of such an order is a foul blot upon the morals of a community. The strength, the glory, the happiness of a nation are all centred in the purity of its morals ; and Institutions founded upon imposture, are the worst of all corruptions, for they poison the public morals at their fountains, and by multiplying the accomplices in guilt, arm them with the confidence of virtue.

Whether your dignity as the head of the Royal
Arch of this Union, is to cease upon your departure
from this country, or to continue during your absence, has not yet been announced to the world ;
but in either event, be assured that neither your
Masonic addresses, nor the proceedings of the General Grand Royal Arch Chapter of the United States,
will henceforth pass without observation into oblivion.

JOHN QUINCY ADAMS.

TO MESSRS. TIMOTHY MERRILL, HENRY F. JANES, MAR-
TIN FLINT, CHARLES DAVIS, EDWARD D. BARBER,
SAMUEL N. SWEET and AMOS BLISS, Committee of the
Antimasonic State Convention, held at Montpelier, in the State of
Vermont, on the 26th of June, 1833.

Quincy, 17 July, 1833.

FELLOW-CITIZENS,—I have received, with great
satisfaction, your letter of the 27th ult., and with
warm sensibility the resolutions which you have
communicated to me of the Antimasonic Convention,
held at Montpelier the preceding day.

The entire character of the Institution of Freemasonry has not yet been displayed to the inspection
of mankind. That it is essentially vicious and
grossly irrational, has been demonstrated beyond all
possibility of reply ; but the extent and degree to

which it vitiates the morals, and prostrates the intellect of its votaries, has not yet been wholly disclosed. It is among the most ordinary symptoms of mental insanity that the faculty of reason is sound and vigorous upon every subject on which it is exercised save one, and at the same time irrecoverably distempered on that one. There are similar aberrations of *moral* principle in the conduct and character of individuals, and it has often been remarked that corporate bodies of men are capable of committing, without a blush, acts from which every individual of the association would shrink with instinctive horror.

The Institution of Freemasonry is founded upon historical imposture ; and can a Christian remark it without disgust, upon imposture foisted upon sacred history? — upon imposture falsifying the most awful truths of the gospel?—upon imposture contaminating with unhallowed step the holy of holies itself?

The fable upon which the first three degrees of Masonry is founded, carries absurdity and falsehood upon its face. There are fraud and duplicity in the oaths and obligations into which the candidates for initiation are unwarily drawn. They are first made to invoke upon themselves the penalties of death and brutal mutilation if they should reveal the senseless secrets to be imparted to them, and then they are told a tale of three Fellow Crafts who like them

16

had invoked these penalties upon themselves, and
upon whom the *penalties had been executed* — not
for revealing the secrets which they had been sworn
to keep, but for murdering the first Grand Master in
the attempt to extort one of the secrets from him.
Ministers of the word of God have the oaths, invok-
ing these penalties upon themselves, administered
to them gratuitously and take them for nothing,
while other poor blind candidates are laid under
tribute for the privilege of burdening their con-
sciences with the same loads. After taking them,
they are told that these have been the standing
penalties *for violation of the oaths of secrecy* which
they have taken, ever since *they were executed upon
the murderers of the first Grand Master.* This first
Grand Master of Masonry, they are told was Hiram
of Tyre, whom the Holy Scriptures declare to have
been a workman in brass ; and they are assured
that he was murdered by three Tyrians with Roman
names three hundred years before Rome existed.

In this tortuous and fraudulent process of administering the oaths, and then delivering a lecture upon
their pretended origin, some apology may be found
for the hundreds of Masons in your State and in
others, who have so stoutly maintained, in the face
of their fellow-citizens, that *they* never had taken
any oaths imcompatible with their duties to God and
their country. To this process may be traced the

utterly groundless *explanation* by which they have confounded treachery with martyrdom, and construed the penalty of death *for* revealing secrets into a sufferance of murder, *rather* than reveal the secrets. The terms of the oaths are plain, explicit and unequivocal. The promise is to suffer death as a penalty, if the swearer reveals the secrets of Masonry, or of Masons. And he is to suffer the death self-invoked, as the Tyrian Fellow Crafts, with Roman names, *did* suffer death for violation of Masonic law. The Tyro-Romans indeed had invoked these penalties upon themselves, after committing murder as well as a breach of Masonic law, and Hiram, the brazier, Grand Master of Masons, had suffered death *rather* than reveal out of time and place the Master's word. Here is a confusion of ideas sufficiently indicative of fraud; and as the administration of the oaths is always oral, and the very writing or printing them was among the promises of the candidates never to do, it is not surprising that thousands of Masons should have taken them, not only without understanding what they were swearing to, but actually believing that their promise was to die like Hiram, the victims of fidelity, and not, like his murderers, to pay the penalties of treachery.

In the promises themselves, however, there is nothing ambiguous or equivocal. They positively contract the engagement to suffer the penalties of death and bodily mutilation, for any one violation of the oaths which the candidate pronounces. The death which a merciful man would not inflict upon a dog, the Masonic candidate for *light*, swears he will suffer as a *penalty*, if he should pronounce the words Tubal-Cain, Shibboleth or Mah-han-bone out of time and place. Nay, if like the abbess of Andouillets and the nun in Tristram Shandy, they presume to halve between them the obnoxious words, to preserve the potency of the spell, without infringing the laws of decorum—not even the syllables Ja—and Chin, or Bo—and Az, can be halved between two Masons, and publicly pronounced out of the Lodge, but upon the penalty of having both their throats cut across from ear to ear. And this, and the like of this, are the *ancient landmarks*, which the Grand Royal Arch Chapter of the United States have earnestly exhorted the Chapters and Lodges under their jurisdiction inflexibly to maintain.

Among the evidences of the true spirit and character of Freemasonry, which are daily disclosing themselves to the world, is this fanatical attachm nt and devotion to these ancient landmarks, which might be more properly denominated these incurable vices of the Institution. To these vices how emphatically may be applied the remark of the moral poet, upon the propensity of human nature, to pass from detestation of vice first seen, to the enduance ana thence to the embrace of vice familiarized to the eye! If any one Legislature of this Union should enact a law, subjecting a citizen of these States, for the most atrocious crime that the heart of man could conceive or the arm of man could perpetrate, to any one of the Masonic penalties, one universal burst of indignation and abhorrence from the Atlantic to the Rocky mountains would redeem the character of the American people from the disgrace inflicted upon it by such a legislative enactment. I hesitate not to delare the belief that not a jury could be assembled in this Union to convict, not a judge could be found to pass sentence upon, a man subjected to such a punishment by the sovereign Legislatures of the land. And yet one of these penalties has been inflicted on a free citizen of this Union — inflicted by the execution to the letter, of the secret, irresponsible, disavowed, and transcendental law of Freemasonry. It has been executed by Royal Arch Masons — executed by the hand of midnight and yet unpunished murder. The fact of this murder has been communicated by one of its perpetrators to an Encampment of Knights Templars in the city of New York, and those Knights Templars, under the seal of the fifth libation, instead of delivering up the criminal to the lawful justice of their country, did, in strict conformity to their Masonic obligations, screen him from the punishment due to his crime, and furnish him with the means of escaping from that punishment forever.

It is therefore, gentlemen, with unmingled satisfaction, that I receive the assurance from you, that the Antimasons of Vermont had determined to *persevere*, in the righteous cause in which they have engaged — namely, that of breaking down the ancient landmarks of Freemasonry — landmarks which are the standing monuments of usurpation and crime. And whatever may be for years to come the fortunes of your cause, *perseverance* alone is the infallible pledge of your final success. We must not flatter ourselves that a moral evil so deeply rooted and of such gigantic dimensions can or will be eradicated in a short time, or by intermitted exertions. We see the Masonic Institution, covered with all its enormities, upheld, by clinging to both the great political parties which divide the nation. We see the Grand Royal Arch Chapter of the United States, taking into consideration the condition of Masonry in the State of Vermont, and pouring forth floods of slander upon you and your associates, asserters of the supremacy of the laws. But you and your accusers are, in the presence of the American people, alike amenable to the definitive tribunal of public opinion. That opinion will ultimately settle into a clear, simple, undeniable moral principle. The code of "Moloch homicide," embodied in the laws of Freemasonry, will pass to its appropriate region in Pandemonium, and one of the sources of error and guilt prevailing in our land will be exhausted and forever drained. For my feeble contributions to effect this happy consummation, your approving voice is to me a precious reward. As a fellow-laborer with you for the extinction of the brutal penalties of Freemasonry, my voice, so long as it has power to speak, shall not be silent to an honest call, and when silenced, as it soon must be, by a summons to another world, my testimony of abhorrence to those penalties shall descend as an inheritance to my children and to my country.

Accept, gentlemen, for yourselves, and for the convention, whose resolutions you have communicated to me, the respect and the thanks of your friend and fellow-citizen,

JOHN QUINCY ADAMS.

TO JAMES MOREHEAD, ESQ., Secretary of the Meadville (Penn.) Antimasonic Convention.

Washington, 14 December, 1833.

SIR, — Your letter of the 30th of August last, communicating to me a copy of the resolution of thanks, from the convention held at Meadville on the 28th of that month, to my respected friend

Mr. Rush and myself, for our services to the cause of pure morals, against the Institution of Freemasonry, was received at my residence in Massachusetts, at a time when 1 was absent from it. Circumstances occurred immediately after my return, inducing me to believe that there might be a propriety in deferring for some time the acknowledgment of the receipt of your letter, and the expression of my grateful sensibility to the approbation of the convention declared by their resolution, coupled as it was with a cheering exhortation to *perseverance* in the cause.

Believing that perseverance — unremitted, undeviating perseverance — is the only and the indispensable requisite, for securing the final, the complete and most desirable triumph of the cause of Antimasonry, I trust that so long as the faculty of reason, and the sense of justice, shall be extended to me by the indulgence of my Maker, I shall be found neither indifferent nor recreant to the cause. That cause, I understand to be the abolition of the oaths, obligations and penalties administered and taken for admission to the general degrees of Freemasonry — obscurely indicated by the mandate of the General Grand Royal Arch Chapter of the United States, held at Baltimore in November, 1832, to the Chapters and Lodges under their jurisdiction; indicated with an injunction of adherence to them, under the

denomination of the ANCIENT LANDMARKS OF THE
INSTITUTION.

The total demolition of these *ancient landmarks*
I take to embrace the whole cause of Antimasonry
—and for the obvious reason, that they are en-
croachments upon the common rights, and invasions
of the common interests of the rest of mankind—
that they are impious, if not blasphemous invocations
of the name of God—that they are fraudulent pal-
terings with a double sense, saying one thing and
intending another—that they are brutalities of
thought and language, shameful to be uttered by the
lips of Christian men, and other objections to them
of no trifling consideration to those who believe that
the first inroads of corruption, consist in familiarizing
the mind to vicious thoughts, and the mouth to polluted words: But it is the common rights and common interests of mankind, that are invaded by the
ancient landmarks of Freemasonry ; and it is the
common interest of all, that they should be, as public
nuisances, *abated.*

And that they will be abated, depends upon perseverance alone. As sure as the daily revolution of
the earth shall bring the source of light to ascend
from the east, so surely shall perseverance sweep
from the face of the earth, as common nuisances,
the ancient landmarks of Freemasonry. Nor is it
necessary to this result, that what is commonly

called political Antimasonry, should be always, or
even generally successful. Political Antimasonry is
but one of the modes, though hitherto undoubtedy
the most efficacious one, of combatting the Masonic
Institution. It is one of the exceptions to this
mode of operation, that it necessarily manifests
itself in the form of opposition to *persons*, and in
the shape of punishment. It enlists therefore
against itself, not only the whole body of Masonic
influence, but all the sympathies of friendship, and
all the weight of individual character and meritorious service. Its success then must and will be
variable — fluctuating with the vicissitudes of tran-
sient popular opinion, and susceptible sometimes by
its failure of retarding, as at others by success it
may advance, the consummation devoutly to be
wished. But I trust it may be considered by Antimasons as only *one* of their weapons against the
common enemy — used with reluctance, and to be
laid aside whenever Masonry herself shall be ban-
ished from the polls.

At the same time I fervently hope that the
Antimasons of the free States of this Union will
not be satisfied with the mere cessation of the
meetings of Lodges, Chapters and Encampments;
nor become indifferent to the cause, even when
justice shall require of them to discard the question
from the field of election. There is no question

but that the Masonic oaths are all *unlawful*. But as in most of the States there is no specific penalty annexed to the administration of extra-judicial oaths, the law itself is outraged by it with impunity. In the States of Rhode Island and Vermont, statutes have recently been enacted, annexing adequate penalties to the administration of extra-judicial oaths; so that in those states Masonry will no longer have the subterfuge to plead that her oaths are *not* unlawful, *because they are null and void.* If I am to credit the newspapers, there has been a decision amounting to this, even by magistrates upon the bench in your State of Pennsylvania. Those magistrates, it is stated, were, all but one, themselves Masons; and if I understand the written opinion, reported as having been given by them, it was that without deciding whether the Masonic oaths were not lawful, they held them to be voluntary promises, which could have no operation contrary to law, and therefore that a man who had taken those oaths was quite competent to be an impartial juror between Mason and Antimason. Now, although there is much *ingenuity* in this argument, and in the conclusion drawn from it, there is another conclusion to which it may lead other minds unilluminated with the floods of light which pour upon the pilgrim of the lodge room. If there were specific penalties annexed to the administration of

all extra-judicial oaths, Masonic judges would be
relieved from all judicial non-committal, whether
the Masonic oaths are lawful or not, and it would
require one step further of Masonic *co-operation on
the bench,* to decide that a man bound by unlawful
oaths, exclusively to favor one of the parties to a
suit of law, is a very impartial juror between those
parties, because the oaths he has taken, exclusively
to favor one of them, ARE UNLAWFUL.

Sir, 1 wish the members of the Convention who
did me the honor to pass the resolution which you
have communicated to me, to accept my thanks,
and a hearty reciprocation with them of the Antimasonic password, "PERSEVERE." It is the un-
conquerable spirit of all energetic virtue — the
impregnable fortress, founded upon the Rock of
Ages..

I am, with great respect,

Your friend and fellow citizen,

JOHN QUINCY ADAMS.

TO R. W. MIDDLETON, GETTYSBURG, PA.

Quincy, 27 October, 1835.

DEAR SIR, — I have received your letter of the
19th instant, with the Star and Republican Banner
of the same date. Amidst the vicissitudes of alter-
nate success and defeat, which in a very remarkable
manner have attended the cause of political Antimasonry, I have witnessed, with warm feelings of
sympathy and of admiration, the *Perseverance* with
which it has been pursued in Pennsylvania, through
good and evil fortune, to its signal triumph at this
time, in the election of Mr. Ritner as Governor of the
Commonwealth, and if I am to credit the public
journals, of a decided majority of avowed Antimasons
to the Legislature.

Hitherto, the Antimasons of Pennsylvania, though
armed with a principle as pure as any that ever
animated the heart of man ; though struggling
against an Institution foul with midnight murder,
perpetrated in strict conformity to soul-ensnaring
oaths and obligations, have yet been a feeble and
persecuted minority — persecuted for uttering the
cry of indignation at a series of atrocious violations
of the laws of God and man — persecuted, for sum-
moning the energies of virtue in the hearts of their

fellow-citizens, to extinguish a secret and lawless conspiracy in the heart of the community against the equal rights of their fellow-men.

I trust the days of this persecution are past in Pennsylvania—that the government of that Commonwealth, by the will of a decisive majority of its people, will be in the hands of Antimasons, and that by the wisdom and moderation of their measures, they will redeem the State from the pollution of Masonic morals, and restore in triumph the supremacy of the laws.

I am, with great respect, Dear Sir,

Your obedient servant,

JOHN QUINCY ADAMS.

ADDRESS TO THE PEOPLE OF MASSACHUSETTS.

In the autumn of the year 1833, Mr. Adams was unanimously nominated at a large Convention of members of the Antimasonic party, a
candidate for the office of Governor of Massachusetts. The call thus
made upon him, he did not feel at liberty to decline. The result was
a triangular contest at the election, between the three political parties
into which the people were divided, and the failure of a choice of
Governor by the requisite majority. According to the provisions of
the Constitution of Massachusetts, the election then devolved upon
the Legislature about to meet in January, 1834. But no sooner was
Mr. Adams made aware of the state of the popular vote, than he
determined to decline to be further considered a candidate for the
post. The reasons for his course, as well in accepting at first as in
withdrawing afterwards, he decided to submit in an Address to the
people of the Commonwealth, which he caused to be published at the
same time that he notified his decision in a letter directed to the
Speaker of the House of Representatives, at the opening of the session. The following is the Address.

TO THE PEOPLE OF THE COMMONWEALTH OF MASSACHUSETTS.

FELLOW-CITIZENS : — For the first time within
nearly half a century, you have been so far unable
to agree upon the person to whom the office of
serving you in the capacity of your Chief Magistrate
should be committed for the ensuing year, that no
one of the candidates presented by previous nomina-

tions to your favor has obtained a majority of your suffrages, and the case has occurred, in which, by the provisions of the constitution, your House of Representatives will be called to present to your Senate two of the four citizens, having the highest number of your votes, and of these two, the Senate will be charged with selecting one, as the Governor of the State.

Of the four candidates, having the highest number of votes, my name stands the second, and supposing it from that circumstance probable, that it might be one of the two offered by the House of Representatives for the choice of the Senate, I have deemed it my duty to withdraw from the canvass, and to request the members of the House of Representatives to withold their votes from me, with the assurance of my determination, founded on the sense of my own duties, not to accept the appointment, should it be conferred upon me.

I have not thought it necessary or proper to assign to the Legislature the reasons which have brought me to this determination. For the exercise of their functions it was only necessary that they should know the fact, and it would have been an unwarrantable consumption of *their* time, which is *your* property, to lay before them an exposition of motives, upon the correctness of which it would not be their province to decide, and which would neither require nor admit of any deliberative action appropriate to them.

This exposition of motives is, however peculiarly due to that portion of my fellow-citizens, who honored me by their nomination, and whose nomination I accepted. It is also due to you all; all having an interest in the issue of the election; and all being entitled to know, wherefore I have felt it justifiable to interpose between the provision of the constitution prescribed for the contingency which has occurred, and its absolute execution.

In accepting the nomination of the Antimasonic Convention at Boston, I was aware of the dissensions which agitated the Commonwealth, and which I had witnessed with deep concern. I knew that the Antimasons as a party constituted a minority of the people of the Commonwealth. That they were for the most part a detachment from that portion of the people, who, in recent times, had been denominated National Republicans, and who under that denomination had embraced at least three-fourths of the people of the State. That their views of general policy, both with regard to the administration of the General Government, and to that of the Commonwealth, still coincided with those of that party, and I believed it an object of the highest importance to your welfare, and most especially with reference to your interest and influ-

17

ence in the affairs of the Union, that this breach should be repaired, and this discord restored to harmony. The Masonic controversy was the only point upon which the two divisions of the party were separated, but that separation I feared was irreconcilable. The party in opposition to the State government, and friendly to the present federal administration, was necessarily Masonic, by adherence to their chief; himself illustrious with Masonic acquirements and dignities. The National Republicans were Masonic, by the declared adherence of their chief to the same Institution of which he was a distinguished member, and indications were not wanting that all the differences of principle between those two parties, ardent and bitter as they were, would be swallowed up, in the transcendent common interest of Freemasonry. So it had emphatically proved in the State of *Vermont*, and such was, in my apprehension, likely to be the issue in Massachusetts. It was with extreme reluctance that I consented to be placed within the wind of this commotion, for I saw that it would bring me in collision with the party then still wielding the power of the State, and with whose general principles and policy my own were in full accord.

I had recently been re-elected, by the co-operation of that party, in the congressional district where I resided, to a seat in the House of Represen-

tative of the United States. I had previously
been nominated by a convention of the members
of that party, as well as by an Antimasonic, and
also a Republican convention, to represent the
District of Plymouth in the last Congress. At the
expiration of that term of service, I was again
nominated by an Antimasonic, and also by a National
Republican convention, to represent the District
as newly constituted in the Congress now assembled. Those nominations were both accompanied
with resolutions, approving in the strongest and
most gratifying terms, the manner in which I had
executed the trust of representing Plymouth District ; and although the District, as newly organized,
was but partly the same with that which I had
before represented, I was re-elected by a majority
equally decisive with that of my previous election.

I had freely avowed my opinions of Masonry and
Antimasonry, when the people of the District
selected me to represent them in Congress. They
were not the opinions of a majority of the people
whom I was to represent, and they were sustained
by a very small, though highly respectable minority
of the people of the Commonwealth. They were
unpopular opinions, and therefore not the ground to
be occupied by persons aspiring to popularity, or to
its rewards.

The legislator of the most illustrious democracy of ancient times, Solon, made it a crime, punishable with .death, for any citizen to shrink from taking his side upon any great political question, which agitated and divided the people. Without approving the severity of this law, I consider the principle of its obligation as the vital spirit of republicanism. Republican government is essentially the government of public opinion, and it is good or bad government, in proportion as public opinion is right or wrong. Public opinion is the aggregate of individual opinions, and the constitution, which secures to the citizen the right of *voting*, makes it his duty to form opinions by which the exercise of that right shall be governed. Every vote is an opinion manifested by free action, and whoever votes contrary to his opinion, or shrinks from the avowal of the opinion upon which he votes, is actuated by no republican spirit. In forming his political opinions every citizen must be governed by his own honest judgment, enlightened by consultation with others, and by such measures of information as he can obtain. But as this measure of information must necessarily be possessed by different persons in different degrees, the opinions of every individual must, in great multitudes of cases, be influenced by his confidence in others. To obtain the information necessary for forming a correct opinion upon political questions is a duty specially incumbent upon those who possess in any degree the *public* confidence; and having been one of those honored with the confidence of a large portion of my fellow-citizens, I have thought it my indispensable duty to make myself acquainted with the facts and the principles involved in the controversy relating to the Masonic Institution.

The authentication of the facts, and the development of principles resulting from them, was necessarily slow and gradual. The struggle between the common rights of the people, and the exclusive privileges of an oath-bound association, organized for extensive secretly concerted action, has been long protracted, and there is no present prospect of its termination. The kidnapping and murder of William Morgan, for merely avowing the intention to reveal the secrets of Freemasonry, was the first act which roused the attention of the people to the nature and character of this Institution. In the transaction of that tragedy, nine or ten of the most atrocious crimes that can be committed by men, were perpetrated, by deeds to which several hundreds of men were accessory — men not of the class of criminals instigated to guilt by poverty, ignorance, or ferocious individual passions, but men in the educated and influential conditions of life, many of them men in all their other relations to society, of exemplary lives and conversation.

At the time of the murder of Morgan I was exercising the office of President of the United States. Neither the penalties of Freemasonry, nor the practical execution of them, by the Masons who murdered him, were known to the public in general, nor to me. Freemasonry exercised an absolute control over all the public journals edited by members of the Institution, and over many others by terror and intimidation. Months and years elapsed before the murder itself was fully proved — nor has it been judiciously proved to this day. The names indeed of the men who took him from his dungeon on the 19th of September, 1826, and closed a torture of nine days' duration by sinking him in the middle of Niagara river, are perfectly well known. It is known that one of them was, according to Masonic law, upon avowal of his crime under the seal of the fifth libation, and under hot pursuit by the officers of justice, furnished by an Encampment of Knights Templars in the city of New York, with the means of escaping from this country. But the witnesses to all these transactions are Freemasons — and as accessories to the crimes of which they are cognizant, refuse or evade giving judicial testimony, on the express ground that they might thereby criminate themselves. There are clouds of witnesses, but they are participators in the guilt, and thus it is that Masonry protects itself from the judicial authentication of its crimes, by the very multitude of its accomplices, all bound by the invisible chains of secrecy.

But the trials of the Masonic outrages in the State of New York have exhibited other expositions of Masonic law. Masonic juries have been packed by Masonic sheriffs, for the express purpose not only of screening the guilty from punishment, but of falsifying the facts by presentments and verdicts known to themselves to be untrue. Masonic witnesses have refused to testify, and suffered imprisonment rather than disclose the facts known to them, even when they did not criminate themselves. Nor is this all. When conscience, bursting the bands of Masonry, has constrained Masonic witnesses to testify to crimes in which they themselves shared, and to the secrets of the craft, solitary Masonic jurors have refused their assent to verdicts, upon which all their fellows were agreed, on the avowed resolution that they would not believe any testimony of a seceding Mason.

The extent to which the public justice of the country had been baffled, and the morals of the people vitiated by Freemasonry, was therefore disclosed to me gradually, and by a slow process of time. Absorbed by other cares, and with time engrossed by the discharge of other duties, I was for years very imperfectly informed either of the laws of Masonry, or of the ascendency they were maintaining over the laws of the land, or of the deep depravity with which they were cankering the morals of the people. Morgan's book was not published till some months after his death — and when published, the Masonic presses long labored in their double vocation of suppressing truth and propagating falsehood, by representing the disclosures of that book as false. Yet Morgan had revealed the secrets only of the first degrees, and the deepest of Masonic abominations were yet screened from the public eye. It was not until the 4th of July, 1828, that the Convention of seceding Masons, held at Le Roy, made public the secrets, oaths, obligations and penalties of the higher degrees — nor were the proceedings of that Convention made known to me till I found them in David Bernard's Light on Masonry.

To that book, and its author, permit me, my fellow-citizens, while recommending it to your perusal and meditation, to offer the tribute of unfeigned respect — a tribute the more richly deserved, for the slanders which Masonic benevolence and charity have showered upon them. Elder David Bernard was a minister of the Genesee Baptist Association in the State of New York. He was a man of good repute, and of blameless life and conversation. Like many others, he was ensnared into the taking of fifteen degrees of Masonry, and was the intimate Secretary of the Lodge of Perfection. He was one of the first seceders from the Order, and from that time underwent every possible persecution from Masons, and the frequent danger of his life. Among the most interesting documents demonstrating the true spirit of Masonry, which have appeared in the course of this controversy, is the plain and unaffected narrative of the treatment which he received, and of the scenes which he witnessed at the meetings of Lodges and Chapters, *before* the murder of Morgan, as well as after, from the time when it was projected in them. That it was so projected is established by his testimony, confirmatory of numerous other demonstrated facts.

To David Bernard perhaps more than to any other man, the world is indebted for the revelation of the most execrable mysteries of Masonry — nor could he, as a minister of the word of God, have performed a service to his country and his fellow-Christians, more suitable to his sacred functions. It was principally by his exertions that the Le Roy Convention of seceding Masons assembled and published the oaths, obligations and penalties of the higher degrees of the Order.

From the time of that publication, the whole

system of the Masonic laws, and their practical operation, having relation to the disclosure of their secrets, have been gradually unfolding themselves, and the law and its execution have been continual commentaries upon each other. When the murder of Morgan was first perpetrated, the instances were frequent of its being openly justified by members of the Institution, as being but the execution of a *penalty*, to which he himself had assented — as it certainly was. Another class of Masons, somewhat less resolute, contented themselves with maintaining that he was a perjured wretch for violating his oaths, and if he had been put to death, had only suffered what he deserved. A third class sturdily denied the facts even after every thing but the last act of murder had been proved in regular judicial trials ; and a fourth, intrenching themselves in ignorance, which they took care always to preserve, by turning away their eyes from all evidence of the facts, rested their defence from the charge of Morgan's murder by professing *that they knew nothing about it.*

From the time when I first perused Elder Bernard's book, I became convinced that it was impossible for me to discharge my duties, as a citizen, to my country, by knowing nothing about it. By a constant comparison of the laws of Masonry with their practical execution, from the robbery of Morgan's manuscripts, and the abortive attempt to burn Miller's house, to the escape of Richard Howard from justice and from this country, a great multitude of facts combined to demonstrate the pervading efficacy of all the Masonic obligations. Measures always enfeebled and thwarted by Masonic influence, were taken by the Legislature and Executive of the State of New York, to detect and bring the offenders to justice. The trials of the criminals were in progress — I endeavored to obtain information of their course and termination. The Letters of Col. Stone upon Masonry and Antimasonry, were addressed to me, in consequence of inquiries made by me, to another person, and communicated to him. With regard to the facts ascertained by those trials, the reports made to the Legislature of New York, and the proceedings of the first Antimasonic Convention, held at Philadelphia, with the essays of William Slade upon the Masonic Penalties, and the *defence* of Masonry by the Grand Lodge of Rhode Island, all concurred in furnishing a mass of information from which my conclusions were deduced.

I saw a code of Masonic legislation, *adapted* to prostrate every principle of equal justice, and to corrupt every sentiment of virtuous feeling in the soul of him who bound his allegiance to it. I saw the practice of common honesty, the kindness of

Christian benevolence, even the abstinence from atrocious crimes, limited exclusively, by lawless oaths, and barbarous penalties, to the social relations between the brotherhood of the Craft. 1 saw slander organized into a secret, wide-spread and affiliated agency, fixing its invisible fangs into the hearts of its victims, sheltered by the darkness of the lodge room, and armed with the never-ceasing penalties of death. I saw self-invoked imprecations of throats cut from ear to ear, of heart and vitals torn out and cast forth to the wolves and vultures, of skulls smitten off, and hung on spires. I saw wine drank from a human skull with solemn invocation of all the sins of its owner upon the head of him who drinks from it. And I saw a wretched mortal man dooming himself to external punishment (when the last trump shall sound) as a guarantee for idle and ridiculous promises. Such are the laws of Masonry, such their indelible character, and with that character perfectly corresponded the history of the abduction and murder of Morgan, and the history of Masonic Lodges, Chapters and Encampments, from that day to the present.

To this general assertion, numerous exceptions must be made, not only of individual Masons, but of whole Lodges and Chapters. I wish I could say of Encampments, which have surrendered their Masonic charters, or silently dissolved themselves.

Other Lodges and Chapters have ceased to hold their meetings, and I have heard of yet others, which still holding their meetings, have ceased to administer any of the oaths. Besides these, there are numbers of individual Masons, who have silently seceded and withdrawn from that Institution without renouncing it. It is probable that these exceptions include one-third of all the Masons in the free States of this Union ; and to them, no observation of censure which I have made upon Masonry or upon Masons, can apply. Their bearing is only upon adhering Masons and Masonry.

But of that censure, the Grand Encampment, the Grand Chapter and Grand Lodge of New York must take their full share. Their opinion of the laws of Masonry, and of their true exposition, is the same as mine. They have proved it by their deeds. They knew that the kidnappers and assassins of Morgan, the robbers of his manuscripts, the slanderers who falsely charged him with larceny to seize upon his person and accomplish his destruction, the incendiaries of the house of Miller; that the sheriffs who packed Masonic juries, the juries who falsified their verdicts, the witnesses who refused to testify, or deliberately testified to falsehood ; they knew that all these had but acted in strict conformity and faithful obedience to the letter and the spirit of the Masonic laws. So well did they know it, that far from expelling any one of these criminals from the fraternity, they have hailed and recognized them as worthy brothers of the craft, have cheered them with consolation in their sufferings, indemnified them with money for their imprisonment, and spirited away one at least of the ruffians, whose hands were reeking with the blood of murder, from the public justice of their country.

All this, fellow-citizens, have I seen, through a succession of time, now extending to more than seven years. To inform myself of the facts I deemed a duty of paramount obligation upon me, as a man, a citizen, and a Christian ; especially after my release from the arduous duties of public office. Had I been actuated by no other motives than sympathy with the feelings of my own immediate neighborhood and friends, I trust they would have needed no apology. It happened that the attention of the inhabitants of my native town of Quincy, had been drawn to the facts of the Morgan tragedy and of the laws of Masonry, years before I came to reside among them. There is a Masonic Lodge in that town, and many of its members are among the worthiest and most respected citizens of the place. Several of them are my personal friends and kinsmen. When the Masonic controversy first made its way into this Commonwealth, the people of that town were among the first who became acquainted with the Masonic laws as they were divulged, and with the Masonic crimes in New York, their natural progeny. A large majority of them became Antimasons, and so I found them upon my return among them. The spirit of Antimasonry had already pervaded the counties of Norfolk, Plymouth, and Bristol ; and the secession of the Rev. Moses Thacher, and the controversies, ecclesiastical and political, in which that step had involved him, occasioned much agitation among this portion of the people in the Commonwealth.

In these dissensions I took no part ; but I should have been insensible to all my duties, had I closed my eyes to facts or turned my ear from argument, and smothered the sense of justice in my soul, for the privilege of blinking the public question, which was convulsing the neighborhood in which I lived, by professing *to know nothing about it.*

Yet I did not intrude myself as a volunteer in the controversy. It had been erroneously stated in a newspaper, edited by a high Masonic dignitary in Boston, that I was a Mason. In answer to an inquiry from a person in New York, whether I was so, I had declared that *I was not, and never should be.* This letter, without my knowledge or consent, crept into the public prints ; and from that day the *revenge* of Masonic *charity*, from Main to Louisiana (I speak to the letter) marked me for its own.

At the critical moment of the Presidential election, in the counties of New York where Antimasonry was most prevailing, a hand-bill was profusely circulated, with a deposition upon oath, attested by a Masonic magistrate, of an individual, real or fictitious, swearing that he had been present at two different times (the dates of which were specified) with me at meetings of a Masonic Lodge at Pittsfield, — a town, in which I had never entered a house in my life.

This was the first punishment inflicted upon me by Masonic law, for declaring that I never should be a Mason. The influence of Masonry upon that Presidential election was otherwise exerted with considerable effect ; and of the more recent election it decided, perhaps, the fate. I never noticed either the false annunciation in the Boston Centinel that I was a Mason, or the oath of the worthy brother of the square and compass, that he had twice met me at the Lodge in Pittsfield. They were both calumnies, as strictly conformable to Masonic laws as to Masonic benevolence, and have been followed up by slanders coined at the same mint, and circulated through all the fraternizing presses of the land.

I have stated to you, fellow citizens, the reasons and motives which have actuated me in the part that I have taken in the Masonic and Antimasonic controversy. To obtain an accurate knowledge of the facts, and of the *real* laws of Freemasonry, and to bring them to the test of pure moral principles, I believed to be my indispensable duty, and having done that, it was no less my duty to bear my testimony on every suitable occasion both to facts and principles.

Col. Stone's Letters contained an exposition of Masonic law, from a Knight Templar, who had withdrawn, but not seceded from the Order — an exposition as favorable as the hand of a friend could make it, consistently with the candor of truth. It was palliative, excusatory, apologetical, for Masonry in its fairest colors; and it first put forth the avowal, that the Masonic obligations were *not* among the secrets of Masonry. This was a point upon which the most eminent dignitaries of the craft differed among themselves; but in the mean time, the obligations were *kept* secret. They never had been divulged till the publication of Morgan's book since the forgotten revelations of Jachin and Boaz, the author of which is understood to have suffered the same fate as Morgan.

Col. Stone gave the original oath, obligation, and penalty, the only one taken at, and long after the primitive institution of the Order. He also referred in his book to a manuscript of the oaths, obligations, and penalties, of the first seven degrees, including the Royal Arch, as they have generally been admin-

18

inistered in the Lodges and Chapters of New England ; and he afterwards, at my request, transmitted to me the manuscript, which is now in my possession. It is a complete, though abridged, summary of Masonic law to the degree of Royal Arch; and the volume of Col. Stone gives the fair and full history of the execution of that law, in its conflict of five years with the sovereign authority of the State of New York.

In those letters Col. Stone had also referred to an opinion, previously expressed by me to him in conversation, that the first step in Freemasonry, the initiatory rite, the Entered Apprentice's oath, was vicious, immoral, and unlawful. By this publication of my opinion, which I had not authorized, but to which I could have no objection, I felt myself called upon to expose, by a strict analysis of the Entered Apprentice's oath, the reasons upon which I had passed that summary sentence of condemnation upon it. I addressed therefore to Col. Stone, for publication in the paper of which he is a joint editor in New York, the four Letters on the Entered Apprentice's oath. which have since been extensively circulated, but which, such is the power of Masonry over the periodical press, it required no small exertion of fortitude and intrepidity in him to publish.

I shortly afterwards received from Benjamin

Cowell, a citizen of Rhode Island, a letter, asking my opinion in what manner this vicious and immoral Institution could most effectively be put down. In my answer to him, I suggested two obvious modes of effecting that object. The one, that the Masons themselves should abolish or cease to administer the oaths, obligations, and penalties ; and the other, that the administration of them should be prohibited under adequate penalties by legislative enactment in the several States.

That they should be voluntarily abandoned by the Masons themselves, was my first wish, because that would have been a meritorious act, — an act now sanctioned by the example of the Lodge of my own constituents at Plymouth, to the members of which I tender hereby my warmest thanks, and which, if followed by all the Lodges, will, I have no doubt, (as it should,) put down all political Antimasonry within the Commonwealth forever. But the General Grand Royal Arch Chapter of the United States, at a meeting held at Baltimore, had just issued an edict, forbidding this voluntary consummation ; and there were numerous other indications, that however multitudes of individual Masons, Lodges and Chapters, were disposed to yield to the voice of reason, of religion, and of law, and to cease from the further administration of their hideous vows, this was not the temper, or intention of

the high and leading members of the Institution ;
and it was apparent that the principle of subordina-
tion, so essentially woven into the texture of the
Order, would deter most of the inferior and affiliated
associations of the fraternity from breaking their
fetters and dissolving their bands. I believed,
therefore, that the aid of legislative prohibition with
penalties, would be indispensable for abating this
moral nuisance in the community ; and I recommended that the administration of the Masonic
oaths should be prohibited by law, upon penalties of
fine, and imprisonment, adequate to *deter* from the
administration of them in *future.*

I take this occasion, fellow-citizens, to justify
myself before you from an aspersion, which the
committee of the convention of National Republicans at Worcester, (who resolved that their party
must be a majority of the people, not only of the
Commonwealth but of the Union,) did not disdain,
in their zeal, to make that majority cast upon me
in their address to you. The committee assured
you that Antimasonry was not a proper ground for
political controversy, and as it did not suit their purposes fairly to state to you the real question between
Masonry and Antimasonry, they presented you a
fictitious one, invented in the lodge room, and
adopted by them as their own. They told you that
Antimasonry was a persecuting spirit, the object of

which was to deprive Freemasons of their rights;
and by quoting with inverted commas, a passage of
my letter to Mr. Cowell, they perverted it into an
assertion that I had recommended a law to punish
men with "fine and imprisonment" ' for being
Masons. I recommended no such thing ; but as I
know that some of the members of the committee
who signed that address have learned to read, and
as some of them may peradventure in times past
have professed to be my friends, I take the liberty of
a friend in recommending to them, the next time
they shall be charged with addressing you, in behalf
of a party which *must* have a majority, to respect
you, if they will not respect themselves. To respect
you, by abstaining from the slander of a political
adversary, not less by a palpable misrepresentation
than by wilful falsehood.

I have great satisfaction in observing that within
two months after the publication of the extracts of
my letter to Mr. Cowell, the Legislature of Rhode
Island did, with great unanimity, enact a law prohibiting the administration of extra-judicial oaths,
upon penalties of fine and political disfranchisement,
which last is rather more severe, but more appropriate to the offence, than that which I had proposed.
It is to be presumed that while that law remains in
force, the General Grand Royal Arch Chapter of
the United States, which is to meet again at the

City of Washington in December, 1835, will not
again enjoin upon the Chapters and Lodges under
their jurisdiction, at least within the State of *Rhode
Island*, a rigid adherence to the *ancient landmarks*
cf the Order ; that is, to these very extra-judicial
oaths. They will, I trust, abstain also from repeat-
ing the same injunction to the Chapters and Lodges
in the State of Vermont, where a similar law, prohibiting in substance the administration of the Masonic
oaths, has lately been enacted. It happens that these
same two States of Rhode Island and Vermont, are
the identical States in which the report of the Committee of the General Grand Royal Arch Chapter of
the United States, affirmed that Masonry had triumphantly sustained itself, and with regard to Rhode
Island that it had been *sustained by the Legislature*.

Fellow-citizens, I indulge the hope that before
the next meeting of the General Grand Royal Arch
Chapter of the United States, YOUR statute book
will present for their consideration, the same disposal of the "ancient landmarks" of Freemasonry.
For when YOU shall have set *your* seal of repro-
bation upon those abominable appeals to the name of
God, these atrocious obligations, those butchering
and blasphemous penalties, and when the Freemasons of your Commonwealth shall *submit* to your
will, in this enactment, Antimasonry within *your*
borders will be extinct — mine at least will "die

away." There is not a Freemason in the State, to whom I bear personally a particle of ill will. There are many for whom I entertain a warm and cordial friendship, even of those who have declared to you that Freemasonry *knows* no penalty beyond admonition, suspension and expulsion. I am willing to believe that they did not understand, so well as the murderers of Morgan, the oaths they had taken. Even of those who have been slandering me without measure and without stint, I am ready to allow that they are only fulfilling their Masonic obligations, and following their vocation, and that they have the example of *my friends* of the National Republican Worcester Convention committee, to sustain them. Whatever of evil there is in Antimasonry is but an aggravation of the sins of Masonry herself.

I am aware of the objections to what is called political Antimasonry, which have hitherto deterred a large majority of you from resorting to it as an extinguisher to the baleful light of Freemasonry. One of the most fascinating allurements of the "handmaid" has been her influence in promoting the political advancement of the brethren of the craft. Silent and secret in her operations, she raised them with invisible hand to place and power, and one of the first discoveries made by Antimasonry was, that three-fourths of all the offices within the range of the cable-tow, were occupied by

Masons. This had become in fact the great and absorbing employment of Lodge, Chapter, Encampment and Consistory; not while the Tyler with drawn sword was at the door—not while the Master, Grand Master, High Priest, or Illustrious Sir Knight was reading lessons of benevolence and charity, from the pages of Holy Writ—not while the slipshod, hoodwinked, haltered, poor blind pilgrim was perambulating the Lodge with pointed dagger at his breast, in search of *light*—not even in the passage from labor to refreshment, nor in the chorusses of Masonic minstrelsy, so congenial to that *decent* mimicry of the ineffable Jehovah in the burning bush. All these were but the types and shadows of what was to come—all this was but the outward shell to the kernel of Masonic brotherhood. The principle of preference established by the Masonic code of politics, was, that a brother of the craft was to be preferred to any other of *equal* qualifications. It was the *odd trick* of the game, and it shuffled all the *honors* into the hands of the Masonic partner.

This statute of Masonic law was in the year 1816 promulgated under the seal of the compass and square, by a Master Mason in the Boston Centinel, the same paper which afterwards so *veraciously* declared me to be a member of the Order. Little attention was paid to this political pass-word at the time. It was taken for a mere common electioneering paragraph. Its operation was neither seen nor suspected. The obligation had not then been sharpened into a positive promise upon oath, clinched as usual with the penalty of death ; but as a general portion of the law of exclusive favor to the brethren of the craft, operating unseen, and visible even in its effects only to the initiated ; it was as it always must be, a conspiracy of the few against the equal rights of the many; anti-republican in its sap, from the fruit blushing at the summit of the plant to the deepest fibre of its root.

It was, perhaps, this monopoly of public office, by the Masonic guide to the ballot box, which first suggested to the Antimasonic party, the expedient of counteracting its effects by adopting the same principle and reversing its application. It needed nothing more. If the Mason was bound, between candidates of equal qualifications, to prefer the brother of the craft, the Antimason was but turning upon him his own tables, in giving the same preference to the brother Antimason. Yet this is the principle openly avowed as a fundamental law of the Masonic fraternity, but which turned upon themselves, raises an universal outcry of proscription, disfranchisement and persecution.

Fellow-citizens, there is in my mind an objection to the principle itself. It is but a modification of

the seifish, intolerant and exclusive principle of party
spirit. In the Masonic code and practice it has the
additional vice of *secret* operation. When Antimasonry first raised its head in New York, it found
three-fourths of all the *elective* offices in the State
in the hands of *Masons*. The proportion of Masons
to the whole population was not one fiftieth part.
How is it with you now? Look to the delegation
from your city in your House of Representatives.
Boston, to speak in round numbers, has ten thousand citizens qualified by your constitution and laws
to serve as Representatives in the General Court ;
of these ten thousand, one thousand may be
Masons. Boston had last year sixty-three members
in the House. Of these, by relative proportion of
numbers, there should have been six, or at most
seven Masons. How many were there? Nearly
thirty. Of the number this year elected, the Masonic proportion is not less. Here are then nine
thousand citizens of Boston, qualified to serve as
Representatives in the Legislature, virtually dis-
franchised, that is, deprived of the enjoyment of
their rights, by the preference of brother Masons
over others of equal qualifications, and the exclusive selection of Masons to fill the seats, the access
to which ought, by your constitution and laws, to be
enjoyed equally by all.

Look to the delegation in your Senate from the

county of Worcester, the very throne of Masonry
in the Commonwealth. There are in that county
say ten thousand citizens eligible to the Senate.
One-tenth of that number may be Masons — one
member in the Senate would be more than their
fair proportion of the representation. They have
five out of six. Now if the Freemasons of Worcester county were, like the patricians of ancient
Rome in her early days, an order of nobility,
exclusively eligible to seats in the Senate, what
would be the difference of the result from that
which is here effected, by the Masonic preference of
a brother of the craft over others of equal qualifications?

I shall not now inquire what influence this combined action of Masonic agency, by the united nu-
meric power of the city of Boston and the county of
Worcester in your legislative councils, has, and must
have over the administration and policy of the whole
Commonwealth. Its power will be pre-eminently
conspicuous in the proceedings of your Legislature.
I only invite your attentive observation of its effects.
Watch the movements of your General Court,
especially upon every subject connected with the
supremacy of Masonry, and observe the issues, as
they may affect your own interests, of the Masonic
sympathies between the delegations from the city of
Boston and the county of Worcester.

The preference at elections, of Antimasons for candidates of their own opinions, is nothing more than the application of the Masonic rule and practice of electioneering to themselves. It is only justifiable as a defensive measure, and as a means of counteracting the rapacious grasp of Masonry at all the offices of the land.

In my letter to Mr. Cowell, I did not express my approbation of political Antimasonry even to the whole of this extent. I confined my approbation to the election of members to the State Legislatures ; and to them, only until statutes prohibiting with adequate penalties the administration of Masonic oaths should be enacted. The Legislatures of Rhode Island and Vermont *have* enacted such statutes, and if the Masons in those two States *submit* to them, Masonry within them must ultimately die, as corporations are extinguished, by the death of all their members.

A far manlier and more honorable course would be that proposed by Samuel Elliot, a Royal Arch Mason, of Vermont, a stranger to me, but a man who deserves well of his country, who had the intrepidity to call upon his brethren and companions of the Order to yield to the unequivocal voice and wishes of their fellow-citizens ; to lay down their childish pageants and preposterous dignities ; to cast away their paper crowns and lackered sceptres ;

their globe and cross-crowned mitres, and their
harlequin wooden swords of knighthood ; and to
emerge from the tawdry honors of Grand Kings
and High Priests, and Princes of the royal secret,
and resume the plain, unembroidered, laceless, but
comfortable and decent garb of Republican citizens.
This proposition was indeed perilous to him who
made it, and the floodgates of slander, according
to the ancient usages of the Order, were immediately opened upon him. But it was regularly considered and debated at a meeting of the Grand
Lodge of Vermont, at which were present one
hundred and twenty members delegated from the
several secular Lodges in the State. Of these, forty-
one voted for accepting the proposal of Mr. Elliot,
one third of the whole number ; and it was before
the act of the Legislature prohibiting the administration of extra-judicial oaths. Let the moral Antimasons who concur in the opinion that the Masonic
oaths and obligations are vicious and immoral, but
who are unwilling to manifest this opinion at the
ballot box, reflect upon this fact. Immediately
before it occurred, the two great political parties
had combined together, and burying all their dis-
tinctive principles, and distributing prospectively
between them all the offices and honors of the
State — had united in one great and convulsive effort
to put down Antimasonry. It failed ; the atmos-

phere of the Green Mountains diffuses around them not only a physical but moral and political air too pure for the contamination of political prostitution. The people at the ballot boxes basterdized the fruits of this unnatural union, and prostrated both the parties to it before the lofty spirit of Anti-masonry.

The immediate consequence of this event was the convocation of the Grand Lodge of the State, to consider the proposition of the Royal Arch companion Elliot, and although it did not then succeed entirely, one important step to the dissolution of the order was taken. The Grand Lodge did grant a permission to the secular Lodges under their jurisdiction, to dissolve themselves; a process which it is earnestly to be hoped that they will generally pursue. For let the Institution but be once formally extinguished by the voluntary act of its members in one State of this Union, and I harbor not a doubt that it will very shortly vanish from the land.

It is to this voluntary relinquishment of the whole system of Freemasonry by its own members, that I look for that great moral and political reform, which will be effected by the extinction of the Order. To this sacrifice of their prejudices and their pride, of their vanities and their follies, they must be brought by the power of permanent and quickening public opinion. I have approved of the ballot box as *one* of the modes of manifesting this opinion; and this the more readily, because it was at the ballot box that the maleficent power of the Masonic trowel was cementing the edifice of the polluted Temple. But I have not deemed the ballot box the only, or even the favorite weapon of Antimasonry. I have sanctioned the partial resort to it with reluctance; and would rejoice to see the day when it should be no longer necessary. I have indeed never resorted to it myself, by interfering in any election against a Masonic candidate, and have in the discharge of my own duties, preferred other modes of operating, to the extent of my poor ability, upon public opinion.

It was this last motive that induced me to publish the four letters to Col. Stone, upon the Entered Apprentice's oath, in which, by a minute analysis of it in all its parts, the appeal to God, the promise and the penalty, it was my purpose to prove it *wrong*, vicious, unlawful and immoral—contrary to the principles of Christianity, of humanity, of law, of eternal truth and justice. To those letters, now fifteen months published, not one word of reply has ever appeared.

When the General Grand Royal Arch Chapter of the United States, at their last triennial meeting, issued their mandate and exhortation to the Chapters

under under their jurisdiction, and their subordinate
Lodges, to turn themselves into lyceums and schools
of useful knowledge, but adhere to their *Ancient
Landmarks* — meaning their oaths, obligations and
penalties, I saw in their proceedings a new occasion
for an appeal to the moral sense of the community.
EDWARD LIVINGSTON, then Secretary of State of
the United States, was re-elected their Grand High
Priest, an office which he had occupied for the three
preceding years. The personal relations between
this gentleman and myself had uniformly been of a
friendly character. As the legislator of a criminal
code for Louisiana, and as on more than one occasion a sound expositor of the principles of our
National Constitution, he had acquired my esteem,
my admiration, I had almost said my veneration.
In his code for Louisiana, he had proposed the total
abolition of the punishment of death, and in his
report to the Legislature had supported this proposition with a power of reasoning and of eloquence,
which, without entirely convincing my judgment,
had been viewed by me as at once the proof of a
vigorous mind and the pledge of a benevolent
heart. It appeared to me impossible that such a
man could read the letters on the Entered Apprentice's oath, without either assenting to their argument, or perceiving the indispensable necessity to
the Institution of refuting it. I could not believe

it possible that HE should deliberately consider the oaths, obligations and penalties, which it was yet his official duty to administer, either innocent, or harmless deceptions; speaking, in the name of God, one thing and meaning another. As the General Grand High Priest of Masonry in the United States, he was bound .to be the ófficial defender of the Institution against any serious charge of unlawfulness or immorality, and he had, perhaps inconsiderately, assumed not only that character, but that of an accuser of Antimasonry at the bar of public opinion, in his inaugural address at his first installation. I sent him, therefore, a copy of the letters on the Entered Apprentice's oath, and addressed six letters to himself, calling upon him to defend his Institution or to purge it of its impurities; to maintain his charges against a numerous and respectable class of his fellow citizens, or to retract them.

There are men upon whom the consciousness of having done great wrong to others, produces little remorse, unless awakened to the sense of their own injustice by feeling the application of the scourge from another hand. I did not believe Mr. Livingston to be a person of such a character. I gave him credit for honest and generous feeling. I believed that if reminded of a gross injury committed inadvertently by himself in the form of erroneous imputations upon others, he would hasten to repair

19

it. The voluntary reparation of its own injustice, is one of the most glorious features of true magnanimity. Mr. Livingston did not notice my letters; not even by acknowledging the receipt of them. Had they been upon any other subject, I have reason to know that they would have been received with friendly acknowledgment and courtesy. But you will recollect that in his inaugural address upon his installation as the Grand High Priest of the General Grand Royal Arch Chapter of the United States, to his brethren and companions, he advised them — that if the CAUSE and the EFFECT; if the oaths, obligations and penalties of Masonry as the *cause;* and the literal execution of them upon Morgan and Miller as the *effect;* followed by the baffling of the sovereign authority of the State of New York in all its exertions to bring the murderers and incendiaries to justice; if the throat-cutting, embowelling, heart and vital-tearing, skull-smiting, hanging, drowning, quartering, double and treble eternal damnation of the penalties on one side, — and if on the other, the apathy of the Masonic executive government of New York, the packing of Masonic juries by Masonic sheriffs, the perjuries and prevarications of Masonic witnesses, the grants of Masonic funds by the Grand Lodge and Grand Chapter of New York to the convicted and confessing kidnappers of Morgan, under the demonination of Western Sufferers; if the illustrious and successful achievement of the Encampment of Knights Templars in New York, in rescuing from the gibbet, and conveying beyond the seas, one of the murderers of Morgan; — if all this should be pressed home and hard upon the fraternity, they should meet it all with DIGNIFIED SILENCE!

I could not be surprised, therefore, at finding him practice upon his own precept; or at discovering the difference of *moral principle*, between Edward Livingston the legislator of Louisiana, and Edward Livingston the General Grand High Priest of the Royal Arch Masonry of the Union.

You will observe, fellow-citizens, that neither in my letters to Col. Stone, nor in those to Edward Livingston, was there one word of political Anti-masonry. The object of the letters to Col. Stone was to prove by plain and unanswerable argument, that the Masonic Institution in its first rite of initiation, is radically and incurably vicious — that of the letters to Mr. Livingston was to prevail upon him to exercise his great and powerful influence to discard those oaths, obligations and penalties, which are the indelible disgrace of the Order. To these letters no answer has been made or attempted.

When my letter to Mr. Cowell was first published, it was in like manner left unnoticed; but when the recent election came on, then came the season for revenge; then it was that a part of my letter to Mr. Cowell was produced, published and trumpeted abroad; and by the same process which in Masonic logic and language expounds a throat cut across from ear to ear to mean *expulsion* from a Lodge—a declaration that I would, if a member of a State Legislature, vote for the enactment of a statute prohibiting upon pain of fine and imprisonment the administration *in future* of the Masonic oaths—was represented as a recommendation to cast into prison every Freemason to whom the oaths have been administered heretofore. And this Royal Arch *mistake*, the committee of the Worcester Convention did not disdain, in addressing you, to adopt and make their own.

Before entering upon the field of the Masonic controversy, I had not only deemed it my indispensable duty to possess myself of the facts and principles material to it, but to contemplate the consequences which would, and those which might, result from being involved in it myself. In the district which I was then to represent in Congress, about two-fifths of the population were Antimasons; but the political majorities in both the counties of Plymouth and of Norfolk, were Masonic, or at least adverse to Antimasonry. Throughout the Commonwealth, the Antimasons were in numbers scarcely one-fifth, and in Boston not more than one-tenth of the voting citizens, while the combined concentrated action of the three Masonic strong holds of the State — Boston, Worcester and Salem — had already succeeded, in accordance with the mandate of the General Grand High Priest of the Royal Arch Chapter of the United States, in raising clouds of obloquy and persecution against the cause of Antimasonry itself, and against all who espoused it. I saw very distinctly that Antimasonry was not the path of ambition. It was certain to give umbrage to a large majority of the people of the State under their *then* existing impressions. It would probably displease three-fifths of my own constituents, whose displeasure might soon be manifested at the ballot box. Their suffrages had not been solicited by me, nor had I the most distant imagination that I should ever appear as a candidate for the suffrages of the people of the State, as their Chief Magistrate. I had at other periods of my life enjoyed large portions of their favor, and had received recent proof that that favor was not abated. I had nothing more ever to ask of them but their good opinion, and that was inexpressibly precious to me. Why should I expose myself to the risk of forfeiting it altogether, without any earthly object or prospect of benefit to myself?

My only answer to this question is, — It was the

cause of truth and pure morals; it was an abused and calumniated cause; it was a cause deeply interesting to my constituents, to my fellow-citizens, and to my country.

My re-election to Congress, by an undiminished majority of my constituents, had been very gratifying to me, as a token that the portion of my fellow-citizens in that district, opposed to Antimasonry, were so far disposed to tolerate my disagreement in opinion with them upon this point, that they did not consider it as a reason for withdrawing their confidence from me.

The Masonic denunciation and misrepresentation of my letter to Mr. Cowell had been tried against me there, without effect. Neither Masonry nor Antimasonry were subjects of controversy in Congress, and it was enough for me to know that the great mass of my constituents were satisfied that my zeal for Antimasonry had in no wise interfered with the faithful discharge of my duties as their Representative.

The Antimasonic Convention held at Boston in September, were pleased to nominate me as their candidate for your suffrages as Chief Magistrate of the Commonwealth for the ensuing year. I knew that their chief object in tendering to me the nomination, was to make an effort to restore the harmony between the two divisions of the National Republican party, which had long constituted the vast majority of the people of the Commonwealth. They were as yet separated only by that line : I believe there was no neutral ground. Aware of personal prejudices against me existing in a respectable portion of the National Republican party, upon other and long standing collisions between them and me — and the public service in which I was engaged being more adapted to the experience of my past life, and better suited to considerations of interest to me, though of none to the public — I had very sincerely hoped and expected that the views of the Antimasonic party would unite upon some other citizen, as their candidate for the chief magistracy of the State. Their nomination was however placed upon grounds which it was impossible for me to withstand; and as I knew it was on their part a tender of the olive branch to those of their fellow citizens with whom they had long walked in the strength of united councils, and from whom they had parted only at the dictate of a pure, uncompromising *moral* principle; I accepted their nomination in the same spirit in which it was tendered, and in my answer of acceptance, expressed to them my determination, if the suffrages of the people should confirm their nomination, to carry into effect, to the utmost extent of my ability, *their* purpose of restoring harmony to the Commonwealth, and of promoting, as far as possible, that of the Union.

But in this acceptance, you will perceive, fellow-citizens, that there was a condition expressed — and there was also one implied. The expressed condition was, the contingency that the suffrages of the people should confirm the nomination. I was resolved in no event to hold the office of Governor of the Commonwealth, from any hands other than those of a majority of the people themselves — for the obvious reason that it was impossible for the representative of a minority of the people, to be the suitable agent for promoting harmony among them. If therefore a majority of the people should reject the nomination accepted by me, it was clear that the restoration of harmony, if to be effected at all, must be accomplished under happier auspices than my elevation to your highest trust. A failure, therefore, of a single vote short of a majority, constituting me your Governor by your own voice, would have been a decisive indication to me, that *harmony* could only be promoted by me, not by persevering in the contest of an election, but (if in any possible manner) by retiring from it.

The implied condition was dependent upon the same contingency. It was that my election should involve no dereliction of other public duties with which I was charged. I was a Representative elect of the Twelfth District of the Commonwealth in the Congress of the United States. Of the

importance to your interests and to the welfare of the
Union that you should have a full representation in
the popular branch of the national legislature, at all
times and without intermission, I had always had a
strong impression, and have now an impression much
deepened by the painful experience of the last Congress; in which, for the want of that full representation, you suffered in various ways gross injustice,
and particularly by the curtailment of your constitutional right in that representation itself. As the
Representative of the Twelfth District, I held it to
be my duty to enter into no engagement which
should deprive my constituents of their voice in the
national legislature for a single day. If therefore,
even before your annual election was held, I had
seen reason to *expect* that I should be chosen your
Governor by the majority of the people, I should
have resigned my seat in Congress, in ample time
to give my constituents the opportunity before the
meeting of Congress, to elect another Representative
in my place. The Convention held at Worcester
the first week in October, rendered this measure on
my part unnecessary, and in resolving to take my
seat in Congress, I assumed the fulfilment of duties
incompatible with my acceptance of the office of
Governor of the Commonwealth.

In saying this, fellow-citizens, I intend no reflection upon the candidate of the National Republican

party for your suffrages as Governor; nor do I mean to say or insinuate that he is, or should be bound by the principles of conduct which my sense of duty prescribes to me for the government of mine. He was nominated by a convention, who, instead of tendering or accepting an olive branch, resolved that they *must* have a majority, and set all other parties in the Commonwealth at defiance. He had no call from them to promote harmony; and if in the event of his election he should, as I hope and trust he will, do so, it will be in the indulgence of his own fair and honorable spirit, and not by following the impulse of that convention, who, representing the remnant of a party which once had a majority, seem to have persuaded themselves that it must necessarily last forever.

He has besides this, a vote of the people, by several thousands, larger than mine; and although by the provisions of your constitution, this is not sufficient for his election, nor even to control the choice of your representatives in the Legislature, it is yet amply sufficient reason for me to withdraw from a contest with him, but not calling upon him to withdraw from a contest with me, or with either of the other candidates, nominated by the convention.

He is also the Representative of one of your Districts in the Congress of the United States, and his acceptance of the office of Governor will necessarily vacate his seat, and leave his constituents for a time (I hope a very short one) unrepresented.

Mr. Davis does not estimate the evil and danger of incomplete representation in the Congress of the United States, as of so great magnitude as I do; and I regret to say, that your opinions upon this subject, appear to correspond more with his sentiments than with mine. There is a great defect in your laws, relating to the election of members of the House of Representatives of the United States. They require an absolute majority of all the votes returned, and make no provision for the contingency frequently occurring when such majority cannot be obtained. This is one of the cases in which practicable good is sacrificed to theoretic perfection; a principle unsound in morals and mischievous in politics. The consequence of it is, that by adhering to it inflexibly you voluntarily deprive yourselves of the full representation to which you are entitled.

At the commencement of the last Congress, two of your Districts were thus unrepresented, and the immediate consequence of that was the choice of a Speaker, assuredly not favorable to *your* interests. Had those two vacancies been filled, another person, less hostile to you, would have been chosen. Committees would have been appointed with more regard to impartiality, and you would not have been deprived by political management of one-thirteenth

part of your right in the representation, as you
have been, for the next ten years. Nor is this
the only or the greatest wrong you are suffering
and will suffer by your perseverance in stripping
yourselves of your own right. At the time to
which I allude, your whole delegation in the
House, with the exception of Mr. Davis, were so
impressed with the importance of this defect in your
laws, that they addressed a joint letter to Governor
Lincoln, requesting him to recommend a revision of
them to the Legislature. He did so — but no effectual remedy was provided. You remained for nearly
the whole Congress unrepresented for one of your
Districts; for nearly the whole of a long and most
important session unrepresented for both; and now,
at this day, shorn of your constitutional right to one
member by a grossly unjust apportionment law, you
are again self-divested of the right to another, by
the neglect of your past Legislature *to provide a rem-*
edy for the evil. To provide such a remedy, I believe to be one of their most imperious duties to you.
That an effectual remedy is perfectly in their power,
the example of nearly every other State in the
Union testifies; and I can only express, as I do, my
earnest and anxious hope, that not one more session
of your Legislature shall be suffered to pass, without
some provision of law, which shall secure to you at
least the remnant of your right to representation in

the councils of the nation which the injustice of the present apportionment law has left you.

Let me not be understood as recommending the principle, though sustained by the example of several States of the Union, that a simple plurality of votes should be sufficient for an election. There is among the temporary laws of the Commonwealth, a statute enacted in the year 1803, which while it lasted did insure to you a full representation in Congress; but it was suffered to expire, rather by inadvertence than from any dissatisfaction that was ever occasioned by it. To the principle of requiring an absolute majority of votes, I would adhere so long as a reasonable hope of effecting it could be entertained; but after two unsuccessful attempts, I believe it would be a safer expedient to terminate the contest even by drawing lots for the choice, than by the protracted collisions and festering irritations of an interminable struggle to turn the elective franchise into an instrument of its own destruction.

Entertaining these opinions and holding these principles, I consider the delegation to me of the authority to represent in the national legislature, the inhabitants of your Twelfth Congressional District, as a trust, to be fulfilled with diligence as well as fidelity. Not one day—not one hour—of *voluntary* absence from the discharge of the duties incumbent on that trust, have I permitted to myself during the

twenty-second Congress, nor shall I permit to myself during the twenty-third. In accepting the
nomination of the Convention at Boston, it was
therefore with the implied condition that it should
in no wise interfere with the fulfilment of my duties
to my constituents of the Twelfth Congressional
District — and from the moment it was ascertained
that an absolute majority of the people of the Commonwealth had not confirmed the nomination of the
Antimasonic Convention, my determination was
taken. And this determination was the more cheerfully made, because the three other citizens, between
whom your suffrages are divided, and who will go
as candidates nominated by you to the Legislature,
are all persons of ability and integrity, with whom I
have the pleasure of being acquainted both in public
and private life, and in whom I have great confidence. To yield to either of them any pretensions
that I might have to your favor or that of your Legislature, costs me not the slightest sacrifice, and after
what I have said of Mr. Davis, it cannot be improper
for me to add, that the preference which I should
without hesitation assign to him, had I a vote in the
election, would be as much in the indulgence of my
own inclination, as in deference to yours ; it being
evident to me from the comparative numbers of the
returns, that in the failure of an absolute majority of
your suffrages for any one, his share of them

approaches the nearest to it and must therefore be considered by me as most deserving of it.

In concluding this exposition of my own motives for assenting to the nomination of the Antimasonic Convention, and now for withdrawing from the contest, let me give the parting advice of a friend to the remnant of the party styling themselves National Republicans, with whom I have generally concurred in opinion upon most of the great interests of the nation and of the Commonwealth — though I have never professed to be one of them or of any other *party.* Let me exhort them to revise the political class book, the elements of which confound the distinction between the meaning of the words *must* and *will.* Let them learn that it is not sufficient for a party to resolve that they *must* have a majority of votes, without using just and proper means to obtain it. Let them especially learn that to put down Antimasonry, it is not enough for them dogmatically to tell you that THEY ".look upon the Masonic fraternity as furnishing no cause for political strife."

The opinions of their addressing committee are no doubt of great weight upon subjects which they understand — but in the utter ignorance of the nature, character and condition of the Masonic Institution which their address displays, it is not from them that you will receive a dictation how you shall look upon it. They speak of Freemasonry as "an inefficient and almost superannuated institution." An institution which, at the moment when thus characterized by them, was convulsing all the free States of this Union; an institution in the support of which, under the transparent mask of neutrality, they were addressing you with pages of invective and slander upon its adversaries ; an institution, under the shadow of whose wings they, and the Convention whose voice they assumed to speak, were as effectively assembled as if every individual of them had drank the cup of the fifth libation ! They tell you in the face of day, that Freemasonry is an inefficient and almost superannuated institution !

And since when is it inefficient and almost superannuated? Had the committee which penned that address heard the eloquent orator of the craft at New London, in July, 1825? He spoke of the then *present time*, and said, "It is powerful -- it comprises men of rank, wealth, office and talent, in power and out of power, and that in almost every place where power is of any importance. And it comprises among other classes of the community, to the lowest, in large numbers, active men united together, and capable of being directed by the efforts of others so as to have the force of concert throughout the civilized world. They are distributed too with the means of knowing one another, and the means of

CO-OPERATING, in the desk, in the legislative hall,
ON THE BENCH, in every gathering of business, in
every party of pleasure, in every domestic circle, in
peace and in war, among enemies and friends, in
one place as well as in another."

Is this the inefficient and almost superannuated
institution of the committee? And upon this
faithful Masonic representation of Masonic power,
did you mark this concerted secret faculty of mutual
recognition for the purposes of co-operation, in the
legislative hall? Did you mark its ascent upon the
very bench of justice? Is this the inefficient and
almost superannuated institution? What *must* be
the result of a mutual secret recognition for the
purposes of co-operation between a judge on the
bench, and a suitor or a culprit at the bar? Inquire
of the records of the judicial tribunals of New York,
and they will furnish the answer.

Has the institution, in the short space of time
since the exhibition of this glowing picture of its
power, been suddenly struck with inefficiency and
superannuation? If the committee had consulted
Masonic authority, they would have found that the
interval of fifteen months between the delivery of
this discourse and the murder of William Morgan,
was one of unparalleled prosperity to the Order and
unexampled multiplication of its members. Since

20

the execution of the law of Masonry upon Morgan, by the co operation, among others, *of the bench*, the Institution has been, and continues to be, a church militant; and if in the prosecution of that warfare it has lost some of its efficiency, to whom and to what is this diminution of its power attributable? To Antimasonry — to *political Antimasonry* alone. All the measures taken to bring the murderers of Morgan and incendiaries of Miller's house to justice, were taken by political Antimasons. Almost all of them were defeated by the power of mutual recognition and co-operation upon *the bench*, and in the jury-box, and on the witnesses' stand. The disclosure of the Masonic oaths, obligations and penalties, was made by political Antimasons, seceders from the Order. Political Antimasonry, and that alone, has prostrated the power of Masonry throughout the whole of that region of the State of New York, where the most atrocious of her crimes had been committed. There, in the very centre of her unhallowed dominion, her sceptre is broken, her voice is silenced, her hand is paralyzed, — she is scotched, not killed, and so entirely does the existence, and of course all the evil, of political Antimasonry depend upon the active and mischievous existence of Masonry herself, that wherever she disappears, even but by hiding her face, political

Antimasonry disappears with her. The people cease to consider either Masonry or Antimasonry as a test of qualification for office. Masons and Masonic adherents share the favor of the people in common with others, and then all the trumpets of Masonry where she still reigns, sound the note of triumph that Antimasonry is "dying away."

Political Antimasonry is founded upon a pure, precise, unequivocal principle *of morals*. That this is the Antimasonic cause, the committee who addressed you against it dare not deny. Moral principle is the vital breath of Antimasonry. That a party thus originated and thus constituted, should be traduced, slandered and vilified by men having any pretension to morality of any kind themselves, is not surprising, only because it corresponds with the general current of history and the ordinary operation of human passions.

Political Antimasonry sprang from the bosom of the people themselves, and it was the cry of horror from the unlearned, unsophisticated voice of the people at the murder of Morgan — at the prostration of law and justice in the impunity of his murderers, and at the disclosure of the Masonic obligations. That cry arose, not from the mansions of the wealthy, nor from the cabinets of the learned or of the great, not even from the sentinels on the watchtowers of Zion;— it came from the broad basis of the population; from the less educated and most numerous class of the community. So it is with all great moral reforms. When the Gospel of Peace itself was proclaimed, who was its Founder? To worldly eyes, the son of a carpenter. Who were its Apostles? Fishermen and toll-gatherers, publicans and sinners. Then the Priest and the Levite — the Pharisee and the Sadducee — the Epicurean and the Stoic — the Roman Governor and Jewish King stood aloof, or *co-operated* in the crucifixion of the Saviour. Not many wise men, not many mighty, not many noble, felt the efficacy of the call; and they who did, immediately became the subject of every persecution and every indignity.

Let me draw no irreverent parallel; but the history of Christianity in its secondary causes, is the history of all reformations of morals. It was by means of the *political* Antimasonic excitement, that the spirit of reformation penetrated from the mass of the people into the bosom of the Lodge, Chapter and Encampment themselves.

The Le Roy conventions were composed of seceding Masons. The Dagan of the Temple fell in the presence and by the hands of his own worshippers. If then Masonry has lost some portion of her efficiency since the boasting celebration of her power by her orator at New London, it is to political Antimasonry alone, that this purification of the public morals must be ascribed. At this moment, between the convulsive struggles of Masonry to maintain in this Commonwealth her empire paramount to the laws, and the persevering efforts of Antimasonry to redeem their supremacy, all the great parties in the State appear to be dissolving into their elements. Your political divisions are becoming petty altercations for men — all community of feeling and interest in public concerns is shivering into rags. You have been unable to concentrate your votes with united energy sufficient to elect the ordinary officers of your government. You have of your own choice, no Governor, no Lieutenant Governor, scarcely a quorum of your Senate, and multitudes of the Representatives of your towns have failed to be elected by yourselves.

A long continuance of this state of things will yield you and your interests to the mercy of those associated with you in the national compact, — yet feeling no sympathy with you, but much rather a disposition to trample you under their feet. Of all this, FREEMASONRY is the cause. Let but the members of that fraternity within your borders, convert their Lodges into lyceums, and cease the administration of their oaths, and you may again be a happy and united people. May it so please the Supreme Disposer of events, prays, with every sentiment of respect and gratitude to you,

Your friend and fellow-citizen,

JOHN QUINCY ADAMS.

APPENDIX.

The following are exact copies of the oaths, obligations and penalties, of the first three degrees in Masonry — the Entered Apprentice, the Fellow Craft, and the Master Mason — extracted from the old manuscript mentioned in Col. William L. Stone's Letters on Masonry and Antimasonry, Letter 7, p. 67; and in the Appendix, p. 3, where it is said that while Morgan was at Rochester, these papers were there, and already written to his hands.

ENTERED APPRENTICE'S OBLIGATION.

I, A. B., do, of my own free will and accord, in the presence of God, and of this right worshipful Lodge, erected to God, and dedicated to holy St. John, hereby and hereon most solemnly and sincerely promise and swear,

That I will always hail, forever conceal, and never reveal, any of the secret or secrets of Masons or Masonry, which at this time, or at any time hereafter, shall be communicated to me as such, except it be to a true and lawful brother, or within the body of a just and regular Lodge, him or them whom I shall thus find to be, after strict trial and due examination.

I furthermore promise and swear that I will not write them, print them, stamp them, stain them, cut them, carve them, mark them, work or engrave them, nor cause them so to be done, upon any thing movable or immovable under the canopy of heaven, capable of bearing the least visible sign, mark, character or letter, whereby the mysteries of Masonry may be illegally obtained.

All this I solemnly and sincerely swear, with a full and hearty resolution to perform the same, without any evasion, equivocation

or mental reservation, under no less penalty than to have my
throat cut across from ear to ear, my tongue plucked out by
the roots, and buried in the rough sands of the sea, a cable's
length from shore, where the tide ebbs and flows twice in
twenty-four hours. So help me God, and keep me steadfast in
this my obligation of an Entered Apprentice. K. once—[kiss the
Bible once.]

FELLOW CRAFT'S OBLIGATION.

I, A. B., do, of my own free will and accord, in the presence of
God, and this right worshipful Lodge, erected to God, and dedicated to holy St. John, hereby and hereon most solemnly and
sincerely promise and swear that I will always hail, forever
conceal, and never reveal, any of the secret part or parts, mystery
or mysteries, of a Fellow Craft to an Entered Apprentice ; nor
the part of an Entered Apprentice, or either of them, to any
other person in the world, except it be to those to whom the same
shall justly and legally belong.

I furthermore promise and swear that I will relieve all poor
and indigent brethren, as far as their necessities require, and my
ability will permit.

I furthermore promise and swear that I will obey all true
signs, tokens, and summonses, sent me by the hand of a Fellow
Craft, or from the door of a just and regular Fellow Craft's
Lodge, if within the length of my cable of tow.

All this I solemnly and sincerely swear, with a full and hearty
resolution to perform the same, without any evasion, equivocation
or mental reservation, under no less penalty than to have my
heart taken from under my naked left breast, and carried to the
valley of Jehosaphat, there to be thrown into the fields to become
a prey to the wolves of the desert, and the vultures of the air.
So help me God, &c. Kiss [the Bible] twice.

MASTER MASON'S OBLIGATION.

I, A. B., do, of my own free will and accord, in the presence
of God, and of this right worshipful Lodge, erected to God, and
dedicated to holy St. John, hereby and hereon most solemnly

and sincerely promise and swear, that I will always hail, forever conceal, and never reveal, the secret part or parts, mystery or mysteries, of a Master Mason to a Fellow Craft, or those of a Fellow Craft to an Entered Apprentice, or them or either of them to any other person in the world, except it be to those to whom the same shall justly and legally belong.

I furthermore promise and swear that I will not be present at the making of a Mason of a woman, of a madman, or of a fool ; that I will not defraud a brother knowingly or willingly; that I will not give the Master's words above breath, nor then except within the five points of fellowship ; — that I will not violate the chastity of a Mason's wife or daughter, knowing them to be such.

I furthermore promise and swear, that I will attend a brother barefoot, if necessity requires, to warn him of approaching danger ; that on my knees I will remember him in my prayers ; that I will take him by the right hand and support him with the left in all his just and lawful undertakings ; that I will keep his secrets as safely deposited in my breast as they are in his own, treason and murder only excepted, and those at my option ; that I will obey all true signs, tokens, and summonses, sent me by the hand of a Master Mason, or from the door of a just and regular Master Mason's Lodge, if within the length of my cable-tow.

All this I most solemnly and sincerely promise and swear with a full and hearty resolution to perform the same, without any evasion, equivocation or mental reservation, under no less penalty than to have my body cut across, my bowels taken out and burnt to ashes, and those ashes scattered to the four winds of heaven ; to have my body dissected into four equal parts, and those parts hung on the cardinal points of the compass, there to hang and remain as a terror to all those, who shall presume to violate the sacred obligation of a Master Mason. Kiss [the Bible] thrice.

These three penalties, the Master of the Lodge, immediately after administering this oath to the recipient Master Mason, declares to him, were *executed* upon the three Tyrian Fellow Crafts, at the building of Solomon's temple, *and have ever since*

*remained the standing penalties in the three first degrees of
Masonry.*

The following form of the Royal Arch Oath, and that of the
Knight Templar, are taken from the Boston edition of Avery
Allyn's Ritual of Freemasonry, printed in 1831, pp. 143, 236.

ROYAL ARCH OATH.

I, A. B., of my own free will and accord, in presence of
Almighty God, and this Chapter of Royal Arch Masons, erected
to God, and dedicated to Zerubbabel, do hereby and hereon,
most solemnly and sincerely promise and swear, in addition to
my former obligations, that I will not reveal the secrets of this
degree to any of an inferior degreee, nor to any being in the
known world, except it be to a true and lawful companion Royal
Arch Mason, or within the body of a just and legally constituted
Chapter of such ; and never unto him, or them, whom I shall
hear so to be, but unto him and them only whom I shall find so
to be, after strict trial and due examination, or lawful information
given.

I furthermore promise and swear, that I will not wrong this
Chapter of Royal Arch Masons, or a companion of this degree,
out of the value of any thing, myself, or suffer it to be done by
others, if in my power to prevent it.

I furthermore promise and swear, that I will not reveal the key
to the ineffable characters of this degree, nor retain it in my possession, but will destroy it whenever it comes to my sight.

I furthermore promise and swear, that I will not speak the
grand omnific Royal Arch word, which I shall hereafter receive,
in any manner, except in that in which I shall receive it, which
will be in the presence of three companion Royal Arch Masons,
myself making one of the number ; and then by *three times
three*, under a living arch, and at low breath.

I furthermore promise and swear, that I will not be at the exaltation of candidates in a clandestine Chapter, nor converse upon
the secrets of this degree with a clandestine made Mason, or with
one who has been expelled or suspended, while under that sentence.

I furthermore promise and swear, that I will not assist, or be present at the exaltation of a candidate to this degree, who has not received the degrees of Entered Apprentice, Fellow Craft Master Mason, Mark Master, Past Master, and Most Excellent Master.

I furthermore promise and swear, that I will not be at the exaltation of *more* or *less* than *three* candidates, at one and the same time.

I furthermore promise and swear, that I will not be at the forming or opening of a Chapter of Royal Arch Masons, unless there be present nine regular Royal Arch Masons, myself making one of that number.

I furthermore promise and swear, that I will not speak evil of a companion Royal Arch Mason, behind his back, nor before his face, but will apprise him of all approaching danger, if in my power.

I furthermore promise and swear, that I will support the constitution of the General Grand Royal Arch Chapter of the United States of America; together with that of the Grand Chapter of this State, under which this Chapter is holden; that I will stand to, and abide by all the by-laws, rules, and regulations of this Chapter, or of any other Chapter of which I may hereafter become a member.

I furthermore promise and swear, that I will answer and obey all due signs and summons, handed, sent, or thrown to me from a Chapter of Royal Arch Masons, or from a companion Royal Arch Mason, if within the length of my cable-tow.

I furthermore promise and swear, that I will not strike a companion Royal Arch Mason, so as to draw his blood in anger.

I furthermore promise and swear, that *I will employ* a companion Royal Arch Mason, in *preference to any other person*, of equal qualifications.

I furthermore promise and swear, that I will assist a companion Royal Arch Mason, when I see him engaged in *any* difficulty, and will *espouse his cause* so far as to *extricate* him from the same *whether he be RIGHT or WRONG.*

I furthermore promise and swear, that I will keep *all* the *secrets* of a companion Royal Arch Mason (when communicated to me as *such,* or I knowing them to be *such,*) *without exceptions.*

I furthermore promise and swear, that I will be aiding and assisting all *poor* and *indigent* companion Royal Arch Masons, their widows and orphans, *wheresoever dispersed around the globe;* they making application to me as such, and I finding them *worthy,* and can do it without *any material* injury to myself or family. To all which I do most solemnly and sincerely promise and swear, with a firm and steadfast resolution to keep and perform the same without any equivocation, mental reservation, or self-evasion of mind in me whatever; binding myself under no less penalty, than to have my *skull smote off,* and my *brains exposed to the scorching rays of the meridian sun,* should I knowingly or wilfully violate, or transgress *any* part of this my solemn oath or obligation of a Royal Arch Mason. So help me God, and keep me steadfast in the due performance of the same. [Kissing the book seven times.]

KNIGHT TEMPLAR'S OATH.

I, A. B., of my own free will and accord, in the presence of Almighty God, and this Encampment of Knights Templars, do hereby and hereon most solemnly promise and swear that I will always hail, forever conceal and never reveal, any of the secret arts, parts or points appertaining to the mysteries of this Order of Knights Templars, unless it be to a true and lawful companion Sir Knight, or within the body of a just and lawful Encampment of such; and not unto him, or them, until by due trial, strict examination, or lawful information, I find him or them lawfully entitled to receive the same.

Furthermore do I promise and swear, that I will answer and obey all due signs and regular summons which shall be given or sent to me from a regular Encampment of Knights Templars, if within the distance of forty miles, natural infirmities and unavoidable accidents only excusing me.

Furthermore do I promise and swear, that I will help, aid and assist with my counsel, my purse, and my sword, all poor and indigent Knights Templars, their widows and orphans, they making application to me as such, and I finding them worthy, so far as I can do it without material injury to myself, and so far as truth, honor, and justice may warrant.

Furthermore do I promise and swear, that I will not assist, or be present, at the forming and opening of an Encampment of Knights Templars, unless there be present seven Knights of the Order, or the representatives of three different Encampments, acting under the sanction of a legal warrant.

Furthermore do I promise and swear, that I will go the distance of forty miles, even barefoot and on frosty ground, to save the life, and relieve the necessities of a worthy Knight, should I know that his necessities required it, and my abilities permit.

Furthermore do I promise and swear, that *I will wield my sword in the defence of innocent maidens, destitute widows, helpless orphans, and the Christian religion.*

Furthermore do I promise and swear, that I will support and maintain the by-laws of the Encampment of which I may hereafter become a member, the edicts and regulations of the Grand Encampment of the United States of America, so far as the same shall come to my knowledge; to all this I most solemnly and sincerely promise and swear, with a firm and steady resolution to perform and keep the same, without any hesitation, equivocation, mental reservation or self-evasion of mind in me whatever; binding myself under no less penalty than to have my head struck off and placed on the highest spire in Christendom, should I knowingly or willingly violate any part of this my solemn obligation of a Knight Templar. So help me God, and keep me steadfast to perform and keep the same. [He kisses the book.]

FIFTH LIBATION.

This part of the ceremony attending the creation of the Knight Templar is deemed interesting in connection with the obligation.

Address of the Master.

Pilgrim, the fifth libation is taken in a very solemn way. It is emblematical of the bitter cup of death, of which we must all, sooner or later, taste; and even the Saviour of the world was not exempted, notwithstanding his repeated prayers and solicitations. It is taken of pure wine, and from this cup. [Exhibiting a human skull, he pours the wine into it, and says,] To show you that we here practice no imposition, I give you this pledge. [Drinks from the skull.] He then pours more wine into the skull, and presents it to the candidate, telling him, that the *fifth libation* is called the sealed obligation, as it is to seal all his former engagements in Masonry.

If the candidate consents to proceed, he takes the skull in his hand, and repeats after the Most Eminent, as follows:

This pure wine, I take from this cup, in testimony of my belief of the mortality of the body and the immortality of the soul; and as the sins of the whole world were laid upon the head of our Saviour, so may the sins of the person whose skull this once was, be heaped upon my head, in addition to my own; and may they appear in judgment against me, both here and hereafter, should I violate or transgress any obligation in Masonry, or the Orders of Knighthood which I have heretofore taken, take at this time, or may hereafter be instructed in. So help me God. [Drinks of the wine.]

The following extracts are referred to in Mr. Adams's fourth letter to Mr. Livingston, page 158.

Extracts from the Report made to the General Assembly of the State of Louisiana on the Plan of a Penal Code for the said State. By Edward Livingston.

"Legislators, in all ages and in every country, have, at times, endangered the lives, the liberties, and fortunes of the people by inconsistent provisions, CRUEL OR DISPROPORTIONED PUNISHMENTS, and a legislation weak and wavering."

"Executions [in England] for some crimes were attended with BUTCHERY THAT WOULD DISGUST A SAVAGE."

"Acknowledged truths in politics and jurisprudence can never be too often repeated."

"Publicity is an object of such importance in free governments, that it not only ought to be permitted, but must be secured by a species of compulsion."

"If he [the culprit] be guilty, the state has an interest in his conviction; and whether guilty or innocent, it has a higher interest that the fact should be fairly canvassed before JUDGES INACCESSIBLE TO INFLUENCE AND UNBIASSED BY ANY FALSE VIEWS OF OFFICIAL DUTY."

"It is not true therefore to say, that the laws do enough, when they give the choice (even suppose it could be made with deliberation) between a fair and impartial trial and one that is liable to the strongest objections. They must do more, they must restrict that choice, so as not to suffer an ill-advised individual to degrade them into instruments of ruin, though it should be voluntarily inflicted, or of death, though that death should be suicide."

"The English mangle the remains of the dead [by suicide.] The inanimate body feels neither the ignominy nor pains. The mind of the innocent survivor alone is lacerated by THIS USELESS AND SAVAGE BUTCHERY, and the disgrace of the execution is felt exclusively by him, although it ought to fall *on the laws which inflict it.*"

"The law punishes, not to avenge, but to prevent crimes. No punishments, greater than are necessary to effect this work of prevention, let us remember, ought to be inflicted."

"Although the dislocation of the joints is no longer considered as the best mode of ascertaining innocence or discovering guilt; although offences against the Deity are no longer expiated by the burning fagot; or those against the majesty of kings, avenged by the hot pincers and the rack and the wheel; still many other modes of punishment have their advocates, which, if not equally cruel, are quite as inconsistent with the true maxims of penal law."

"As to the authority of great names, it loses much of its force, since the mass of the people have begun to think for themselves."

"Where laws are so directly at war with the feelings of the people whom they govern, as this, and many other instances prove

them to be, these laws can never be wise or operative, AND THEY
OUGHT TO BE ABOLISHED."

Extracts from detached parts of the projected Code.

" No act of legislation can be, or ought to be, immutable."

"Vengeance is unknown to the laws. The only object of
punishment is to prevent the commission of offences."

" Penal laws should be written in plain language, clearly and
unequivocally expressed, that they may neither be misunderstood
nor perverted."

" The law should never command more than it can enforce.
Therefore, whenever, from public opinion or any other cause, a
penal law cannot be carried into execution, it should be repealed."

" The legislature alone has a right to declare what shall constitute an offence."

Made in the USA
Lexington, KY
23 January 2015